The Architecture of Oppression

The SS concentration camp system has been one of the most widely researched institutions of National Socialist Germany. Yet the fact that many of the forced-labor concentration camps were initially established around stone quarries and brickworks has received little attention. In *The Architecture of Oppression*, Paul B. Jaskot takes up this issue by asking the following question: why did the SS choose to focus so many of its forced-labor concerns around the production of building materials? Through an analysis of such major Nazi building projects as the Nuremberg Party Rally Grounds and Albert Speer's plans for the rebuilding of Berlin, Jaskot ties together the development of the German building economy, state architectural goals and the rise of the SS as a political and economic force. In so doing, he argues that the architectural history of Nazi Germany is inextricably linked to its most punitive institutions.

This book re-evaluates not only the architectural history of Nazi Germany but also the development of the forced-labor concentration camp system. Further, the author sheds new light on Speer's relationship to criminal state policy by fore-grounding his involvement with the SS and the German monumental building economy. As a result, *The Architecture of Oppression* contributes to our understanding of the conjunction of culture and politics in the Nazi period as well as the agency of architects and SS administrators in enabling this process.

Paul B. Jaskot is an Assistant Professor in the Department of Art and Art History at DePaul University in Chicago. His work focuses on the relationship between politics and culture in modern European Art and Architecture.

THE ARCHI*TEXT* SERIES

Edited by Thomas A. Markus and Anthony D. King

Architectural discourse has traditionally represented buildings as art objects or technical objects. Yet buildings are also social objects in that they are invested with social meaning and shape social relations. Recognising these assumptions, the **Architext** series aims to bring together recent debates in social and cultural theory and the study and practice of architecture and urban design. Critical, comparative and interdisciplinary, the books in the series will, by theorising architecture, bring the space of the built environment centrally into the social sciences and humanities, as well as bringing the theoretical insights of the latter into the discourses of architecture and urban design. Particular attention will be paid to issues of gender, race, sexuality and the body, to questions of identity and place, to the cultural politics of representation and language, and to the global and postcolonial contexts in which these are addressed.

Framing Places
Mediating power in built form
Kim Dovey

Gender Space Architecture
An interdisciplinary reader
edited by Jane Rendell, Barbara Penner and Iain Borden

Forthcoming titles:

Moderns Abroad
Italian colonialism and construction
Mia Fuller

Architecture and Language
Thomas A. Markus and Deborah Cameron

Spaces of Global Cultures
Anthony D. King

Paul B. Jaskot

The Architecture of Oppression

The SS, forced labor and the Nazi
monumental building economy

London and New York

First published 2000
by Routledge
11 New Fetter Lane, London EC4P 4EE

Simultaneously published in the USA and Canada
by Routledge
29 West 35th Street, New York, NY 10001

Routledge is an imprint of the Taylor & Francis Group

Typeset in Frutiger by Solidus (Bristol) Ltd
Printed and bound in Great Britain by St Edmundsbury Press, Bury St Edmunds, Suffolk

British Library Cataloguing in Publication Data
A catalogue record for this book is available from the British Library

Library of Congress Cataloging in Publication Data
A catalogue record for this book has been requested

ISBN 0-415-17366-3 (Hbk)
ISBN 0-415-22341-5 (Pbk)

TO MY FAMILY

Contents

Illustrations

Acknowledgments

It goes without saying that a book, as an accumulation of knowledge, is a social product. It is with great pleasure that I take this opportunity to thank many of the people who supported my project and its development.

My study of the relationship between art and politics in National Socialist Germany began with my dissertation research at Northwestern University. I am most grateful for the help, support and critical engagement of my advisors, O.K. Werckmeister and Peter Hayes. Peter introduced me to the vast historical literature on National Socialist Germany and the SS concentration camp system. He has never failed in demanding intellectual rigor and engaging in a lively scholarly debate on my topic. Karl, my principal advisor, led me through the thicket of National Socialist art history and was a constant supporter of my research. Further, his work on art and politics in modern Germany as well as his commitment to a critical art history were an inspiration for many of the ideas worked out in this book. I am happy to say that my debates with Karl and Peter continue to aid in my intellectual development.

In the late 1980s, Northwestern's Department of Art History emphasized issues within the social history of art which greatly influenced my work. I would particularly like to thank the critical contributions to and professional support of my topic by S. Hollis Clayson, Nancy Troy and David van Zanten. Further, my colleagues offered an environment of debate and discussion which proved invaluable for the formulation and finishing of the project. For that intellectual support, I am particularly grateful to: Alex Alberro, Priya Jaikumar, Sherry Lindquist, Julie Lindstrom, Jonathan Maskit, Diane Miliotes, Kevin Murphy, Kristin Sazama and Kathleen Wilson. Ellen Christensen also offered useful criticisms of key parts of the final text. In addition, I remain indebted to the continuing exchange of views on German art history offered by: Isabel Balzer, Keith Holz and James van Dyck.

Three scholars in particular deserve special thanks for their support in seeing this manuscript to its conclusion: Michael Thad Allen, Barbara McCloskey and Jonathan Petropoulos. Allen's work on the SS administration has helped me to clarify many of the more complex issues addressed particularly in Chapter 2. Petropoulos has never wavered from an interest in my project and has provided much crucial criticism of the final text. And for her willingness to read and critique multiple versions of my work, I cannot thank McCloskey enough. However, these three have not only offered advice and support but also friendship for which I am very grateful.

Many of the major themes in this work were developed while completing the research in Germany or in discussion with other art historians. At a crucial stage of my research in Koblenz, several friends offered almost daily advice on the significance of particular aspects of the project. Many thanks in particular to Tiziana Carrozza, Lisa Heineman, Peter Kirchgraber, Maria Mitchell, Patty Stokes, Guillaume de Syon and Kathy Tumpek. I appreciate as well the professional and intellectual support of my work by Eckhardt Dietzfelbinger, Richard Etlin, Winfried Nerdinger and Wolf Tegethoff. In addition, I thank the participants in the discussion of my work at the Winchester School of Art, the University of Reading and the University of London. I am obliged to Andrew Hemingway for arranging those discussions and for his continued commitment to debates concerning Marxism and art history.

In the Chicago area and at DePaul University, several individuals have greatly contributed to the development and support of this project. I wish to thank Glen Carman, Shawn Gillen, Deborah Mancoff, Darrell Moore, Alex Papadopoulos, Inca Rumold, Ann Russo, Julia Sneeringer and Robert Bürglener. For their encouragement and support, I would also like to acknowledge my colleagues in the Department of Art and Art History, especially Steve Harp, Liz Lillehoj, Marlena Novak and Mark Zlotkowski for their comments on my work.

For their early interest in and help with completion of the manuscript, I am indebted to the support and advice of my editors, Anthony King and Thomas Markus. Further editorial guidance was given to me by the editors at Routledge, Jody Ball, Sarah Lloyd and Caroline Mallinder, as well as my copy editor, Sophie Richmond. Their assistance and patience proved invaluable.

Partial funding of this project was received from the Deutscher Akademischer Austauschdienst and a Northwestern University Dissertation Year Grant. DePaul's Office of Sponsored Research and the University Research Council provided additional funding. I am obliged to these institutions for their support.

For the reproduction of specific photographs, permission has been provided by the Archive of the Mauthausen State Memorial and Museum, the Nuremberg City Archive, the German Federal Archive, the Rijksinstituut voor Oorlogsdocumentatie and Ullstein Bilderdienst. I am grateful for the courteous help in finding and reproducing particular images offered by the staffs at the photo archives of the US Holocaust Memorial Museum and Northwestern University's Special Collections.

Finally, my thanks to my family without whom the present project would never have been completed.

Chicago, 1999

Abbreviations

AGKBZHwP	Archivum Glowna Komisja Badonia Zbrodni Hitlerowskich w Polsce (Archive of the High Commission for the Investigation of NS Criminals in Poland)
Arge	Arbeitsgemeinschaft (association)
Arge Nürnberg	Arbeitsgemeinschaft Natursteinlieferungen Reichsparteitags-bauten Nürnberg GmbH (Reich Party Rally Buildings Natural Stone Supplies Association)
BA	Bundesarchiv Koblenz (Berlin; formerly Federal Archives Koblenz)
BA, Potsdam	Bundesarchiv, Abteilung Potsdam (Berlin; formerly Federal Archives Potsdam)
DEST	Deutsche Erd- und Steinwerke, GmbH (German Earth and Stone Works)
DöW	Dokumentationsarchiv des österreichischen Widerstandes (Documentation Archive of Austrian Resistance)
DWB	Deutsche Wirtschaftsbetriebe GmbH (German Economic Concerns)
GBBau	Generalbevollmächtigter für die Regelung der Bauwirtschaft (General Plenipotentiary for the Regulation of the Building Economy)
GBI	Generalbauinspektor für die Reichshauptstadt Berlin (Inspector General of Building for the Reich Capital Berlin)
Gestapo	Geheime Staatspolizei (Secret State Police)
HAHuB	Hauptamt Haushalt und Bauten (SS Central Budget and Building Office)
HAVW	Hauptamt Verwaltung und Wirtschaft (SS Central Administration and Economic Office)
IfZ	Institut für Zeitgeschichte (Institute for Contemporary History)
IMT	International Military Tribunal, Nuremberg

KL	Konzentrationslager (concentration camp)
LA	Landesarchiv, Berlin (Berlin State Archive)
NSDAP	Nationalsozialistische Deutsche Arbeiterpartei (National Socialist German Workers' Party)
ÖDMMA	Öffentliches Denkmal und Museum Mauthausen Archiv (Archive of the Mauthausen State Memorial and Museum)
OKH	Oberkommando des Heeres (Army High Command)
OKW	Oberkommando des Wehrmachts (Military High Command)
OT	Organisation Todt (Organization Todt)
RGBl.	*Reichsgesetzblatt (Imperial Law Gazette)*
RSHA	Reichssicherheitshauptamt (SS Reich Security Main Office)
SA	Sturmabteilung (Storm Division or Storm Troopers)
SAN	Stadtarchiv Nürnberg (Nuremberg City Archive)
SS	Schutzstaffel (Guard Squadron)
WVHA	Wirtschafts- und Verwaltungshauptamt (SS Economic and Administrative Central Office)
ZRPT	Zweckverband Reichsparteitag Nürnberg (Reich Party Rally Grounds Association Nuremberg)

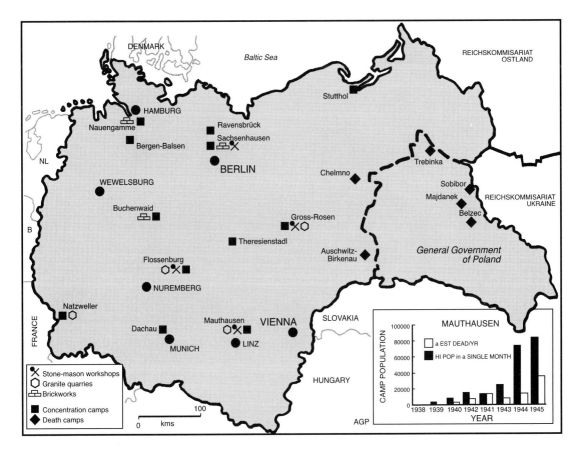

Concentration Camps in the German Reich and General Government (1942 borders) with the SS forced-labor stone quarries, mason shops, and brickworks indicated

Chapter 1: Introduction

The Architectural Policy of the SS

In present-day northern Bavaria, near the Czech border, lies the small isolated town of Flossenbürg. Here among the idyllic Fichtel Mountains and in the shadow of the ruins of a medieval castle that once belonged to the Holy Roman Emperor Friedrich Barbarossa, the SS established a concentration camp (Konzentrationslager [KL]). The question is, why did the SS site the camp in such a place? When Flossenbürg opened in 1938, the SS had already situated the other major camps near concentrated population centers. But KL Flossenbürg was not conveniently located; it was neither particularly close to a major rail line for transport of prisoners nor in the vicinity of a large city. The camp's location, however, was highly significant for this moment in the economic development of the SS, for the surrounding hills were the source of rich supplies of high-grade granite deposits suitable for Hitler's monumental building projects. For his building plans particularly in Nuremberg and Berlin, Hitler paid close attention to the kinds of materials being used, especially in his choice of stone. While the SS established Flossenbürg like the other camps to punish political and ideological enemies of the state, it also adapted the process of punishment to the massive demand for stone in the monumental building economy. Thousands of prisoners lost their lives in the forced-labor quarries, realizing the political function of the camp. Yet this forced labor also served an architectural function: the largest single patron for Flossenbürg granite was Albert Speer's office for the rebuilding of Berlin. In pursuing such a patron, the SS attempted to establish at the camp an economically productive use for forced labor. The location of KL Flossenbürg was not haphazard.

SS control of forced-labor concentration camps after 1936 linked state architectural policy to the political function of incarcerating and punishing supposed enemies of National Socialist Germany. Due to the polycratic structure of the Nazi regime, the SS developed its plans for the camps with relative freedom even though its economic goals often competed with those of other state, Party and private institutions. Pursuing both the economic and political interest in making the camps permanent institutions, Heinrich Himmler and his staff systematized the camp administration and drove it towards the production of huge amounts of building materials. Part of this attempt to secure the role of the camps in German society was the orientation of forced labor to the specific demands of the monumental building projects of Berlin and Nuremberg. Brick making and, especially, stone quarrying became the daily experience of the prisoners. These prison populations expanded during World War II with the extension of SS policing authority over more and more people and ever larger geographic segments of Europe. Because of such a nexus of architectural projects, economic interests and political oppression, we can say that the SS developed a distinct architectural policy. Once the decision had been made to re-educate (as the SS commandants would say) the inmates with the production of building materials, monumental architecture in Nazi Germany became inextricable from its most punitive institutions.

An examination of National Socialist architecture and the concentration camp system demands a new understanding of the intersection of art and political history. Art historians of the Nazi period have investigated the aesthetic significance of particular buildings, the biography of high-profile architects and the conditions of architectural practice.[1] This book builds on this work, especially that of critical scholars such as Barbara Miller Lane, Wolfgang Schäche and Alex Scobie. Nevertheless, the resulting ideological and institutional critique taken up by previous art historical scholarship has been carried out separately from a systematic analysis of the political history. That is to say, while propaganda strategies and particular political events have become essential markers for this art history, the relationship between architectural policy and the development of other seemingly non-artistic social, economic and political conditions needs further research and clarification. At its extreme, this art history has over-generalized what was in fact a highly differentiated set of competing interests, interests that were mediated by material conditions, institutional developments and particular agents.[2] The result has been an art historical analysis that sees politics largely as an expression of ideology rather than as the functional implementation of policy. Analyzing the SS interest in the monumental building economy depends on such a functional understanding of political history. This political history of art is less dependent on how, for example, specific architectural careers can be used to interpret singular works; rather it is more interested in how architectural production – from inception to design to construction – influences other state and Party policies. An extended political history of art comes from an analysis of the *process* by which the SS adapted specific ventures to the monumental building projects, not from a static evaluation of the finished structures.

The architectural policy of the SS poses particular problems for both historians and art historians of the period. For art historians, including an evaluation of the SS means reassessing the scholarly conception of Nazi cultural politics. Such a reassessment involves extending the definition of historically significant architecture to take into account not only major projects like Speer's plans for Berlin but also buildings like the guard towers at Flossenbürg which the SS administrators considered to be monumental and important structures as well. Further, this analysis involves the incorporation of specific political economic conditions into art history to make sense of the SS interest in the monumental building economy. For historical scholarship, on the other hand, including how aesthetic decisions influenced oppressive policy calls for a re-evaluation of the development of the forced-labor concentration camps. An examination of SS architectural policy complicates the standard scholarly discussion of the pre-1941 camps as predominantly punitive institutions. Cultural goals were not ancillary but integrated into the punitive process. These goals drove the implementation of specific oppressive labor practices or influenced the timing of institutional decisions. Clarifying the relationship between the SS and the monumental building economy thus extends our historical understanding of forced-labor enterprises while demanding at the same time a more critical political history of art.

The significance of such a project can be induced from a brief summary of the historical scope of this book. Scholars have previously noted that the SS used its forced-labor enterprises to link its steadily increasing political authority to the privileged position of architectural policy, but they have never systematically analyzed the phenomenon.[3] After the reorganization of the concentration camp system in 1936, Himmler began developing his interest (carried out by his administrative chief, Oswald Pohl) in establishing new SS economic concerns. In 1938, this planning resulted in the foundation of the German Earth and Stone Works (Deutsche Erd- und Steinwerke [DEST]), an SS firm set up to exploit forced labor in the quarrying of stone and brick making. Pohl's administration of DEST, the largest SS enterprise, proved most successful in the early years of World War II when the influx of political prisoners and the presumption of a quick end to the *Blitzkrieg* allowed for the extension of economic and architectural policy. The formation and expansion of DEST developed in relation to this broader political economy of Germany. Particularly during the war years, the conditions of the building economy promoted an emphasis on productivity which the SS took up in its quarry and brick-making concerns. Such an emphasis led to variations in camp labor policies which in turn were influenced by political decisions within the SS hierarchy.

As a producer of building materials, DEST managers promoted the economic use of forced labor by attempting to gear the output of specific facilities to particular projects, notably the publicly proclaimed, large-scale, state and Party structures that defined the monumental building economy. Hitler and his chief architect, Speer, made aesthetic decisions that had a direct effect on the quantity and kind of materials being produced in this market. DEST administrators endeavored to mobilize their competing political and economic interests to take advantage of opportunities available through the production of building materials for such privileged plans as the Reich Party Rally Grounds in Nuremberg. With Nuremberg, the SS attempted to expand and differentiate the work in the camps to make forced labor indispensable to architectural policy. This differentiation of forced labor kept DEST abreast of broader changes in the German monumental building economy. The flexibility to adapt to these conditions allowed for the pursuit of SS economic goals at crucial moments in the late 1930s and into the war.

Yet, as its enterprises expanded, the internal organization and development of the SS administration both contributed to and hindered the implementation of economic objectives. The function of the camps – to abuse the labor population but also to exploit its productivity – were sometimes conflicting, sometimes complementary goals. As a result of this uneven process, historians have generally dismissed DEST concerns as inefficient and therefore secondary to the punitive function of the camps in spite of their ability to maintain contracts with such important sites as the Reich Party Rally Grounds.[4] But before 1942–3, when German military victories began to turn into defeats, efficiency was a consideration to the SS only in so far as it seemed to affect the power to produce. This focus on output helped maintain relations between the SS and Speer's office of the Inspector General of Building for the Reich Capital Berlin (Generalbauinspektor für die Reichshauptstadt Berlin [GBI]), which was a regular and politically powerful patron of DEST enterprises. By separating a concern for labor efficiency from an emphasis on quantitative output, DEST could maintain a productive focus on providing materials for Speer's monumental building site, all the while avoiding a disruption of the primary purpose of the forced-labor camps in punishing ideological and political prisoners of the Party and state. How the SS imagined and planned its economic development indicates the success and failure of DEST in dominating segments of the German building economy and receiving building material orders for state and Party projects.

With the Berlin building program, it was not only a matter of DEST taking advantage of the material needs of specific monumental projects but also, conversely, of the GBI at times calling on the SS in order to carry out its architectural plans. In the bureaucratic organization of the Nazi state, the interests of individual administrations both conflicted and came together at key moments in the development of oppressive policies in the camps and the monumental building economy.[5] Architects became active agents and, at times, politically involved in the expansion of DEST enterprises. While Speer and Himmler separately jockeyed for more administrative power by appealing to Hitler, their respective long-term architectural or economic goals brought them together to pursue short-term interests.[6]

Such a dynamic between variable interests and developing conditions also demands going beyond the selectivity of a canonical architectural history, a scholarly limitation that overlooks the political importance to the SS not only of Hitler's major projects but also of the institutional architecture of the SS itself.[7] In the DEST facilities, the oppression of individuals because of their political affiliation or imagined ideological impurity developed through a complicated and often erratic practice of physical annihilation. Oppressive circumstances – from beatings to murders, from health conditions imposed on the inmates to the psychological effects of their incarceration – were often directed towards specific individuals and groups, linking the forced-labor camps to the extermination policy later developed for the death camps. As camp construction in particular depended on forced labor, an analysis of the building process at KL Flossenbürg and KL Mauthausen testifies to the direct connection at the camp site between punitive policy and architecture.[8] In carrying out the ideological concerns of the leadership, the SS focused special attention on the design of the permanent facilities at KL Flossenbürg and the building of the walls at KL Mauthausen. Both were massive complexes distinct from other pre-war concentration camps in their architectural form and punitive conditions. The investigation of how individuals experienced the practice of extermination in these camps relates the history of the forced-labor enterprises and architecture to the most criminal elements of National Socialist Germany.

This summary of the SS interest in the building process indicates that the conjunction of architectural projects, SS economic goals and oppressive policy in the camps came about and then began to dissipate in the short but crucial four-year period from 1938 to 1942. In their analyses of these years, art historians tend to end their accounts with the beginning of the war on 1 September 1939. Yet paying closer attention to the process of production extends this chronology into the early war years and brings the political function of architecture more clearly into focus. As Dietrich Neumann has observed, "To this day, the complex general conditions of architectural production have received far less attention than they deserve. We still do not know enough about how modern buildings actually came about, how the participants in the building process interacted, how building materials were invented and promoted."[9] A historical concern with production is important in determining DEST's decision-making process as well as in analyzing the preconditions and effects of forced-labor quarrying and brick-making operations. Such an analysis clarifies the relationship between cultural goals and the ability to implement specific policies. It avoids seeing National Socialist architecture as an expression of a monolithic ideology and instead puts emphasis on the political function and, hence, the political history of the SS involvement with the monumental building economy.[10]

A brief overview of the changing conditions of the building economy and their influence on both architectural and labor policy demonstrates the importance of paying attention to the production process. When Hitler came to power in 1933, construction was used as a means of work creation that resulted in much road building and many public structures but very few monumental building projects. Yet as the Nazi leadership consolidated power over the government and the economy, so too was there a corresponding political promotion of monumental architectural policy. By 1938, the systematization of monumental architectural production in such key "Führer cities" as Berlin and Nuremberg prospered thanks to the strong personal support of Hitler. In this period, Hitler's backing guaranteed that workers and funds were obtained even though the broader German economy was suffering a labor shortage exacerbated by the political decisions made to expand armaments production and prepare for war. With the war itself, this politically driven economy was further prioritized in order to maximize the labor, infrastructural and material needs of the German military effort and *Blitzkrieg* strategy. Due to Hitler's continued interest in architecture, this prioritization also affected the monumental building economy as the majority of state and Party projects were shut down while the remaining few large-scale projects were able to concentrate resources within the building economy to sustain their design and construction efforts. This situation continued until the complete mobilization of the German war economy with the readjustment from the *Blitzkrieg* strategy to total war in 1943. DEST adapted to and, at specific moments, tried to influence these political economic conditions in order to further the economic goals of the SS.

Central to DEST's ability to adapt was its control over ever extending quantities of forced laborers. Forced-labor policy in general and the SS use of forced labor in particular have been subject to much scholarly debate. At issue is how to make sense of the structural contradiction between the implementation of political-ideological goals (destroying designated inmate populations) and the needs of the increasingly stretched German economy into the war (the necessity to maximize all labor potential). In relation to the DEST concerns, Enno Georg's early influential work and, more recently, the writings of Hermann Kaienburg thematize the connection of economic concerns to political considerations through the attempted link of forced labor to the building economy.[11] Yet both scholars offer a schematic view of the pre-1942 history of DEST, and they lack detailed research on the stone-quarry operations. Thus, they de-emphasize the importance of architectural policy to the SS. Kaienburg in particular pushes his analysis to an extreme by contending that the practice of "destruction through work" was the only serious goal of forced-labor operations before 1942 when the SS became involved with armaments production. Such an interpretation places an undue burden on the political function of the camps to the exclusion of a more differentiated analysis that takes into account both the cultural and economic goals served by the political oppression of the inmates.

As Ulrich Herbert and Michael Allen have pointed out, forced-labor policy should be discussed less as "destruction through work" but, more accurately, as "destruction and work." That is to say, a more systematic account of the institutional development of the SS use of forced labor leads to an investigation of how economic and political goals, labor and oppression, were simultaneously implemented rather than administratively integrated policies.[12] Herbert in particular analyzes how state and Party institutions (including but not exclusive to the SS) made use of or devalued forced labor depending on developing structural conditions, different motivations and the political or ideologically designated status of the worker. At stake in both accounts is the central historical question of the exact relationship between ideological goals and oppressive policies, even if each author under-analyzes the adaptation of SS political and economic interests to the monumental building economy.[13]

In essence, an attention to the process of production is crucial to a specific analysis of the integration of forced labor, the building economy and monumental architectural projects. Both before and after the founding of DEST, architectural considerations conditioned and influenced the timing and enactment of particular economic, political and cultural goals for the quarry and brick-making forced-labor concentration camps. These subtle and developing dynamics of the conditions of production require a consideration of the changing significance and function of architecture in National Socialist Germany. To limit art historical research to the investigation of the propagandistic function or the ideological interpretation of the monumental buildings of the Party and state is to avoid delineating either policy decisions that combined architectural and political goals or the interest of government and Party institutions in the production process. A focus on the development of SS architectural policy rejoins the political function of art with its ideological critique.

Methodologically, this emphasis on the creation, timing and implementation of policy depends on the integration of art historical interests with historical political economy. By focusing not on the fantastic claims made for architecture but on architecture's operative political function, different questions need to be answered in terms of the relationship between political and economic conditions.[14] Where one puts the stress in this relationship is, of course, crucial. Whether the historian analyzes political choices as a means of establishing an economically efficient society, or, conversely, whether economic conditions are seen as contextually related to political interests, significantly influences the scholarly assessment. The former position emphasizes the causal relationship between political decisions and economic outcomes whereas the latter stresses the conditional interdependence of political and economic forces and interests.[15] I argue for the use of this second model as it can be derived and induced from the material evidence of political economic goals and developments.

Such a general historical political economy must also deal with the debates and questions concerned particularly with fascism. Does the rise of fascism between the world wars mark a break with democratic capitalism or is it an extension of pre-existing circumstances? Is it best characterized by a specific political philosophy or should we see fascism as implementing a set of distinctly new structural economic conditions? Is it a coherent and international political force or a disparate and loosely analogous series of separate national movements? Certainly, these dichotomies are not all mutually exclusive positions but rather indicate some of the central issues in the analysis of fascism. In art history, scholars have focused on fascism as a political philosophy characterized by a systematic commitment to, for example, a nationalist, racist, militarist and anti-Marxist world view. National Socialist Germany, especially with its virulent anti-Semitism, is most often seen as an exceedingly brutal extreme of a fascist society. Having thus defined fascism ideologically, scholars then proceed to relate the interests of the Party and state to the cultural production under its control.[16] Art historians concentrate their analyses on a critique of the ideological content of particular works or on the *Gleichschaltung* (coordination) of artistic institutions.[17]

But this emphasis on ideological concerns needs to be extended to include an understanding of the developing political economic conditions that are key to analyzing the rise of fascism. The following pages demonstrate the centrality of the building economy as a factor in the consensus and contradiction inherent in the Nazi administration. Generally speaking, National Socialist leaders did not work from a consistent economic policy, implemented when Hitler came to power in 1933 and destroyed with the end of the war in 1945. Rather, for all their anti-capitalist rhetoric, the Nazi economy maintained essential components of the Weimar economic system (such as property relations). Throughout the 1930s and early 1940s, state and Party officials attempted to guide the economy through a series of crises and consolidations. Specific economic plans were adapted only over time and never completely to various ideological goals. In this sense, it is more accurate to talk of a nazification of the economy (including the building economy) rather than a structural transformation of capitalist conditions into fascist ones. This does not mean that we cannot discuss a fascist economics. Rather it means that the nature of fascist economics was adaptive and hence implemented in different ways depending on chronological developments and political strategy.[18]

In relation to an architectural history of the period, these political economic distinctions are necessary. To clarify the dynamic conflicts that characterized the development of the Nazi state helps to explain the radicalization of political involvement in the building economy.[19] By the late 1930s, the politicization of the building economy led to the privileging of specific materials as well as to struggles over labor markets. Multiple agencies exerted influence over this politically driven building economy, particularly as these agencies attempted to work around a system rife with labor and resource crises. Hence, to implement a large-scale architectural plan, architects had to become involved with the political regulation of the building economy; further, they tried to resolve many of the crises that affected their production process through direct policy initiatives. Hence, the political function of architecture is imbedded here in the economic conditions. This dynamic cannot be separated out from an art history of the period. A more comprehensive evaluation of political economy in relation to architecture is also a means of arguing for a fundamentally more comprehensive analysis of the function of art.

Situating the political function of architecture in a history of the conditions of production is not, of course, an issue specific to Nazi Germany or the SS. Production is, after all, about the mobilization of labor and resources in order to enact a particular goal, a process that extends to all the arts. Relevant here, how-ever, is how the production process concerning monumental architecture was limited or enabled by individual policies or structural conditions; in turn, it is a question of how that developing production process influenced seemingly non-artistic policies. This involves analyzing how specific individuals and agencies acted in relation to a changing array of structural political economic conditions. In National Socialist Germany, this process was an essentially polycratic one charac-terized by crises and conflicts of administrative interest but also consensus at particular times to promote specific shared goals.[20] Thus the structural and chronological analysis of production presented here must also include a critical evaluation of the agency of individuals and groups within this process.

As should be evident from this emphasis on production, my analysis develops from a Marxist tradition of historical materialist scholarship. Understanding the importance of production to a history of art foregrounds the struggles over access to resources and labor that characterize and differentiate various social epochs. Political and economic decisions by DEST administrators often derived from conflicts over the distribution of specific materials and sources of labor within the building economy. This process requires critical analysis of the conditions and the individuals who influenced its development, as well as the new contradictions or new crises produced as a result. In this case, to clarify the history of SS forced-labor enterprises is to understand the function of architecture in influencing the scale and timing of SS involvement in the architectural production process. The development of SS economic enterprises was extremely volatile and, more often than not, responsive to particular crises that occurred in the building economy, domestic programs and foreign policy. The SS attempted to resolve these crises through the application of more violence; this led, ultimately, to the self-destruction of its economic ventures. Issues concerning the function of production need to be foregrounded in order to clarify this dynamic for the DEST enterprises in the forced-labor camps. As Tim Mason observed in a different context, "The present wave of doubts about and within Marxism has many justifications, but none of them should lead to a wholesale abandonment of the basic *questions*, however many of the fascist answers may need to be radically revised or abandoned."[21] I would argue that the importance of the "basic question" of production needs to be considered not only in Nazi art historical studies but in art history as a whole.

An analysis of SS architectural policy contributes to a more comprehensive political history of art in National Socialist Germany. If we are to promote a critical political history of art, we must emphasize the functional relationship between art and politics, not just art's propagandistic or institutional significance. In this way, we can analyze the historical influence of artistic decisions on other state and Party policies. For the DEST enterprises, the design and construction process for the rebuilding of Berlin, the Party Rally Grounds at Nuremberg and the SS's own institutional architecture became crucial factors in their economic development. Certainly, the role of the SS as the extreme of the state's oppressive institutions warrants that it be thoroughly examined in any political history of Nazi Germany. That the SS also established economic goals in relation to the monumental building economy makes its absence from an inclusive political history of art impossible.

This question of the relationship between art and politics is not simply one of method and historical accuracy but takes on renewed urgency in the face of ongoing efforts to come to terms with the legacy of World War II and, more insidiously, to recuperate the careers of Nazi cultural figures (such as Arno Breker, Leni Riefenstahl and Albert Speer). Art history cannot be in the business of forgetting this past by separating cultural products from the implementation of state and Party policy. To confront such attempts, the following chapters analyze not only the architectural policy of the SS but also the pivotal role Speer occupied in this history. One final example highlights the importance of this political history of art: in 1985, the prominent architect Leon Krier published an expensive volume of

Speer's drawings with accompanying essays. In the frontispiece for this volume, Krier stated: "This book cannot disculpate the crimes of a regime or a man. Classical architecture and the passion of building are its only subject, its sole justification."[22] In spite of Krier's ideological and rhetorical caesura between architecture and politics, it was precisely the passion of building that was structurally related to the criminal capacity of the SS to carry out state policy in the forced-labor concentration camps under its control.

Chapter 2: The Interest of the SS in the Monumental Building Economy

As Albert Speer has written, the SS never efficiently maximized its use of forced labor even after 1942 when forced-labor operations were made a key part of centralized government wartime economic policy.[1] But such a retrospective assessment misrepresents a crucial point: while SS economic managers and on-site camp administrations never *efficiently* used their forced-labor population, this population nevertheless was coerced into functioning *productively*. The SS did not temper the punitive and brutal goal of the camps in suppressing supposed enemies of the Party and state in order to address the individual needs of the forced-laborer to make him more efficient. Rather, it was through the day-to-day oppression of individual prisoners that the productive goals of SS administrators came together with the punitive initiatives of the on-site camp personnel.

But for what end were productivity and punishment combined? From the founding of major forced-labor operations in 1938 until their reorientation to the armaments industry in 1942–3, the predominant answer to this question is: to provide materials for the monumental building economy. The building economy in general was one of the most dynamic sectors of growth in National Socialist Germany. Monumental projects favored by Hitler provided a high-profile symbolic focus to contemporary discussions concerning the strength of the German economy. As one of Hitler's major peacetime initiatives, the reconstruction of specific cities on a massive scale and with particular aesthetic materials (above all, stone) helped revive particular segments of the building economy, a revival that was thoroughly integrated with the broader policies of the state. Hence, an analysis of the involvement of SS companies in the production of building materials for individual monumental projects necessitates a triangulation of political, economic and architectural conditions. The effectiveness of the SS in linking its control over larger concentration camp populations, the productive output of these populations and the need for specific building materials can be critically assessed as material conditions for this moment in the political history of art. How these sometimes complementary, sometimes conflicting conditions developed is the subject of this chapter on the SS interest in the Nazi monumental building economy.

A history of the German Earth and Stone Works (DEST), the largest SS economic concern, affirms the connection of forced labor to state and Party architecture. DEST was set up in April 1938 to oversee the economic exploitation of concentration camp forced labor in the production of bricks and quarrying of stone. Through an institutional history, DEST's development as an important influence on the reorganization of the camps after 1936 comes most clearly into focus with its expansion in the early war years. DEST economic activity stepped up in this period due to increased numbers of prisoners from the occupied territories and SS attempts to wield more power in the National Socialist political hierarchy. KL Flossenbürg and KL Mauthausen, the first and largest stone-quarry concentration camps respectively, were used to assert SS authority both by producing stone for specific projects and by punishing various peoples designated as enemies of the state. By orienting DEST's production to the monumental architectural projects of Hitler and Speer, the SS competed in the expanding market for building materials and in the volatile political spheres of the Party and state.

Crucial to the development of the building materials enterprises in the concentration camps was the advantage DEST administrators took of developing political and economic conditions in the late 1930s and during the war. Oswald Pohl's SS economic managers worked opportunistically to secure any leverage that extended the SS's economic or political sphere of influence and to fight off encroachments on their authority from other administrations.[2] For it was only by taking advantage of changing conditions that the long-term goals of ensuring the permanence of concentration camps could be pursued. The permanence of the institutions would guarantee, by extension, the endurance of the SS itself as a political and economic force in National Socialist Germany. Simply put, SS policy for the labor camps remained somewhat flexible in order to adapt to changing circumstances and to use its increasing political authority most effectively.

After 1936, the SS set up the concentration camps to punish physically those deemed ideologically or politically threatening to the state and, in the process, to build up a stable position within the German peacetime economy. The production of building materials in these camps was an attempt by the SS to make a brutally inefficient operation economically viable. Concerns for the individual laborer were rarely addressed in this period whereas the potential productivity of the entire inmate population was of greatest interest to DEST's managers. Only through increasing production rates at camps such as Flossenbürg and Mauthausen could the decimation of the labor force continue to be justified in economic terms. The shrewd decision of Himmler and his advisors to target early on the privileged state and Party architectural projects as a potential market allowed for the focus on productivity late into the war. While other industries were forced to curtail their production or turn their enterprises over to armaments tasks, the SS retained its building materials industry through both its undiminished political authority and its economic orientation towards architectural policy. That this occurred at the expense of thousands of lives in the forced-labor camps is also part of the architectural history of National Socialist Germany.

THE DEVELOPMENT OF THE SS AND THE CONCENTRATION CAMP SYSTEM

The choice of the building economy was not a predictable one for SS admin-istrators; further, the use of forced labor for productive economic ends was of course neither an initial goal of the SS nor an impetus for the founding of the concentration camps. Rather, the interest in persecuting perceived enemies of the Party was only adapted to economic purposes after changes in the organization and administration of the camps as well as the development of the monumental building economy. The rise of forced labor as a driving force for the formulation of specific oppressive policies depended on key aspects of these early changes in the management of the camps.

A brief overview of the initial years of the concentration camp system indicates which developments would condition the introduction of DEST's forced-labor operations. When the National Socialist government came to power in 1933, the three main Party-controlled policing forces of the Gestapo, the SS and the SA all opened temporary concentration camps to incarcerate individuals opposed or threatening to the NSDAP. These camps allowed the Party to avoid the potentially hostile government response that would have resulted had Party members resorted to the state's established judicial and penal system. In the early stages of the concentration camps, the prisoners held there were almost exclusively political enemies from the German Communist Party or Social Democrats and union officials. Some felons were also put in the camps, though the politicals made up the vast majority of prisoners. The turn towards the secret police, the SS and the SA to crush the strongest elements of political opposition established early on the authoritarian character of the National Socialist state.[3]

German policing institutions, whether controlled by the state or by various Party groups, competed with one another for primacy in these years. By 1933, the SS had evolved from a small cadre of guards who protected Hitler in his appear-ances at public meetings in the Weimar Republic to become a formidable counter-balance to the SA. The year 1934 proved to be crucial for the SS in its pursuit of increased political authority in National Socialist Germany. In April, Hermann Göring made Himmler head of the powerful Gestapo in Prussia, and, after the purging of the SA in June of that year, Hitler elevated the SS to the status of an independent Party institution. As a result of these orders, the SS achieved total control over the concentration camps, securing the foundation of the eventual integration of the SS into the German state as the dominant policing force.[4]

When the SS took over the concentration camp system in 1934, the main camps were Columbiahaus, Dachau, Ersterwegen, Fuhlsbüttel, Lichtenburg, Oranienburg and Sachsenburg. Many of these camps were nothing more than warehouses acquired for the purpose of having detention centers separate from the German police. But Dachau became a model for subsequent larger con-centration camps because of its construction as an independent complex outside of a major urban area and its centralized administration. Dachau had early on been established as the training center for guards (the Death's Head Squads [SS

Totenkopfverbände]) under the leadership of Theodor Eicke. Himmler appointed Eicke in July 1934 to head the office of the Inspector of Concentration Camps and SS Guard Units (Inspekteur der Konzentrationslager und SS-Wachverbände [Inspekteur der KL]). In this role, he was responsible for preparing the guards and commandants and overseeing the administrative organization of the camps. Through the Inspekteur der KL and the Death's Head Squads, SS on-site camp personnel were trained in a quasi-military environment that emphasized the ideo-logical goals of camp punishment separate from considerations of administrative efficiency. Eicke, because of his influence in setting up Dachau, would be crucial for providing the model for further concentration camp development after 1936.[5]

Work at the camps was rarely systematically organized before 1936. Dachau formed the exception to this rule. In this camp, Eicke introduced cultivation and peat collecting in the moor by summer 1933, while also in that year various labor details were set up to provide for the general maintenance of the camp. At this stage of development, work served the purpose of making the camp as self-sustaining as possible. The SS also occasionally contracted out some small groups of prisoners to private firms. The labor details within the camp were headed by Kapos, that is, prisoners (usually drawn from the criminal population) who oversaw the work groups. Kapos retained their position as long as the labor details remained productive. If not, they were replaced or disciplined.[6]

Unrelated to the concentration camps, the SS also began early on to acquire private businesses which legitimated the ideological goals of the SS and promoted its independent position in the state. In December 1934, the SS purchased its first firm, the Nordland-Verlag, responsible for publishing SS tracts and other texts. A porcelain manufacturer, Porzellan-Manufaktur Allach, was also taken over by the SS in 1936 and used private labor for its concern near Dachau (though some prison labor was used later in the 1930s). Allach was one of Himmler's favorite projects and produced various figurines (soldiers, animals, etc.) to compete in the small but profitable German porcelain market. Throughout its history, the SS acquired a wide range of enterprises including works that produced mineral water, clothing, flower pots and other goods.[7] Enterprises that relied on private labor, however, were not the focus of SS economic activity after the reorganization of the camp system and the beginning of the production of building materials.

The increase in the size of the SS administration and its interest in private economic activity resulted in the organization of a new office in June 1935. Administratively part of Himmler's Personal Staff, the SS Administrative Office (SS-Verwaltungsamt) was created to deal with all budgetary considerations, economic enterprises, construction tasks, housing, clothing and other daily necessities of the SS. Himmler gave the leadership of this office to Oswald Pohl, who entered the SS in February 1934. Up until this time, Pohl had served as a naval officer and administrator. His political convictions were clear, however, as he had joined the NSDAP early on in 1926. With the development and extension of the Verwaltungsamt through the 1930s, Pohl began his quick rise to become one of the most powerful men in the SS (after Himmler and Heydrich).[8]

By 1935, the concentration camp system was organized and centralized in the SS offices in Berlin. Pohl had established control over a separate economic and administrative office for the potential exploitation of forced labor beyond the self-sustaining needs of the camps, and the SS as a policing institution was rapidly expanding its influence in Germany. In 1936, Hitler appointed Himmler as head of the German police force (controlled by the Ministry of the Interior) thus centralizing the state and Party policing apparatus. In the same year, the concentration camp system was reorganized on the Dachau model. The SS was clearly marked as an integral part of the National Socialist state. The question is, then, why did the SS specifically decide to use the output of forced labor for the monumental state and Party building projects, a decision that would affect both the enactment of economic goals and the consolidation of policing authority through the con-centration camps?

THE GERMAN BUILDING ECONOMY, 1933–8

The centralization of the SS administration and the systematization of the con-centration camps happened simultaneously with but separate from the resurgence of the German building economy. The German economy in general began sluggishly but significantly to pull out of its 1929 crash in the fall of 1932, months before Hitler came to power. In the initial recovery, however, unemploy-ment remained high, and National Socialist candidates made the issue central to their campaign promises and criticism of the Weimar Republic. Employment had significant political import because by 1932–3 only two out of every five people with a job in 1929 were still working. This ratio was even higher in some geographic areas of Germany with strong building industries. In the southern state of Bavaria, for example, rural crises and a disenchantment with the parliamentary democratic system proved influential in turning citizens to vote for the NSDAP in the 1932 elections (with support at just over 37 per cent in July 1932). But economic distress and unemployment became crucial factors as well for voters rejecting the republican political parties. As the largest sector of the Bavarian industrial economy, the building trades suffered from the Depression at even higher rates than many other comparable industries; according to the 1933 census, 39 per cent of building trade workers were unemployed.[9] A crucial campaign issue, the unemployment situation provided fodder for NSDAP leaders in general, and for propaganda aimed specifically at sectors of the building economy.

As a major concern of the new NSDAP regime, the unemployment situation and stimulation of production formed the core of economic policy as they had in the previous republican governments. From 1933 to 1936, work-creation schemes and the stimulation of trade were astonishingly successful in aiding the recovery of the German economy. But, as Richard Overy points out, this was less a result of instigating any particularly new kind of "fascist" economic policy as it was due to Hitler's decision to stimulate growth through directed government spending with the "linkage effects it produced and the stimulus it offered to particular areas of private business."[10] Such a policy was undertaken by any number of different political systems, from democratic to fascist. As with other regimes, Hitler also promoted the construction industry as a central component of this directed spending effort. In this regard, while no one sector of the economy was sufficient on its own for causing the recovery, construction grew at a much higher rate than the economy as a whole. As of 1932, RM 2 billion were invested in construction; by 1936, that number had multiplied to RM 9 billion with a concomitant employment of 2 million workers. The bulk of this construction was in new housing and road construction (particularly the *Autobahn*), but industrial and commercial construction as well as a few high-profile public buildings made a significant contribution to the overall economic effect. Government expenditure in the construction industry not only had the desired economic impact of stimulating businesses related to and reliant on building activity but also helped achieve the political goal of marking the NSDAP as the party that had brought Germany back from the economic brink.[11]

Through such means as work creation and directed state investment, the employment situation was eventually stabilized by 1936. At that time, the reverse problem arose of an increasing demand on the available labor pool. Public works projects (particularly the *Autobahn* and building construction) and the growing importance of armaments production as a percentage of total economic output strained the labor market even further.[12] NSDAP National Treasurer (Reichsschatzmeister) Franz Xaver Schwarz pointed out the continuing problem in a memorandum of 1939: "The lack of manpower, especially in the building economy, demands a planned use of the available manpower."[13] The competition for labor in these years had considerable influence on decisions concerning state and Party construction projects and there was infighting over labor allocation between government administrations pursuing individual and institutional interests. The emphasis on labor-intensive industries such as construction solved the unemployment situation but created other problems for the productivity of the German economy.[14] The worker shortage became a primary condition that affected the SS mobilization of forced labor in the concentration camps.

In addition to tight labor markets, the intensification of production in certain sectors of the economy led to shortages of key materials. By 1936, as preparations for war began to dominate state economic policy, attempts were made to correct these problems through the centralization of the distribution of material resources as well as the work force through Hermann Göring's Office of the Four Year Plan. In April 1936, Hitler appointed Göring to organize the economy and put all available state and Party institutions at his disposal. This resulted in Göring's Four Year Plan (announced at the Party Rally in September 1936) which promoted a rapid militarization of industry. The centralization of the allocation of workers and materials – the key to the plan's success – also increased the influence of the large private conglomerates involved in the military and economic drive. Though the German economy continued to operate under competitive market conditions, the conjunction of increased political control over the economy and the interests of the larger conglomerates tended towards a highly managed economic system, distinct from that of democratic industrial states and socialist economies.[15] This tendency helped a politically powerful institution like the SS to pursue its economic goals.

The same process of centralization affected the building industry, most intensely by the reduction of its access to iron and cement as well as the stricter control of labor markets. In addition to the implicit effect that the allocation of materials and labor for military industries had on supplies of each for other trades, the building industry became an institutionalized part of the Four Year Plan when Göring on 9 December 1938 named Fritz Todt as the General Plenipotentiary for the Regulation of the Building Economy (Generalbevollmächtigter für die Regelung der Bauwirtschaft [GBBau]). Todt, who had previously organized the building of the West Wall (a series of bunkers and defenses on the western border of Germany), became responsible for the construction of all necessary military projects, important armaments factory sites, canals, *Autobahn*, railroads and housing estates for workers in Four Year Plan firms. The GBBau also secured materials and workers for those concerns determined crucial to national defense. Finally, Todt's administration was meant to manage the construction of the designated monumental building projects in Berlin, Nuremberg and Munich. Though Speer saw to it that Todt was never able to bring the control of the city rebuilding projects under his jurisdiction, Todt's grip on the iron market and worker allocation in particular made the GBBau central to monumental building schemes in Germany.[16]

As a high-profile segment of the building economy, monumental Party and state construction prospered from the initial impetus to direct government spending towards building; yet after 1936, such construction was also restricted by the crisis in labor markets and limitations on materials. Hence, aesthetic choices combined with political economic policies. This situation can be elucidated by looking at the stone industry, stone being the key aesthetic material promoted by Hitler and his architects. Paul Ludwig Troost's House of German Art (Haus der deutschen Kunst [Figure 1]) in Munich, Hitler's first major commission after he came to power in 1933, relied on vast quantities of German limestone for its façade, a material Hitler had chosen himself. Hitler also influenced Werner March's use of stone instead of steel and glass in his re-working of the initial design for the Olympic Stadium (1936 [Figure 2]) in Berlin. In these cases as in others, Hitler's belief in the permanence of stone and its connection (unlike modernist structures) to a craft tradition which he associated with powerful political regimes and a "German" style obviously influenced aesthetic choices made by state and Party architects. Though many types of buildings and materials were used throughout the National Socialist period, the high-profile projects of the Party and state remained exclusively stone buildings with modified neo-classical forms.[17]

Moreover, the most important projects were constructed almost in their entirety from granite, limestone and marble. In Nuremberg and in Berlin, Hitler's direct approval via Speer was required for major designs, and they both consistently favored granite or limestone façades with marble interiors or detailing, as was the case with Speer's New Reich Chancellery. These preferences for stone led to a

Figure 1
PAUL LUDWIG TROOST, HOUSE OF
GERMAN ART, MUNICH, 1933–7
Source: G. Troost, *Bauen im neuen Reich*, 1938

Figure 2
WERNER MARCH, OLYMPIC
STADIUM, BERLIN, 1936
Source: G. Troost, *Bauen im neuen Reich*, 1938

strong revival of the quarrying industry up to the outbreak of war in 1939, but only for specific types of stone. For example, in a letter of April 1937 from the Labor Ministry to the NSDAP administration for Koblenz-Trier, the local basalt industry was cited as one area of stone production where conditions were becoming worse because of a lack of government contracts.[18] The building materials market, when it came to stone, depended on aesthetic decisions made by Party and state leaders who, in turn, took their cues from Hitler and his architect Speer.

But in spite of exceptions, the stone industry prospered with the broader state economic policies. By 1936, industry specialists had already noted a significant increase in the production of marble, granite and limestone as a result of state-directed funding. Further, one critic noted that the reliance on foreign stone imports had been greatly reduced in favor of a renewed emphasis on production within Germany itself (autarky being one of Hitler's key nationalist policies).[19] Such optimism was tempered only after 1936 when even architectural-quality stone had to be registered with the state to monitor its production, and the work force came under the same pressure as in other industries in the German economy. Particularly of concern was where the new generation of laborers was going to come from, i.e. the apprentices for stone masonry, quarrying work and construction.[20] The conclusion that we can reach from this situation is that the increase in the political management of the economy resulting from Göring's Four Year Plan significantly affected seemingly non-military industries that nevertheless also relied on labor-intensive work and the use of specific materials. Clearly, by the late 1930s, the stone industry and architects working on monumental projects were feeling just such an effect.

All in all, then, when the SS set up its economic concerns, the building industry was subject to political manipulation by state and Party institutions greatly stressed by the huge demands of rearmament and architectural policy. Gradual centralization of the industry allowed for the protection of fewer and fewer projects and for a concentration on those enterprises deemed absolutely crucial to the state. Further, the pressure on employment markets left the private economy and state projects eager for ways to maximize the output of a limited labor force. A building economy faced with restrictions on its workers and the kinds of materials available for construction as well as expanding in all sectors provided an opportunity for an institution like the SS that unilaterally controlled people in its camps. It indicated a potential choice for SS economic administrators newly concerned after 1936 with directing the abuse of those people to the broader German economy.

SS CONCENTRATION CAMPS AND THE FORMATION OF DEST

Demands placed on the German economy due to the Four Year Plan came about just as the SS had consolidated its power over the entire police force of Germany and was reorganizing the concentration camp system. When Hitler appointed Himmler to head the German police in June 1936, Theodor Eicke had already been working for two years on planning the construction of large institutions throughout the Reich based on the model of KL Dachau. These plans for consolidation and expansion were fully implemented after Himmler's appointment. By August 1936, the camps at Oranienburg, Fuhlsbüttel, Esterwegen and Columbiahaus had been consolidated into the facility at KL Sachsenhausen just outside of Berlin. A year later, the SS closed down Sachsenburg and moved its prisoners to the new camp at KL Buchenwald near Weimar. Buchenwald and Sachsenhausen were modeled after Dachau in their administrative structure and their capacity to hold up to 8,000 prisoners each. The other remaining camp, KL Lichtenburg, had been reserved exclusively for women since the summer of 1937.[21]

The extension of the camps and choice of sites indicate that Himmler's goal was not simply to set up an effective penal system but to establish the long-term viability of the camps as political and economic tools of the SS. Inmate populations in 1934 and 1935 had been steadily decreasing as the initial political prisoners arrested after January 1933 were released. Planning for larger camps depended in 1936–7 on a view of their permanent importance to the state as well as on the potential prison populations determined from ideological criteria. Economically, Sachsenhausen and Buchenwald were chosen for their proximity not only to population centers (Prussia, Saxony/Thuringia), but also to clay deposits suitable for brick making. Early on, the SS oriented these camps to their potential production of materials for the building industry. In the case of Buchenwald, for example, the location near Weimar was suggested by the Thuringian Geological Provincial Examination office (Thüringische Geologische Landesuntersuchung) because of the availability of clay deposits. It was only after this suggestion that Eicke and Pohl made a visit to the site in May 1937 and approved the location of a camp here.[22] In 1937, these economic plans remained vague in terms of how they were to be implemented; nevertheless, the interest in the economic use of forced labor for the building economy influenced this extension of the concentration camp system.

For Eicke, and seemingly for Himmler as well, the founding of Buchenwald and Sachsenhausen was first and foremost a manifestation of the political gains achieved by the SS in 1935–6. Economic goals remained secondary (and Pohl remained in the background) while the SS consolidated its power to regulate German society through policing institutions. Himmler had fought off the Justice and Interior Ministries' attempts to establish authority over the concentration camps and had received Hitler's approval to make the camps permanent institutions. Finally, the extension of arrest categories after 1936 enhanced the necessity for the KL by drastically increasing the numbers of inmates. The largest extension of categories occurred only after Himmler gained control of the police and reorganized the camps in 1936. Through a series of orders and laws from 1937–8, the SS began defining and arresting occupational criminals, so-called asocials (beggars, Sinti and Roma [Zigeuner], vagrants, prostitutes, alcoholics and others), homosexuals and Jehovah's Witnesses. Himmler based these extra-juridical arrests on the Law for the Protection of the People and State (Gesetz zum Schutz von Volk und Staat) of February 1933. First enacted to legitimize the arrest of large numbers of Communists after the burning of the Reichstag, the SS used this law to lay its hands on all people who were seen as destructive to the Party or state. The exact categorization of those arrested was left up to the local police and Gestapo officials. With Hitler's approval in hand, the SS had gained not only an established control over policing institutions but also had increased its ability to punish and incarcerate greater numbers of people cast as political or ideological enemies.[23] Through such means, the SS legitimated once again the need for the concentration camp system which it unilaterally controlled.

The political authority won by the SS allowed for the pursuit of other interests that would contribute to the consolidation of the concentration camps as integral institutions in the German state. By 1937, Himmler, through his administrator Pohl, began to place increasing emphasis on securing the permanence of the camps by adapting them to a comprehensive economic program. It was already clear to Himmler that larger camps would be needed in times of war, but a growing emphasis on economic enterprises would give the SS a reason to expand the camps in peacetime as well. Though the intent to exploit penal labor was part of the organization of the camps from the very beginning, it was only in 1937–8 that the SS addressed the economic potential of forced labor as a key means of guaranteeing its role in a peacetime Germany. After regulations concerning who could be taken into custody were broadened, the SS could and did actively target prisoners who met its economic needs. The opening of KL Buchenwald, for example, was aided by a direct order in June 1938 from Reinhard Heydrich, chief of the SS-Reich Central Security Office (Reichssicherheitshauptamt [RSHA]), to the effect that every local police district arrest at least 200 male so-called asocials who also were considered ready and able to work. Through such measures, Buchenwald's population rose from an initial 2,295 inmates in August 1937 to 7,776 one year later.[24] Prepared as they were to select prisoners based on political, ideological and economic criteria, the SS could attempt to maximize its economic potential. This policy was also clearly in line with the need to extend the productivity of all labor as defined by the state's economic goals and those of Göring's Four Year Plan.[25]

Extending the function of the camps to include grander schemes of developing an economic empire occurred first with the brickworks established at Buchenwald and Sachsenhausen in 1938. It was in 1937–8, again a time when severe labor and material shortages were common, that the SS began seriously to orient forced-labor operations to the building materials market. At first, SS brickworks were linked only to the necessities of the Four Year Plan. For example, Hellmuth Gommlich (Minister of the Interior in Thuringia) wrote in a letter of 24 April 1937: "The camp inmates should be occupied, within the framework of the Four Year Plan, with the production of bricks."[26] Yet by the time construction began on the brickworks in 1938, the SS had turned to the more exclusive and increasingly powerful patronage of Speer by linking the quarries and some of the brickworks to Speer's needs as head of the Inspector General of Building for the Reich Capital Berlin (Generalbauinspektor für die Reichshauptstadt Berlin [GBI]).

The decision to focus the majority of forced-labor operations on the production of large-scale brickworks and stone quarries came at the initial meeting of Speer, Himmler and Hitler, that occurred after Buchenwald opened in July 1937 but before Pohl's trip to Flossenbürg and Mauthausen in March 1938.[27] With the support of Speer and Hitler, the use of the prisoners to make bricks and to quarry stone became institutionalized in the founding of DEST on 29 April 1938. The business was officially registered on 10 June 1938 under the management of SS-Obersturmbannführer Arthur Ahrens (who in September 1938 appointed

SS-Standartenführer Walter Salpeter as deputy manager). Two agents (procurators) were also named, SS-Hauptsturmführer Hans Mummenthey and SS-Untersturmführer Hans Clemens Tietjen. On paper, the business always had a double organization. DEST personnel administered the concern as a private enterprise but, as SS members, they were also politically responsible to the SS-Verwaltungsamt under Pohl, although at this stage Pohl played little more than an overseeing role in the firm.[28]

The goals of DEST were spelled out in the corporate resolution (*Gesellschaftsvertrag*): (1) the opening of stone quarries and quarrying of natural stone;[29] (2) the production of bricks; (3) street building (later dropped as a potential assignment); and (4) the running or acquiring of other enterprises related to quarrying or brick making. These goals were set up not only to "re-educate" the inmates of the concentration camps but also, in the process of punishment, to serve the massive demands of the German construction industry. Mummenthey, in a report on the organization of the administration of DEST in July 1940, stated the goal succinctly: "In the general interest, its [DEST's] task primarily consists in employing the labor power of the concentration camp prisoners for the job of the production of building materials."[30]

But such a company was of dubious legality as it involved a Party institution getting involved with the private economy, a point that had been ignored with the small-scale operations prior to 1937–8 but now became of crucial importance to the NSDAP Treasurer Schwarz as the SS expanded into national building materials markets. The German state had such a restriction on economic activity precisely because, among other reasons, a political institution was perceived to have an unfair advantage and, hence, must be banned from investing in the private market. SS administrators avoided this criticism by using the loophole that their concerns were not, like private businesses, engaged in maximization of profit but rather served the dual political goals of punishing or "reforming" inmates through labor as well as providing needed materials for the monumental building projects prioritized by Hitler. Specifically, Speer's plans for Berlin (Figure 3) were continuously cited by the SS in its reports and contracts as a justification for the unlawful entry of a Party institution into private business. For example, in a memorandum of 15 June 1938 sent to Schwarz from his staff, Pohl is quoted as defending the legality and purpose of the brickworks at Buchenwald and Sachsenhausen. Pohl declared that the SS entry into the brick-making business was justified in two ways: (1) to keep the inmates busy, especially as the recent annexation of Austria had greatly contributed to the number of prisoners; and (2) to supply Speer with building materials for the "Führerbauten," as the output of the German brick-making industry could meet only 18 per cent of Speer's need of 2 billion bricks a year.[31] The memorandum indicates how the SS justified its economic operations by pointing to Speer's special needs as well as casting its enterprise in terms of the political function of managing the prison population. With this cultural and political legitimization, no mention need be made of legal debates.

Figure 3
ALBERT SPEER, MODEL OF THE
NORTH–SOUTH AXIS, BERLIN,
c. 1940
Source: Ullstein Bilderdienst

Administratively, DEST was organized at first under Pohl's SS-Verwaltungsamt. However, with the rapid expansion of the economic enterprises, this office quickly developed into the SS-Central Administration and Economic Office (Hauptamt Verwaltung und Wirtschaft [SS-HAVW]), established 20 April 1939 on the organizational model of Heydrich's RSHA. Unlike the SS-Verwaltungsamt, which only had jurisdiction within the SS itself, a Hauptamt had a dual status as a Party position (e.g. overseeing the administrative organization of the SS and its concerns) and a position within the Ministry of the Interior (e.g. administering finances of the state for the formation of an SS army and the KL). The HAVW had three divisions corresponding to Pohl's areas of authority: legal, economic and a department for the inspection of all SS administrations and concerns. The economic division oversaw the bureaus that managed the SS-controlled businesses. Eight of these bureaus existed by 1940, covering the building materials firms in the Reich and occupied territory, the porcelain works, the mineral water works and the other SS concerns.[32] DEST itself made up Amt W III A/1 in the economic division.

This reorganization came also as Pohl was professionalizing the managerial staff of the SS economic division especially in the face of bungled operations in the first year of DEST.[33] Although he was a brickworks owner before he came to the SS, Ahrens proved to be a disaster as a leader of DEST, and in 1939 Pohl replaced him with Salpeter, a man who came to the job prepared with administrative and financial management experience. Salpeter, assisted by Mummenthey, directly administered the enterprise. Amt W III A/1 was further broken down into the two main divisions of the brickworks under the leadership of Erduin Schondorff, and the granite works under Heinz Schwarz, both of whom were technical professionals in their fields. The administrative breakdown indicates the way the SS rationalized management of production and centralized the direction of the enterprises in its economic administration. While ideologically committed to the punishment of inmates, Pohl's economic administrators also focused on ways of increasing the output of DEST by concentrating on the economic organization of the operations.[34]

Although set up in April 1938, DEST lacked significant funding for development in the concentration camps until a major contract was signed with the GBI on 1 July 1938. This was to be the first of many contracts, large and small, that the SS made and attempted to make with the GBI, establishing a predominantly architectural orientation to DEST's economic concerns. The GBI agreed to extend RM 9.5 million in credit to DEST in 1938 in exchange for deliveries of at least 120 million bricks annually over a ten-year period from the brickworks at KL Sachsenhausen. So clearly connected was the enterprise to state architectural policy that Speer even took credit for suggesting the construction of a brickworks for Berlin when funding became an issue with the Economic Ministry after the initial contract was signed. (Notably, Speer repeatedly emphasized in his post-war work that SS economic aspirations were entirely motivated by administrators within the SS. He avoided in his writing all mention of GBI initiatives with the SS.)[35] The delivery of bricks was to begin by October 1938. However, due to problems that immediately beset production at Sachsenhausen, the GBI had paid less than RM 6 million of its promised support. In a renegotiated contract signed by Speer, Pohl, Salpeter and Mummenthey on 27 August 1940, the terms of the original agreement were somewhat altered. The GBI promised to pay DEST RM 10 million (minus what had already been paid) on annual deliveries of 100 million core bricks and 20 million façade bricks. This new contract came at a time when the confidence in victory during the war reached its peak and the viability of the KL firms had to be reasserted after the failure of the new brick-making technology at Sachsenhausen. Whereas the original contract simply listed the terms of agreement, the later contract specifically linked the public interests of the SS and state architectural policy: the brickworks at Sachsenhausen was set up to "occupy" the prisoners of the KL and, simultaneously, to "help out" with the great pressures placed on the building materials industry by the rebuilding of Berlin.[36]

The GBI was the first and largest single patron of DEST during its entire history as a provider of building materials. Beginning with base payments in 1938 for pre-approved brick orders and additional payments through 1941 totaling over RM 9 million, no other customer was so crucial to DEST's success. Though credit funds were received from other sources including the Reichsbank, the GBI retained its role as the predominant architectural client through its payments to the SS.[37] Financing the enterprises at the camps rested largely on the advantage taken by the SS of the GBI's need for an ever larger share of the building materials market in Germany.

Bank credits and advances from the GBI allowed the SS to build and develop its ventures from 1938 to the beginning of the war in September 1939. Construction had begun on the brickworks at KL Sachsenhausen and Buchenwald by the summer of 1938 and the initial quarries at KL Flossenbürg and Mauthausen were either leased or acquired by this time. The 1938 annual report shows a loss, but in 1939 the operating budget jumped and a small profit of RM 135,850 was achieved. These initially optimistic figures were compromised by the mistakes made at KL Sachsenhausen, but nevertheless reflect the growth of the concerns. Payments were also received in these years for relatively small orders from (among others) the *Reichsautobahn* and the "Buildings at Adolf Hitler Platz" Association in Weimar. Both of these orders were for stone, the brickworks not yet being operational, and indicate the relative success of the granite works in this period (profit of over RM 390,000) in relation to the brickworks (loss of more than RM 390,000).[38] Thus, by the time the war began, four of the six concentration camps were producing or being readied to produce building materials, some of which were already making their way to the monumental building projects of the Party and state. The SS attempt to obtain a major share of the building materials industry in Germany was well under way before September 1939 due to consistent financial backing and the increased authority to arrest extended categories of people. With Speer's GBI and the centralized organization of the seemingly unlimited forced labor, these concentration camps were filled and the inmates put to work.

DEST AND THE MONUMENTAL BUILDING ECONOMY DURING THE WAR

The outbreak of war in September 1939 did little to dampen the development of DEST and the pursuit by the SS of a share in the German building economy. Not only did the SS expect the war to end quickly, but it had been exempted from turning over its economic operations to armaments industries. Hence, DEST extended its operations, acquired new quarry sites and brick-making facilities and directed its production to specific monumental projects. Punishing prisoners through the development of the forced-labor camps continued at a rapid pace.

Three periods of economic activity can be distinguished, which correspond to state architectural policy, economic conditions and military circumstances. First, the quarries and brickworks went through a phase of accelerated expansion geared to the production of architectural materials (1939–42). Second, DEST, in its attempts to be flexible in the face of military setbacks, extended only particular works based on the shrinking number of architectural projects (1942–3). Finally, DEST redirected labor and resources towards the armaments industry economy, though it still had access to the occasional commission for architectural materials (1943–4). With its authority extended through greater policing powers gained during the war, the SS took advantage of the crucial importance of architectural policy to the state and adapted to the economic crises and priorities inherent in a wartime market economy.[39]

With the intent to achieve Nazi ideological and military goals, the war led to further political management of the private economy. The regulation of wages, costs of basic materials, etc., became central factors for the military economy. But the difference between pre- and post-1939 was significant; not only were certain production costs fixed but the state also implemented increasingly stringent measures in terms of the prioritization of "useful" projects. That is to say, a clear hierarchy was established based on determining the necessity of the project to the war effort and, from the business side, the effectiveness of the firm at carrying through the project. A firm's ability to compete was based less on competitive pricing and more on productivity. In such a situation, the larger firms – particularly the cartels – were favored as they had the means to maximize productivity with their expansive use of resources and mobilization of labor.[40]

The building economy was no different. In the optimistic war years before 1942, articles in the architectural trade journal of *Der Deutsche Baumeister* emphasized the need of architects to become more knowledgeable about the use of diverse building materials, the availability of building materials and the relation between the building economy and the war effort. But as most materials were already regulated by the GBBau, the variable of greatest concern to the building economy was the labor force. Already within the first war year, the state encouraged architects and construction professionals to maximize labor output at all costs. While the curtailment of peacetime building projects during the war (excepting after June 1940 Hitler's favored projects for Berlin, Nuremberg, Munich, Linz and Hamburg) led to some relief from the worker shortage in other areas of the building economy, construction was seriously threatened by the loss of skilled and unskilled workers to the military. Replacements needed to be found, and state officials discussed publicly the use of more foreign civilian labor from occupied territories and the use of prisoners of war. In article after article, professionals emphasized the quantity and quality of the labor force as the most pressing need in the war economy and, up to 1942, for the presumed post-war needs of the monumental building projects which seemed to be only a battle victory or two away. Thus, in the early war years, the efficient use of regulated materials as well as the expansion and maximization of labor productivity dominated the concerns of the state and its architects. At least up until the clear military setbacks on the Eastern Front, such concerns were used to urge architects and construction managers to prioritize their efforts in order to pursue the goals both of the wartime building economy and Hitler's favored architectural projects.[41]

Such an emphasis on productivity and specific monumental projects proved useful for DEST administrators in their efforts to expand their economic operations. In contrast to other industries that were immediately affected by restrictions due to the war, SS ventures were negatively influenced more by the failure of the new brick-making process implemented at the KL Sachsenhausen facility (named Oranienburg I) than by external factors. This brickworks' technological failure resulted in the need to rebuild the facility and became the basis for the formulation of SS economic strategy in 1939–40. For example, in July 1940, Pohl decided on the advice of Salpeter and Hans Hohberg to collect the majority of SS firms in a holding company called the German Economic Concerns (Deutsche Wirtschaftsbetriebe GmbH [DWB]). The immediate purpose of the organization was to offset DEST's losses at Oranienburg I with the collective profits from other SS firms. The reorganization allowed the SS to reduce taxes on the individual profit-making concerns. Hohberg more generally introduced modern accounting techniques and other practices gained from his pre-SS knowledge of management and administration.[42] Thus, the SS rationalized its enterprises in 1940, becoming more efficient by using business practices of private industry (like the holding company) to cut costs and raise levels of production.

This rationalization helped the development of DEST, though it faced a loss based on the performance of the brickworks. The operating budget gained in relation to the previous year, and monthly production at Mauthausen and Flossenbürg slowly increased. Both of these camps began to show a profit well above the proceeds of the brickworks. The GBI agreed to pay an additional RM 5 million in credit towards DEST's operating budget, RM 1 million of which was designated for the granite works in May 1940. Further payments were agreed upon for the brickworks in a new contract of August 1940 between the GBI and DEST. The augmentation of funds, and small but growing profit in the granite works, contributed to the general optimism among the officials of DEST in this first war year, leading Himmler in October 1940 to order an increase in production. At the end of the budget year, Salpeter stated that the leadership of DEST had operated on the assumption that the war would end victoriously by late fall 1940 and be followed by an unimaginable rise in the need for building materials. DEST attempted to position its firms to take advantage of this need.[43]

As the GBI financing indicates, much of the development costs of DEST and the promise of its continued success during the war was linked to the brickworks and their potential capacity to provide a stable basis of productive activity for the peacetime years to come. Aside from the Oranienburg work at Sachsenhausen and the Berlstedt work at Buchenwald, the SS had also acquired a brickworks near Hamburg in 1938 that led to the planned development and creation of KL Neuengamme in 1940. Two other brickworks within the Reich were purchased in the first years of the war near KL Stutthof (Danzig) and Prambachkirchen near Linz. Prambachkirchen, however, did not use prison labor and quickly focused its production on armaments tasks.[44]

Hitler furthered the SS expansion into the brick industry when he appointed Himmler to the post of Reich Commissioner for the Consolidation of German Nationhood (Reichskommissar für die Festigung Deutschen Volkstums) in December 1939. In this position, Himmler was given exclusive authority over all brickworks in the occupied territories that were not owned or controlled by German citizens or by people of German descent. Salpeter administered the takeover of these properties through the new concern of the East German Brickworks (Ostdeutsche Ziegeleibetriebs GmbH). By May 1940, the works included those at Bielitz, Kalisch, Posen, Zichenau and the ghetto at Lodz (Litzmannstadt). Though not centered around concentration camps, the eastern brickworks nevertheless often had brutal labor conditions and extreme production schedules carried out by Polish civilians or Jewish forced labor. The SS planned to use these brickworks particularly to establish building brigades later in the war for its own construction projects in the occupied territory. As in 1935–6, the increased political authority of the SS was followed by grander schemes for economic development.[45]

Bricks were important to the German building industry because of the restrictions placed particularly on iron first by Göring's Four Year Plan and then the material needs of the war economy. Ideologically, the construction of brick buildings was often associated with local architectural projects (such as those in Hamburg) or with particular "German" academic traditions (most notably, that of Schinkel). However, SS production never centered on high-quality bricks necessary for façade work except at KL Neuengamme, where the clay deposits were particularly good. Though aspiring to tap the market for façade bricks, the SS quickly reconciled itself to producing bricks in most of the works that would mainly serve as structural material.[46]

Whereas the brickworks provided the impetus for the SS's entrance into the building materials industry, the stone quarries were more specifically aligned with particular building projects. As a result, they had a greater rate of success in meeting DEST's economic goals. In addition to Mauthausen and Flossenbürg, KL Natzweiler and KL Gross-Rosen were also set up around quarry systems in 1940. A quarry at Marburg was acquired by DEST in 1942, though it employed only civilians. DEST, under the guidance of Speer's administration, also set up a stone-processing center (Oranienburg II) in 1941 near KL Sachsenhausen. Oranienburg II used prisoners to cut stone in preparation for the monumental building projects in Berlin. The SS created similar stone-mason programs for inmates at Flossenbürg, Gross-Rosen and Natzweiler.[47] Himmler and Pohl's decision to erect a system of quarries connected to concentration camp labor was quite practical in relation to the overwhelming importance of stone to the monumental buildings in National Socialist Germany. It also corresponded to the general conditions of the early-war building economy in which Hitler continued to privilege his high-profile projects.

It is thus hardly surprising that DEST quarries were sited on high-quality granite deposits. The SS specifically targeted the monumental representational building sites, acquiring contracts for (among others) the German Stadium in Nuremberg and the Soldiers' Hall in Berlin. Speer also advised DEST managers in choosing sites based on the type of granite for Natzweiler and Gross-Rosen, and possibly for Flossenbürg and Mauthausen as well. The focus of quarrying efforts on Hitler and Speer's major projects also provided a reason for justifying further developmental funds for DEST, funds which could be related only to the potential output of the brickworks. From 1938 to 1943, the total turnover of the granite works was at least double that of the brick producers.[48] Though bricks were always a crucial component of the production plans, DEST's quarries were connected more consistently with specific monumental state and Party projects. This optimism concerning the productivity of the quarries and the expansion of DEST's concerns coincided with enlarged camp populations resulting from the extension of Gestapo and police authority to arrest individuals for reasons of "internal state security during the war."[49] The political function of the camps coincided with the economic adaptation of DEST enterprises to the military situation and the wartime building economy's focus on labor and productivity.

Nevertheless, the simultaneous expansion of DEST enterprises and centralization of administration at the beginning of the war did not go unchallenged. In 1940, the Finance Ministry confronted Pohl with the need to raise SS payments to the state for support of prisoners engaged in laboring for SS concerns. This issue was central to the ability of the SS to use almost all of its revenue for development rather than for the welfare of the laborers. Discussion of this issue took place at a meeting between the SS and the Finance Ministry on 20 October 1940. Until this time, SS payments to the state of RM 0.30 per inmate per day were meant as a means of funding the upkeep of the inmates and institutions. Finance Ministry representatives compared SS payments to the RM 3.00–4.50 per prisoner per day paid by the judicial prison system in an attempt to convince the SS that it, too, had to raise its support. They also noted that prisoners hired out to armaments firms and private businesses netted the Waffen-SS RM 5.00–6.00 per day. This amount went directly into funds controlled by Pohl. Though the Finance Ministry wanted to limit SS revenue and force it to abide by restrictions like the judicial penal institutions, the meeting produced only a promise to take the matter up in the 1941 budget year.[50] That the issue was raised at all, however, indicates the kind of administrative maneuvering typical of the National Socialist government which, in this case, attempted to limit the growing economic power of the SS – in vain, as it turned out.

In addition to the administrative and technical challenges faced by the SS in 1940, Germany's failure to defeat the British air force in the fall indicated that the war would continue for some time. Yet, throughout 1941, DEST persisted in expanding its economic activities in order to position itself more strongly in the market for building materials. As long as the military successes (especially in France and at the beginning of the Soviet campaign in 1941) were more frequent than defeats, building professionals could still talk about the demands of the monumental building projects, and SS economic administrators remained opti-mistic about the extension of their empire. In a report from the HAVW early in 1941, goals continued to be set confidently, not only in relation to the development of the enterprises but also to the German building market as a whole. DEST meant to increase production of stone in the granite works by 30 per cent, securing a 12.5 per cent share of the German granite industry, the largest of any firm. The stone-processing center of Oranienburg II and the quarry at Natzweiler were also scheduled to open this year. The HAVW set goals for the brickworks as well: Oranienburg I at Sachsenhausen was to be brought up to half its total production capacity, Buchenwald's output was to increase qualitatively and quantitatively and Neuengamme was to be completed.[51] DEST requested funding for these developments from the Deutsche Golddiskontbank through the Reichsbank, receiving an RM 8 million credit in May 1941.[52]

Production increased noticeably, though not at the rate projected by the HAVW. Mauthausen doubled its rate while Flossenbürg remained relatively even. Gross-Rosen continued to develop but slowly, and the brickworks still had technical problems though they were producing. DEST, on the basis of sales and develop-ment, resumed talks with the GBI for further stone contracts. At this stage, as Salpeter wrote to Mummenthey, top priority was given to making the concerns ready to take advantage of the rush on the building materials market expected as soon as the war ended.[53] The loss for the year totaled over RM 3.3 million as the costs for rebuilding Sachsenhausen were absorbed, while turnover reached above RM 2.1 million, once again mostly from the granite works.[54]

The SS could continue production in 1941 based on the function of the forced-labor camps as oppressive institutions and on Hitler's decision to favor certain sectors of the monumental building economy. Yet economic exceptions granted to DEST because of the political function of the concentration camps once again came up as an issue in the administrative struggle over tax regulations with the Stone and Earth Economic Division (Wirtschaftsgruppe Steine und Erde) in the Reich Economic Professional Organization (Reichswirtschaftskammer). In January and February 1941, Schondorff, for DEST, wrote to the Economic Professional Organizations that DEST should be freed from paying any export-extraction duties on its products. Schondorff justified this position by stating that DEST represented no competitive threat to private concerns. Prisoners produced bad quality work and the costs such as watch personnel were significantly higher than those in the private sector. Furthermore, DEST should be freed from paying the duties because judicial prisons were not required to pay taxes on goods produced.[55] Whereas previously DEST administrators had drawn a distinction between the concentration camps and prisons of the judicial system (as with prison laborer support payments), now they were relating the two and playing down all notions of income. The flexibility to redefine the enterprises was meant here as before to establish SS control over the largest share of development income available through the manipulation of its labor camps.

The Reich Economic Professional Organization ultimately rejected DEST's request, claiming that DEST was too big and would disrupt the competition in the market whatever the claims to the opposite might be. As a registered private concern, DEST had to follow the rules set up by the Ministry of Economics for other members of the organization. However, as a compromise, a flat-rate payment on earned revenue was suggested for DEST similar to that paid by the air transport industry.[56] But even with this compromise, the Economic Professional Organization showed itself to be fully aware of DEST's potential to achieve the aims that Himmler himself had envisioned: a substantial share in the building materials market.

DEST's expansion and its consistent struggles with other administrations led in September 1941 to the reorganization and further rationalization of the HAVW. All concerns of the SS were placed in Amt W, the granite quarries and brickworks being assigned Amt W I under Salpeter assisted by Mummenthey. (Salpeter had been called up for war duty, so Mummenthey continued as the actual leader.) These changes were short-lived but important for the final manifestation of the SS economic administration in the form of the SS Economic and Administrative Central Office (Wirtschafts- und Verwaltungshauptamt [WVHA]), founded in February 1942. The WVHA united the administrations of the SS Central Budget and Building Office (Hauptamt Haushalt und Bauten [HAHuB]) and the HAVW, forming one organizational entity for all administrative and economic concerns. Such a reorganization corresponded to the unprecedented plans for SS control over expansion and settlement in the east as well as the growing pressures for mass mobilization placed on the German war economy, particularly by the armaments industries. The reorganization was further a result of SS administrators still being optimistic about a potential post-war building market and plans proposed for their own massive institutional building needs in the post-war German order. With the rise in requests for forced labor from armaments industries as well as the expansion of SS enterprises, Pohl could now place the administration of these tasks under a prioritized and rationalized economic policy.[57]

This reorganization proved successful for increasing the ability of the SS to adapt to wartime economic conditions and simultaneously to extend its economic operations. Since Speer turned away from architecture after his appointment in February 1942 as Minister of Armaments and Munitions Production and head of the GBBau, he delegated most of his architectural duties to his staff.[58] The important market planned for SS building materials – especially the state projects of Berlin, Nuremberg and Linz – appeared to be losing support from those planning the wartime economy. Hence, Pohl's rationalization extended his ability to act in all areas of the SS use of forced labor and became crucial as the priority given to architectural policy crumbled in the face of mounting difficulties posed by the war. DEST was still an important component but only one of the myriad and expansive goals set by the WVHA.

In 1942 some monumental building project managers were still ordering materials and the perceived need for stone and bricks in the potential post-war building economy provided enough impetus for the continued development of DEST concerns. During 1942, the SS consolidated its hold on properties that it had previously leased or administered and took over the management of several new concerns. Stutthof, a camp outside of Danzig, was made an independent KL in April 1942 and two brickworks were purchased there and nearby at Hopehill. Stutthof concentrated on brick production, while Hopehill also produced roofing tiles and ceramic pipes. The gravel works at Auschwitz, administered by DEST since 1940, was bought outright in March 1942. DEST also acquired the private quarries at Marburg in February 1942, though they were never fully developed. Thus, 1942 continued to be a year of expansion and consolidation for the building materials concerns of the SS.[59]

DEST had a total turnover in 1942 of over RM 9.1 million, almost 7 million of which came from the production at the granite works alone. Still troubled by the reconstruction of the brickworks at KL Sachsenhausen, the holding company of the DWB absorbed over RM 1 million in losses. Negotiations were begun for setting prisoners to work on armaments production – at Oranienburg II, recycling of cable and machine parts; for Flossenbürg a Messerschmitt works; and Mauthausen inmates were put at the disposal of Steyr-Daimler Puch AG. However, this did not affect DEST enterprises. Their production remained focused on building materials, and above all stone. The SS maintained its building materials market orientation even to the point of displaying the various stones, brick and ceramic products at an industry trade fair in October 1942.[60] Though most accounts of the KL system describe this year as marking a shift towards armaments production, the reorganization and expansion of SS enterprises indicates a consistent effort to maintain the DEST building material operations throughout 1942 even while the WVHA was shifting its organizational focus to armaments tasks under the impetus of Speer's ministry.[61]

It was only in 1943 that the SS succeeded in changing the focus of production from building materials to armaments. Even then, however, DEST still attempted at every turn to expand and develop its building materials concerns. That the SS simultaneously promoted both armaments work and its own building materials firms this late in the war is indicated by a DEST audit report:

> Actually, an *analysis of the profit results* shows that returns for 1943 and 1944, for *the most part*, stem from the *armaments production* taken on by DEST in 1943. But there is likewise no doubt that the *profit situation* also *has improved beyond the scope of the armaments business*; for not only the works in which important military products were made but also the works that have kept to their peacetime production [e.g. granite quarries] show a favorable development of returns.[62]

Even though 1943 proved to be a year of restructuring for the entire forced-labor industry, the SS continued to hold on to a belief in the eventual usefulness of DEST building materials enterprises for architectural products.[63]

The change in emphasis from the production of building materials to armaments work came quickly but with uneven results in the various DEST enterprises. By the beginning of 1943 half of the planned new work at KL Neuengamme was finished and operating, raising the output from 4.3 million bricks in 1942 to 15.2 million in 1943. Notably, the majority of these bricks were of a very high quality, suitable more for the planned rebuilding of Hamburg than simply for the repair of bomb-damaged structures. It was not until the first air raids in Hamburg began in summer 1943 that the bricks from KL Neuengamme were used for reconstruction efforts. Up to that point, they had been saved for the eventual end of the war and continuation of the city's redesign. Orders continued to be filled at KL Mauthausen, KL Flossenbürg and KL Natzweiler as well. Though by this time private quarries (unlike brickworks) were not consistently protected as a war-important industry, DEST quarries received and maintained exceptional status to continue their work throughout 1943. While 33 per cent of Flossenbürg's c. 8,000 prisoners (including Soviets) were working for Messerschmitt by September 1943, 1,000 prisoners continued to quarry stone even in early 1944.[64]

By 1943, the issue of payment to the state to support forced laborers was again brought up and settled in an attempt to improve the output of what no longer appeared to be an unlimited inmate population. Though populations grew rapidly from c. 60,000 in all KL in 1942 to over 300,000 by the end of 1943, increased pressure was put on the camps by both top SS officials and external administrations (particularly Speer's ministry, as well as the Plenipotentiary for Labor Allocation headed by Fritz Sauckel) to make forced labor more productive. Pohl, through an order of 30 December 1942, implemented a new payment support scale that ranged from the standard RM 0.30 per day to RM 2.50 per day depending on the classification of the prisoner. The order sought to obviate problems similar to those brought up by the Ministry of Finance in 1940: the appearance on the part of the SS of having excessive advantage over private firms, and disturbances of the market caused by its undercutting prices. This order changed the overall cost of support for prisoners in many of the camps. As many prisoners who lived through the experience attest, some advantages did accrue directly to them as a result (including allowing them to acquire small quantities of tobacco or receive extra food rations for heavy labor and armaments work in camp canteens) but these supposed advantages were sometimes fictitious or irregular at best. Yet, for the majority, their labor did change from the murderous production of building materials to the relatively more valued armaments tasks.[65]

Although little expansion took place during 1943 in the capacity of the DEST works to direct output towards the monumental state and Party projects, fewer cutbacks in this area were made than the historical literature suggests. While in 1943 much of the remainder of concentration camp labor was turned towards armaments production, the DEST works still produced their highest turnover yet with almost RM 9 million coming from the granite quarries alone. Revenues for DEST also remained high for the first half of 1944, totaling c. RM 6.6 million.[66] However, by 1944, the development of DEST's building materials business was almost entirely stopped. The quarries filled only a few orders and had been idle for the most part, while the brickworks continued producing for air-raid shelters and for the eventual rebuilding of bomb-destroyed cities. Whereas a large clay deposit was purchased in summer 1944 at Zehlendorf for brick production at KL Sachsenhausen, an attempt to buy a quarry previously leased by DEST for KL Flossenbürg was put off until the end of the war.[67]

Yet even the total mobilization of DEST and the other KL concerns for the war economy was short-lived, as the organization of the camps came under increased pressure with the advance of the Soviets on the Eastern Front. By January 1945, KL Stutthof had been evacuated as had other eastern camps, sending thousands of prisoners on a murderous march west to camps like Flossenbürg and Mauthausen or leaving them to die along the road.[68] The orientation of DEST economic enterprises at the concentration camps to the architectural projects of the Party and state could not compete with the total mobilization of the German economy by 1943. As a producer of building materials, DEST quickly faded away, for the military defeats eroded its basis of support in state contracts for the monumental building economy.

What is evident from this institutional overview of DEST is that the SS interest in the production of building materials was subject to the political pressures on the building economy beginning as early as 1936 and extending into the crucial war years. As an important economic sector of pre-war and wartime Germany, the building economy itself was integrated into the developing political economy of the state. But as long as this political economy could be adapted and expanded to include the variable needs of monumental state architectural projects, the pre-war development of DEST around high-quality granite concerns and brickworks could continue. Further, these concerns could be extended during the war due to the increased control of new numbers of forced laborers sent to the concentration camps as a result of military operations. Only in 1942–3 did DEST administrators reluctantly give up this politically determined advantage of controlling the largest labor force of any building materials concern in the German economy. However, just as the wartime setbacks undermined Hitler and Speer's pursuit of architectural construction so too did these wartime conditions promote a further militarization of the German economy including that of the building industry. The results of this institutional development would prove crucial for the day-to-day life of the prisoners in the key forced-labor camps geared to the production of building materials for DEST.

PRODUCTIVITY AND PUNISHMENT AT THE DEST STONE QUARRIES

Having analyzed the development of DEST in relation to monumental architectural policy and the militarized economy, the question remains as to how these developments were affected by the punitive policies implemented in the camps themselves. Because the granite quarry concentration camps were more dependent than the brickworks on the monumental Party and state projects, an analysis of the two major DEST quarry camps – KL Flossenbürg and KL Mauthausen – indicates most clearly how the economic goals of the SS amounted to an architectural policy. It also indicates the extremely variable results of those economic goals. Once the first stages of camp construction and development were completed, both quarry systems became active in producing stone for local and state needs. From 1938 to at least mid-1943, the majority of forced labor performed by the prisoners was devoted to the production of building materials for DEST. Because of the increased flow of prisoners to the camp, the SS was least concerned about the conditions of laborers in this period. Thus, the number of work-related injuries and deaths in the forced-labor concentration camps remained high while DEST pursued its interests in the building materials economy. Output rather than maximization of labor potential remained the primary criteria for the abuse of labor. The productivity of that labor was won not at the expense but as a result of the camp's main function of punishing the inmates. The political practice of policing the prisoners was significantly influenced by the economic policy of productivity.[69]

KL Flossenbürg and KL Mauthausen (Figures 4, 5) were the fifth and sixth concentration camps set up in National Socialist Germany, after Dachau, Buchenwald, Sachsenhausen and (at that time) Lichtenburg. On 24 March 1938, Eicke, Pohl and the building engineer Hubert Karl (SS-Verwaltungsamt) visited the land around Flossenbürg and then Mauthausen. The group decided in favor of both sites for the formation of new concentration camps, above all because of the available granite. In the case of Mauthausen, an additional justification for its location near Linz was the purported need to employ the expected number of new prisoners resulting from the annexation of Austria on 12 March 1938. By 30 March 1938, the Gauleiter for Oberdonau, August Eigruber, triumphantly spoke of the honor Austria had received in being allocated its own concentration camp in a speech picked up by the international press.[70]

KL Flossenbürg originally included three leased quarries with a fourth acquired in 1941, all near the camp itself. The total planned output was 12,000 cbm (cubic meters) of stone a year, 90 per cent of which was to be architectural quality stone while only 10 per cent was to be for street building material. The stone consisted of coarse-grained blue-gray and gray-yellow granite of an average grade. KL Mauthausen was made up of three quarries, all acquired or leased in 1938: Wienergraben immediately outside of the camp complex and leased from the city of Vienna; Kastenhof, also a leased quarry but several kilometers from the camp; and Gusen, the land of which was partly leased and partly purchased from the local quarry firm Poschacher and also far from the camp. The granite was blue-gray, fine-grained and of a higher quality than that of Flossenbürg, though only 42,000 cbm of the planned output of 290,000 cbm a year was suitable for high-profile architectural projects.[71] Since the quarrying industry by definition was heavily reliant on labor-intensive work, achieving such fantastic production goals for both camps would require the effective organization of thousands of inmates. That the political function of the camp would, on the one

Figure 4
WATCH TOWER AT KL
FLOSSENBÜRG, *c.* 1940 (present
condition)
Source: Author

hand, hinder economic effectiveness (through a focus on physical and arbitrary punishment) while, on the other, guarantee control over a large productive labor force did not at the time appear to DEST administrators as a contradiction.

Hitler's and Speer's aesthetics and the massiveness of the ceremonial building projects secured the market for Flossenbürg and Mauthausen granite and its production in quantity. Granite and stone in general had been favored by Hitler even as early as *Mein Kampf* (1925). In his book, Hitler contrasted the worthy endurance of stone monuments of the past with the plaster and temporary tenements and department stores "of a few Jews" in the Weimar Republic. German architects and architectural administrators had argued long before Hitler for the ideological significance of stone, even if what, exactly, stone architecture signified was disputed. Hitler's favored projects posed no less of a contradiction in that stone buildings

Figure 5
SOUTHWEST FAÇADE OF KL
MAUTHAUSEN, *c.* 1942 (present
condition)
Source: Author

could be discussed simultaneously in terms of an imagined reference to Greek society (and, hence, Aryan racist roots) or to Roman precedents (emphasizing a comparison of the contemporary German "empire" with those of the past). But whatever the ideological significance, the importance of certain kinds of stone remained a dominant feature of Hitler's aesthetic commitments and, by extension, a key symbolic component of the German building economy. Because the aesthetic preferences of Hitler and Speer determined the materials chosen for the building projects of the "Führer Städte," the blue-gray granite at each DEST quarry could easily serve these projects. This aesthetic also guided the further purchase of quarries at KL Gross-Rosen and KL Natzweiler.[72]

But the organization and institutional socialization of camp personnel, from the commandant to the guards, worked against the efficient production of stone to fulfill the aesthetic choices of state and Party architecture. Particularly apparent was the contradiction between the economic goals set out by the trained management personnel of DEST's central office and the emphasis placed on punishment by commandants and guards who had worked their way through the ranks of the Death's Head Squad under Eicke's Dachau model. From the beginning, Dachau was known for its random physical abuse of prisoners, a characteristic that was common to concentration camps during their entire period of existence. In the camps, Himmler took care that the punishments would be controlled by SS personnel, away from the interference of the Justice Ministry but also outside of the control of DEST. At Dachau, Eicke early on instituted a standard hierarchy of punishment and an organization of the camp administration that remained relatively constant until the end of the war and de-emphasized an efficient use of forced labor. The use of forced labor was subject to the approval of the commandant, though the camp administration as a whole remained under the authority of the central SS office in Berlin.[73]

The hierarchy of the camp administration indicated the potential means by which the prisoners would be punished and also made productive. Those who determined the lives of the prisoners were organized in the five departments of the inner administration. First was the Kommandantur, including the commandant who was responsible for both the guards and the overall camp administration. After the organization of the WVHA in early 1942, commandants were also meant to manage the economic enterprises at the camps. At both Mauthausen and Flossenbürg, however, management of the works remained mostly under the control of the DEST administrators even after 1942. The second department of the camp was the Political Division controlled by the Gestapo and responsible for the registration of new prisoners and any release of so-called reformed inmates. The camp administration made up another division (including the camp building engineer) and the camp doctor formed a fourth division.[74]

The fifth section, the Protective Custody Camp Leader (Schutzhaftlagerführer), supervised the economic function of the camps. The Schutzhaftlagerführer had the most immediate and direct control over each prisoner's life and was therefore central to the effectiveness of the forced labor in the camps. Because of the size of the camps, more than one person frequently led this division. The Schutzhaftlagerführer oversaw the work assignments as well as the Block leaders and the Commando leaders, who were responsible for the prisoner Kapos. Kapos were directly chosen from the prisoners and held accountable for the inmates under their control. Till 1943, Kapos were invariably German criminals used by the SS to ensure that most day-to-day punishments would be conducted by the inmates themselves. The orders from the central offices of DEST in Berlin went directly to the Schutzhaftlagerführer, then were carried out in the quarries through the work assignments. This process allowed for much abuse of the system, as the Schutzhaftlagerführer was rarely held responsible for any deaths or injuries to the prisoners on the job as long as the assigned task was done.[75] This division of the camp thus embodied the dual goal of the organization of forced labor for economic production and the oppression of the prisoners. While the emphasis on punishment denied the efficient maximization of labor it did not preclude the possibility of productive forced labor used to achieve DEST's economic goals. In this sense, work and the destruction of prisoners were related goals of DEST managers and on-site SS personnel.

But how did this organizational emphasis on production and punishment work in practice at Flossenbürg and Mauthausen? Of the two camps, Flossenbürg opened first at the end of April or early May 1938. The initial Commandant was SS-Sturmbannführer Jakob Weiseborn, who committed suicide in January 1939 and was replaced by SS-Obersturmführer Karl Künstler. Künstler, a career soldier, directed the camp from May 1939 to August 1942 in its most active period of development and success in granite production. However, after a drunken brawl in April 1942, he was strongly censured by Pohl and Himmler at which point he entered the Waffen-SS division Prinz Eugen to fight at the front. He was replaced in September 1942 by the Commandant from Natzweiler, SS-Sturmbannführer Egon

Zill. Zill proved ineffectual in his duties, however, and was replaced in April 1943 by Max Koegel who had been trained, like many, at Dachau. The Schutzhaftlager-führer, SS-Hauptsturmführer Hans Aumeier, also came from Dachau and performed well enough at Flossenbürg to be sent to Auschwitz in the same role at the end of 1941. He was replaced by SS-Hauptsturmführer Karl Fritzsch who held the post till March 1944. The work leader for the DEST quarries was SS-Mann Max Schubert, who was replaced in January 1942 by SS-Obersturmführer Alois Schubert.[76] The socialization of these men was varied, from rural to urban, lower class to middle class, and reflected the general heterogeneity of the SS. However diverse their backgrounds, though, the administration of Flossenbürg provided them with an opportunity to achieve their personal, political or ideological goals by punishing inmates and making them productive.[77]

At the end of April 1938, the first prisoners arrived from Buchenwald and were used to build the camp and prepare the stone quarries. Prisoners were sent from Dachau between May and July, from Buchenwald between August and November, and from Sachsenhausen in late November, bringing the total to 1,500 inmates by the end of 1939. The initial work led by Schubert at the stone quarries was heavy labor with primitive tools, since the modernization of methods did not occur until 1940–1. The clearing of the camp site itself and the construction of necessary buildings for the prisoners also occupied much of the initial stage of forced labor. By the end of 1939, enough of the quarries had been cleared for stone orders to begin.[78]

At Mauthausen, the SS administration was changed less often and the quarries themselves started production for outside contracts earlier than was the case at Flossenbürg. The camp opened under the command of SS-Sturmbannführer Albert Sauer, who lasted only until April 1939. His post was taken over by SS-Sturmbannführer Franz Ziereis, an SS member trained at Dachau, who remained Commandant until the liberation of the camp. Ziereis had been a career soldier since 1924 and was praised by his superiors for his seemingly organized development of the camp. At times, Mauthausen, because of its size and many subsidiary camps, had three Schutzhaftlagerführer, the most important for the quarries being SS-Hauptsturmführer Georg Bachmayer, who oversaw much of the granite production after he came to the camp in January 1939. The DEST work leader was a certain SS-Hauptsturmführer Spichalsky, replaced in March 1941 by a civilian Otto Walther, who entered the SS only in June 1944.[79]

The camp began operations at the end of May 1938 or the beginning of June, when the first work teams were sent from Dachau and began construction on the site. Unlike Flossenbürg, where the majority of prisoners were transported from other camps before the war, Mauthausen quickly received prisoners from Germany and Austria directly. The prisoners were also categorized by occupation as early as March 1939, facilitating the distribution of work duties by the Schutzhaftlagerführer though by no means guaranteeing a rationalized assignment of labor. In 1938, the work at the camp concentrated on the construction of the facilities; the quarries did not begin their full operation until 1939. Between

January 1939 and the end of the year, the number of prisoners working in the quarries rose from 400 to 1,066, reaching c. 40 per cent of the total population. As with Flossenbürg, the work began with arduous manual labor that only later included the use of modern machinery.[80]

Until the outbreak of war, the prison populations at Flossenbürg and Mauthausen were, for the most part, those defined above. With the coming of the war, however, the prison populations increased exponentially as Germany's territorial expansion began in earnest, supporting the optimism of DEST's leaders. Non-German prisoners arrived in KL Flossenbürg for the first time in April 1940, including Czech students and intellectuals as well as Poles, the latter group making up the largest percentage of non-German prisoners. At least since mid-1940, the SS sent some German, Polish and Czech Jews to the camp, who were subjected to especially cruel treatment. By the time Himmler enacted his order of October 1942 sending any remaining Jews to Auschwitz or Lublin, only twelve Jews remained at Flossenbürg to be transported to the death camps. Most Jews sent to Flossenbürg were either executed immediately or died within the first week through abuse while they labored. This situation did not change until 1944 when the necessity of mobilizing labor for armaments also included Jewish labor for Flossenbürg. Receiving similar treatment, 2,000 Soviet prisoners of war were sent to the camp in October 1941, kept in a special section to themselves and not included in the general SS camp registration lists. By February 1943, the camp held 4,004 inmates (not including Soviet prisoners of war) and reached its highest population during the death marches in February 1945 with c. 11,000.[81] Camp populations reflected the military advances of the German army through Europe and the Soviet territory as well as the expanded authority of the SS to control ever larger groups of people.

The concentration camp population at Mauthausen was somewhat different from that of Flossenbürg. As of May 1940, 2,674 German and Austrian prisoners remained at Mauthausen, this number rising in Mauthausen-Gusen to 14,838 by March 1943. Foreign prisoners began arriving in early summer 1940 and, as with Flossenbürg, Poles formed the largest national group that was not German/Austrian. Almost to a person, Polish nationals were placed in the worst work commandos, including site-clearing in the quarry. Mauthausen also received major transports of Soviet prisoners of war, beginning with 2,000 in October 1941, who were given the most difficult work assignments. Soviet prisoners of war totaled 5,000 by early 1942, of whom only 80 were still alive by March. Unlike at Flossenbürg, another national group almost as large as the Poles was formed by exiled Spanish Communists and Republicans, trapped in France after the German invasion in 1940. The Spanish were rounded up and sent to various concentration camps beginning in early 1941. Around 8,000 arrived at Mauthausen in that year, only 1,600 of whom were still alive at the end of the war. French political prisoners, picked up in the "Night and Fog" action on 7 December 1941, formed a significant segment of the population before 1943. Until 1940, Jews made up an even smaller percentage of the population than at Flossenbürg; the first Jew registered in the SS records was a gay man from Vienna who died in the camp in March 1940. Jewish transports began arriving in greater numbers in 1941, the majority of whom came from Holland. Of the 900 incarcerated, only eight were still alive in December.[82] Compared to Flossenbürg, Mauthausen became a center for the internment and punishment of a higher percentage of political prisoners from the variety of SS arrests and actions throughout the occupied territories.

Punishing prisoners was inseparable in the early war years from the development of SS economic policy. Of the five camps existing at the beginning of the war in which economic concerns played a significant role, Flossenbürg was the first and most consistent in producing development income from forced labor. Though the quarries had been worked from the opening months of the camp, it was not until January 1940 that orders began to be filled and deliveries to be made (see Table 1). In 1940–1, the most consistent stone orders were for the rebuilding efforts in Berlin, guaranteeing contracts for camp production as long as architectural policy was still a priority at the state level. In November 1940, stone-mason workshops set up to train prisoners also began providing limited amounts of cut stone for the Party Rally Grounds at Nuremberg, another privileged wartime project. The four quarries and stone-mason training program remained in full production until the first quarry was closed and its workers turned towards the manufacture of armaments in May 1943.[83] DEST goals had to be constantly modified due to wartime economic and military conditions. Nevertheless, DEST could pursue its interests through the attachment of its Flossenbürg enterprises to major state architectural commissions and the extension of production to include stone-cutting to adapt to the German building economy.

Production was, of course, successful in these years for DEST because it was based on the exploitation of a camp labor force that, at this stage in the war, seemed unlimited to the SS administrators. While the guards of the Death Head's

Table 1: Comparison of known stone production at KL Flossenbürg and KL Mauthausen, 1940–2

	Production year	Production in cubic meters
Flossenbürg	1940	2,897.924
Mauthausen	1940	1,017.932
Total 1940		**3,915.856**
Flossenbürg	1941	2,848
Mauthausen	1941	2,635.951
Total 1941		**5,483.951**
Flossenbürg	1942	1,690 (June–Dec.)
Mauthausen	1942	1,111.248 (June–Dec.)
Total 1942		**2,801.248** (June–Dec.)
Total 1940–2		**12,201.055** (minimum)

Source: DEST Annual and Monthly Reports, BA, NS3/341; NS3/1347.

Squad were bent on punishment as an end in and of itself, DEST managers saw punishment as the means of guaranteeing productivity. The contradiction of killing laborers used simultaneously to create an economic empire was maintained as long as the SS continued to increase its political authority over prisoners in the early war years.[84]

DEST's unwillingness to address the conditions of labor during this period meant that both intentional and unplanned injuries and deaths occurred frequently in the stone quarries. Stone quarrying itself was extremely labor intensive, even with the use of machinery, exposing workers to dangerous working conditions where being injured was a constant reality. In addition to the conditions of stone quarrying, the punitive agenda of the guards and the oversight of brutal Kapos resulted in random abuse, ill treatment and frequent beatings used to make the laborers work harder. Further, the brutal weather conditions of the winter months and the lack of basic nutrition or health care were conditions faced regularly in the camp, setting one prisoner against the next in a struggle for survival. Quarry commandos were not only seen as the worst possible job by the prisoners, because of the arduous work and conditions, but they were used as well to carry out reprisals against prisoners especially during Künstler's command. Even the camp doctor, SS-Hauptsturmführer Dr Schmitz, remarked in a memo to the Commandant and Schutzhaftlagerführer in June 1940 that the seemingly accidental injuries to prisoners in the quarries had reached unendurable proportions. This was a situation not in the interest of production or of "the people as a whole" (notably, the doctor is not interested in the individual good of the prisoner).[85] Prisoners marked for punishment were often forced to carry exceedingly heavy stones on their backs from the quarries to the camp at the end of a day, collapsing with fatigue or dying with heart failure from the exertion. Such activity did not stop in the stark winter of 1939/40, when temperatures dropped to −30° Celsius and work was only halted when fog or the depth of the snow made guarding the prisoners difficult. In this period, very few prisoners were exempted from working in the stone quarries. When dysentery broke out at the same time, the quarry was closed for a month but the prisoners received little medical attention; the camp was simply quarantined and, as soon as the epidemic was over, the prisoners were back in the quarries.[86] Yet because of the control over more prisoners (particularly from the occupied territories) in these years, camp administrators still managed to maintain and even increase levels of productivity, in spite of the destructive conditions of labor.

By mid-1940, cranes and machines had been purchased to improve output as the DEST administration demanded an increase of stone production to an eventual 12,000 cbm a year (a comparatively huge amount of stone; note that the major commission of the New Reich Chancellory used 5,000 cbm).[87] To secure this increase, the DEST work leader Max Schubert encouraged the destruction of physically exhausted or injured prisoners. With these persons out of the way, he could use the fittest laborers until they, too, gave out under the strenuous work program. Schubert and other on-site personnel viewed productivity and punishment as the same goal. At the end of 1940, conditions of some prisoners improved with their induction into a training program as stone-masons that included 400 inmates by March 1941. Conditions also changed slightly after Künstler was replaced by Zill in 1942 and the Commandant was required by the WVHA central offices to be the manager responsible for the production of the DEST concern. But the effort to increase output at any cost led to the continued abuse of the prisoners. Finally, by February 1943, when the camp numbered around 4,000 (not including Soviets) and the first 200 prisoners were taken from the DEST concern to work for Messerschmitt, labor conditions seemed to improve.[88] Punishment of inmates by using them to fill orders for the architectural projects of the Party and state was on the wane.[89]

Unlike Flossenbürg's reliance on the Berlin projects, Hermann Giesler and Roderich Fick's monumental redesign of Linz, for which production at KL Mauthausen was initially designated, remained only in the planning stages. Stone was not ordered for this project from the camp in central Austria. However, as with other camps, DEST administrators and the work leaders adapted by taking advantage of other architectural commissions during the war and attempting to link their production to important state projects. Even more so than at Flossenbürg, this was done at great expense to the lives of the prisoners. Heydrich had designated the camp for individuals not intended to be released and this, along with Mauthausen's size, led to correspondingly worse conditions, while punishment and work in the quarries resulted in the highest mortality rate of any of the labor camps.[90]

Production in the three stone quarries of Mauthausen began in earnest by October 1939, when orders were already being filled. By 1940, the quarry at the subsidiary camp of Gusen was producing so much that barracks were set up for the prisoners there rather than losing an hour of productive work by having them walk the 3 kilometers to and from the main camp. Gusen established itself as the quarry where most of the architectural quality stone was produced. Kastenhof and Wienergraben produced some stone, though the majority of their output was used for roads and rough building materials. In 1940–1, Mauthausen quarries noticeably increased their output although production totals were below the planned improvement to 3,500 cbm (see Table 1). Nevertheless, the quarries showed a significant gain for DEST during wartime.[91]

Work continued throughout 1941, abetted by the increase in the number of prisoners sent to the camp since the beginning of the war. In Wienergraben alone, 3,844 prisoners were working by May 1942, though the number was reduced in 1943 to 4,800 in all three quarries. Modern machinery had been brought in to expedite production by 1940, and the training of prisoners as stone-masons began in February 1941. The SS also enlisted specific prisoners designated as specialized skilled labor such as draftsmen and architects from other camps to help with the stone-mason work in 1941. In 1942, DEST purchased more machinery as iron contingents were procured from the GBBau under Todt, probably through the influence of Himmler and Speer. In the same year, DEST began planning to fulfill a potential contract for the rebuilding of Linz although no stone seems ever to have been quarried directly for this project. Orders remained plentiful, though complaints were frequently made by the DEST work leaders of insufficient transportation opportunities due to the necessities of war and the need for more prisoners. By March 1943, however, the armaments industries had begun to dominate production interests.[92]

The continuation of production during these years at KL Mauthausen, as at Flossenbürg, was dependent on the abuse and exploitation of prison labor. After the war began and production increased in the quarries, the life expectancy of the prisoners dropped to an average of six months from the time they entered the camp. The influx of huge numbers of prisoners before this date meant that the SS did not deem necessary any correction of the work conditions as long as production continued to rise. In 1940, Polish prisoners were sorted out for special punishment in the quarries, as were the Spanish partisan fighters. Soviets were also designated for almost immediate execution, though Himmler issued an order as of 15 November 1941 that this should not take place if they were physically able to work in the quarries. However, they, like the Spanish, the Polish and the political prisoners, were inevitably assigned the most arduous tasks in the stone quarry.[93]

Many survivor testimonies describe the actual type of labor and abusive actions that took place in the quarry during the development of the SS economic enterprise. They make clear that the day-to-day punishment in the quarries both inhibited efficiency as well as compelled productivity. For example, Milos Vitek, a university professor sent to Mauthausen in 1941 on charges of revealing information about the armaments industry and attempts to support Spanish partisans, stated:

> On the steps [into the quarry], the Block Leader began to lay into the last five [prisoners in line]. These five, evading the punches, threw the row going in front of them to the ground and the entire group of a hundred formed a tangle of bodies in the stone quarry into which the Kapos struck with clubs. As the quarry was worked in wooden shoes, we lost them repeatedly in the confusion and had to work the whole day barefoot. We Czechs and also the Jews were used mostly for the most difficult work in the Special Commando for Milling, where stones were broken up and which stood under the leadership of the Kapo Nagel. But also with Ritter, Willi Steiner or Bertl it was not better. It was here an awful struggle for the preservation of life, where the person suffered hunger, was weak and was almost dead from exhaustion and, in spite of this, must work, as otherwise he would be beaten. During the summer, we were on our feet up to 16 hours, working daily 10 to 12 hours and the rest we spent at the roll call. Often also at night we were "exercised". So shattered, we lay down at night. . . . The work hours appeared to us endlessly long and indeed when it concerned a very difficult job, we measured the time in minutes. The duration of our lives numbered in weeks.[94]

Vitek's testimony indicates the way certain groups were selected out for the hardest work and how the quarry could be used as a general site for the SS to punish or destroy.

Yet by late 1942, the decimation of the prisoners had become a cause of concern to SS administrators who then carried out several orders designed to ameliorate the conditions under which the prisoners worked. However, these orders were given as a means of increasing output not as a means of maximizing the labor potential of the prisoner. With the move to armament production, conditions were changed and the prisoners grudgingly accorded some improvements. These changes included the limited ability to acquire goods (instituted in December 1943) and a slight improvement of health and nutritional conditions. Yet, increasing productivity still did not guarantee respect for the condemned prisoner's life, only his labor. For example, an experiment run on 370 inmates from December 1943 to July 1944 intended to see which of three different diets kept prisoners alive and working longest. Results indicated that the normal prison meal with 30 grams of a complex B-Vitamin food was best for the "prisoners employed in the camp." While the outcome was used to increase work, 116 inmates who participated in the experiment died in the process including seventeen fed the supposedly better meal. For this experiment, the life of the inmate in general was of no concern but rather the productive capacity of the laboring inmate in scientific nutritional terms became the priority. Productivity was reduced to a medical and numerical problem that was independent of the oppression faced by individual prisoners.[95] The punishment of the inmates remained a priority even while the SS searched for methods to increase productivity.

In both camps there were multiple ways in which these prisoners died or were killed, intentionally and accidentally, by SS personnel and through the planned conditions of the concentration camps themselves. Undernourishment killed the most prisoners in the forced-labor camps, ahead of epidemics and disease. Suicide was also prevalent for prisoners who could no longer stand the physical or psychological punishment, though often such supposed suicides as running into the electric fences surrounding the camps were people cajoled into death by the SS men in charge. By 1939, the average of deaths in the camps stood at more than one per day; by 1942, that number had risen in Mauthausen to almost forty per day. At least 14,293 people died in the camp that year.[96]

Though these averages reflect the intentionally brutal living circumstances of the work camps in general, the quarry camps had significantly more deaths associated directly with the working conditions than did the brickworks. Thus, death at Mauthausen and Flossenbürg often came together with the orientation of the camp economy to the architectural projects of the Party and state. About 10 per cent of the approximately 30,000 deaths at KL Flossenbürg and 25–30 per cent of the 113,575 at KL Mauthausen can be accounted for in the period from 1938 to 1943. These percentages seem low only because the vast majority of deaths at the camps occurred in the last few months of the war when the SS was herding inmates in from the east in huge numbers (with hygienic conditions deteriorating even further). From 1938 to late 1944, however, these percentages were high in relation to deaths recorded after armaments work was begun in 1943.[97]

In these years, the stone quarries were significant in contributing to the conditions that led to physical and psychological breakdown or that exposed inmates to the vagaries of the SS and its designated Kapos. It was not without reason that, in both camps, a prisoner feared being assigned to the stone-quarry work details of DEST, for it implied almost certain death. In the early stages of the war, the symbolic importance of Hitler's building programs could be maintained at the expense of the prisoners' lives. Work conditions were at their worst precisely in those years when DEST policy regarding the production of building materials was being most consistently developed and implemented. Before 1943, the forced-labor conditions at Flossenbürg and Mauthausen indicate the connection of architectural policy to the political function of the camps through the SS pursuit of an economic empire. A productive use of forced labor, the quarrying of high-quality granite and the punishment of prisoners were complementary goals even if they conflicted in practice. In spite of the SS guards' practical disregard for DEST management ideals, the process of punishment led to a level of productivity that sustained SS hopes in developing forced-labor operations through their connection to the monumental building economy.

It is not the case that political interests outweighed economic ones because so many inmates died. Rather, from 1938 to 1943, DEST took advantage of political and economic developments to expand its economic enterprises through the oppression of a seemingly unlimited labor force. Production for the building industry and for monumental building projects in particular was inseparable and achievable only through the physical oppression of the camps. DEST administrators emphasized production totals over any concern for maximization of labor potential while taking advantage of the promotion of architectural policy by Speer and Hitler during the war. The intersection of SS economic interests with architectural policy gave the initial impetus to the reorganization of the concentration camp system after 1936 and facilitated the punishment of prisoners through the production of building materials.

Chapter 3: The Party Rally Grounds at Nuremberg

SS Economic Goals and National Socialist Architectural Policy

Building in Germany depended both on the prioritization of architectural policy by Party and state officials and the ability of architectural administrators to carry out their goals in the face of mounting political and economic constraints. As the German economy was being geared for war by 1936, access to limited material resources and labor for construction became increasingly restricted. Party and state interests centered on a small number of important commissions that required a huge quantity of labor and materials. The Reich Party Rally Grounds at Nuremberg (Figure 6), a prestige project favored by Hitler, operated as a focal point for the competition of construction and materials firms in Germany. The competitive situation intensified during the first few years of the war, as planning and the mobilization of resources for Nuremberg continued while the state closed down other smaller sites. A belief in a victorious outcome to the war propelled the pursuit of architectural goals to the degree that the economic and political situation allowed. It was in this moment of military optimism that DEST linked specific production goals at its forced-labor quarry enterprises to the aesthetic and quantitative material needs of the Nuremberg Party Rally Grounds.

Previous art historical accounts have remained focused on the ideological significance of the complex, exploring issues such as the relation of the building designs to classical sources and Speer's so-called "aesthetic of ruins."[1] All of these studies take the politics of National Socialism as crucial to understanding the project but have limited themselves to interpretations of how the design of the structures expresses a particular programmatic point of view. However, some of the most powerful officials and institutions used the building process at Nuremberg for the implementation of specific policies distinct from propagandistic concerns. Political and economic goals in particular were pursued through the mobilization of the massive resources required for the building process. If an institutional examination of DEST has allowed us an understanding of SS economic operations, a micro history of the building process at Nuremberg leads us to an analysis of the implementation of specific DEST policies as well as to a more comprehensive account of the political function of architecture in National Socialist Germany.

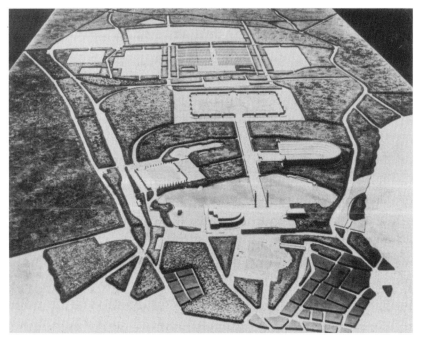

Figure 6
ALBERT SPEER, MODEL OF THE
REICH PARTY RALLY GROUNDS,
NUREMBERG, 1937. Buildings
from bottom to top: LUITPOLD
ARENA, CONGRESS HALL,
ZEPPELIN FIELD, GERMAN
STADIUM, MARCH FIELD
Source: G. Troost, *Bauen im neuen
Reich*, 1938

Key to analyzing DEST's relation to Nuremberg is an explanation of the monumental building economy itself, especially the stone industry. As we have seen, into the war years, the increased political management of the building economy privileged certain kinds of materials. This process was concomitant with Hitler's prioritization of specific architectural projects, above all those at Berlin and Nuremberg. Each of these developments depended on an economic emphasis on productivity and labor. Such an emphasis required a maximization of output by stone-quarry concerns in order to meet the incredible demand for building materials caused by design and construction decisions on site. Explaining this complex and chronologically specific process at Nuremberg helps to clarify the extent of DEST's development. An analysis of the Party Rally Grounds at Nuremberg thus attests to how far the SS wanted to go with its economic policy.

As a result of Hitler's emphasis on a few large architectural projects, agencies and firms involved with the design and construction of the Nuremberg buildings secured a steady and profitable supply of work. The quarrying industry particularly depended on such projects because stone could not be utilized as easily as iron or bricks to meet wartime building needs. DEST quarrying enterprises in the forced-labor concentration camps were no different. SS administrators at the height of their optimism pursued stone orders for Nuremberg and made organizational decisions for the camps in relation to the monumental building economy. By 1941, the SS had secured contracts to provide granite for Albert Speer's German Stadium (Figure 7) at the Party Rally Grounds from the concentration camps at Flossenbürg, Gross-Rosen and, especially, Natzweiler in Alsace. In the same period, DEST also

Figure 7
ALBERT SPEER, MODEL OF THE
GERMAN STADIUM, NUREMBERG,
1937
Source: G. Troost, *Bauen im neuen
Reich*, 1938

organized stone-mason programs at several of the quarry camps to process stone for commissions such as the German Stadium. The question to be resolved here is then twofold: how did specific aesthetic decisions affect DEST's position within the developing monumental building economy and, further, how did this process lead to particular policy changes in the quarry camps including the diversification of labor?

At the heart of these questions is a need to analyze more closely the way Himmler and his DEST managers defined their economic policy and its imple-mentation. In the quarrying and cutting of stone for projects such as Nuremberg, they systematically ignored the relationship that existed in the concentration camps between labor conditions and output, preferring instead to favor a limited under-standing of labor as a quantitative factor in productivity (number of workers) rather than as a qualitative factor which could be differentiated through developing indi-vidual worker performance (labor efficiency).[2] DEST was acutely aware of the advantage of quantitative output, and, particularly in the stone-mason programs, it pursued its interest in dominating various segments of the building economy. As a result, DEST administrators set out economic priorities based on a commitment to productivity. Such a policy was part of both the general hierarchical privileging of projects in the pre-war and wartime building economy as well as the specifically defined political function of the camps in punishing those individuals deemed by the SS as supposed enemies of the state. Thus, analyzing the building process at Nuremberg and its connection to SS forced-labor policy explains how exactly the goal of punishing camp inmates came together with the economic expansion of DEST ventures and the monumental projects of the Party and state.

THE FUNCTION OF THE PARTY RALLY GROUNDS AT NUREMBERG

Why the SS focused some of its forced-labor operations on buildings at Nuremberg has much to do with the aesthetic and organizational development of the site from 1933 to 1939, the point at which DEST operations became involved with the pro-ject. In these years, the Reich Party Rally Grounds became the largest single complex of monumental government buildings ever constructed in National Socialist Germany. Situated southeast of the town center at the site of a memorial to fallen soldiers from World War I, the complex consisted of five major buildings and many minor structures. Construction of all the major buildings was begun, though only two were completed. The grounds themselves were planned around a small lake and along a central axis, providing a vast ceremonial setting for the yearly propaganda festivals of the Party.

More than at any other site in Germany, here the ideological machinations of National Socialism received their epitaph as the "aestheticization of politics," exemplified to our own day by such contemporary evidence as Leni Riefenstahl's *Triumph des Willens*.[3] The staging of propaganda spectacles in order to introduce state policies or reinforce aspects of National Socialist ideological goals was certainly the most public function of the rallies. For example, Riefenstahl's film, like other elements in the annual spectacles, focused constantly on the "Führer cult," where the role of the leader as the embodiment of the supportive German masses was emphasized. Goebbels' Propaganda Ministry furthered this goal by surrounding Hitler and the other Party leaders with pins, flags, trophies, uniforms and other paraphernalia to project the totalized and unified Nazi foundation of this support. Further, the rallies functioned as a means of focusing the attention of the nation on key Nazi policies such as the introduction in 1935 of the Nuremberg Laws, which denied German Jews citizenship rights and defined who was and was not considered Jewish. By the announcement of the Four Year Plan at the 1936 Party Rally, the annual ceremonies were well known and their use as platforms to introduce policy decisions had been established.[4]

But as the design and construction of the Party Rally Grounds progressed in the 1930s and into the war, a functional relationship developed between this building process and other state and Party needs beyond the propagandistic bombast of Riefenstahl's film and the public introduction of policy. Hitler, for example, took advantage of the party rally building projects to solidify his image as an architect and to consolidate his influence over major architectural commissions in Germany. When the NSDAP came to power, Hitler decided that an appropriate and permanent setting should be chosen for the rallies, a setting that was supposed to last for hundreds of years. Though in the Weimar Republic two of the four party rallies had been held there, Nuremberg was not necessarily the only city from which Hitler might choose. Stuttgart also competed for the right to be the site of the party rallies. Nuremberg City Council members presented Hitler with final plans for their version of the grounds on 22 July 1933 in order to win his approval. They chose, naturally, the site used for previous rallies near the zoo, a public stadium and the war memorial grounds. At the July meeting, Hitler agreed to the city's proposal to be the permanent site of the rallies. Hitler's approval, however, was contingent on laying out the grounds to his specifications and not compromising the plans just to save a "couple of old trees" in the Luitpold Grove (Luitpoldhain) arena. Hitler's wishes included not only leveling the field of the Luitpoldhain and getting rid of its small pond but also the construction of the necessary tribunes and stands for the participants and the press. After three days, Nuremberg mayor Willy Liebel pressed the City Council to accept all of Hitler's demands in order to keep the party rallies in Nuremberg. The changes were approved and Hitler showed early on his ability to control his favored architectural projects.[5]

The architecture of the principal buildings, all of which were to be completed in the stripped-down neoclassicism preferred by Hitler for monumental Party and state commissions, also served in the planning phase as a means of bringing together some of the most ambitious architects and administrators in the Third Reich. Most notably, a young Albert Speer was brought to the attention of Hitler through his designs for the 1933 Party Rally. Facing a problem with the Zeppelin Field (Zeppelinfeld [Figure 8]) stands, the Nuremberg City Council called Speer to the site in July 1933 to draw up plans for a temporary structure. Because Hitler himself had to approve the designs, Speer was sent to Munich where Hitler

Figure 8
ALBERT SPEER, ZEPPELIN FIELD,
NUREMBERG, 1934–6
Source: Rittich, *Architektur und Bauplastik der Gegenwart*, 1938

was staying. Hitler began his promotion of Speer's architectural career with the approval of these drawings.[6]

In working on this project, Speer also met Walter Brugmann and K.F. Liebermann, both of whom were to play key roles in the construction of Nuremberg and Berlin. Later in the 1930s, they became important as intermediaries between Speer's office of the GBI and the SS. Brugmann in particular exemplifies how social and political connections between architects and administrators could work to streamline and centralize architectural policy in National Socialist Germany. Joining the city's building administration in 1922, Brugmann steadily rose in the ranks overseeing various building projects (construction and design) in the Weimar Republic. In the Nazi period, he worked on the "restoration," following Nazi principles, of the old section of the city and was given control over on-site construction efforts at the Party Rally Grounds. In this capacity, he and Speer systematically cut off initiatives coming out of the city administration and furthered their respective careers in the process. For his efforts, Brugmann, like Speer before him, was given by Hitler the honorary title of "professor" on his fiftieth birthday in April 1937.[7]

By the mid-1930s, party rallies and construction also served a local economic function by bringing in revenue from the large crowds attending the annual event and for increasing the city's working population. Construction of the buildings and the rallies themselves directed trade as well as government and Party investment to Nuremberg, and, by 1935–6, laborers from all parts of Germany were moving there to find jobs. Furthermore, the Nuremberg project fell under the auspices of work creation programs that were central to the economic recovery of Germany from the world depression.[8] With Hitler explicitly favoring the project and the coordination of labor and resources well under way, the Party Rally Grounds provided an obvious target for a variety of administrative, economic and political interests in National Socialist Germany.

CREATION OF THE ZWECKVERBAND REICHSPARTEITAG NÜRNBERG

At the beginning of 1934, Speer received the commission to replace the temporary bleachers of the Zeppelin Field with a more permanent structure. He then designed the 1,300-foot-long honor tribune, modeled (as he later said) on the Pergamum Altar; Hitler subsequently approved the design. In the same year, plans were requested by Liebel from the experienced Nuremberg architect Ludwig Ruff for a new Party congress building. Ruff readied the initial plans for the Congress Hall (Kongresshalle [Figure 9]) by May and signed a contract in November 1934. With its rounded façade and three tiers of arches, the Congress Hall also had a classical precedent in the Roman Colosseum. In addition, Hitler commissioned Speer to integrate the buildings into a unified complex. Speer received the commission in the fall and the first sketches were ready by October 1934. By December, he had finished the first complete plan of the grounds which featured the basic elements of the Luitpoldhain arena, the Zeppelin Field, the Congress Hall and the March Field (Märzfeld) for the military exercises, all arranged on a central axis (Grosse Strasse). Up until this point, Hitler expected that the city itself, or rather its building administration, would carry out the planning, construction and securing of funds for the project.[9]

Hitler-approved additions to the original plan increased the scale of the Party Rally Grounds and created a need for a more comprehensive architectural and financial administration. Adding the Congress Hall to the projects for the Luitpoldhain

Figure 9
LUDWIG AND FRANZ RUFF,
CONGRESS HALL, NUREMBERG,
c. 1935 (present condition)
Source: Author

and the Zeppelin Field, in particular, proved to be a problem for the already over-extended city building administration. In December 1934, Nuremberg asked the Reich Chancery to create an association between the parties concerned – the city, the state (Bavaria), the government and the NSDAP – in order to spread the financial and organizational responsibilities. The city argued that the massive building of the Congress Hall and the extension of the plans to form an integrated complex would require a much greater building effort and more financing than previously assumed.[10] The appeal of the city and the increase in planning tasks resulted in the founding of the Reich Party Rally Grounds Association Nuremberg (Zweckverband Reichsparteitags Nürnberg [ZRPT]), a public corporation created in March 1935.[11]

The 1935 law creating the ZRPT outlined the various tasks of the organization. The introductory clause, from the drafts to the final version, remained unchanged and detailed the purpose of the organization: "For the construction and maintenance as well as for the operation of grounds, buildings and other facilities for the Reich party rally in Nuremberg an Association is formed."[12] The city of Nuremberg, the state of Bavaria, the Reich and the NSDAP were all to be equally responsible for funding, construction and administration of the site. In cases of any disagreement, participating parties might call on Hitler to resolve the dispute. The law was signed on 29 March 1935, and Hitler appointed the Reich Minister for Church Matters, Hans Kerrl, to head the ZRPT, though the position was largely symbolic. Board members met for the first time in April.[13]

Discussion amongst the concerned parties leading up to the creation of the law focused almost exclusively on each administration's financial responsibility, delineated in the seventh clause of the draft. Though apparently each party would contribute equally to the construction, the Finance Minister, Lutz Schwerin von Krosigk, quickly pointed out that the plans' high costs could result in an undue strain on the Reich that would force the curtailment of other, "more pressing" state political tasks. Interior Minister Frick, who was overseeing the passage of the law, settled on a compromise after meeting with Schwerin von Krosigk on 25 March 1935 to discuss the problem. The final version of the law set no specific financial burden on the four parties involved: "The costs of the Association are to be raised through donations and contributions."[14] Nevertheless, while vague, the discussion and the ensuing law clearly identified the main function of the ZRPT, i.e. as an institution that would guarantee funding of the project.

In practice, however, Schwerin von Krosigk's fears turned out to be well grounded, especially as the tasks of the ZRPT grew under the monumental plans set forth by Speer. The ZRPT did prove to be necessary precisely as the Nuremberg city administration had predicted; neither the city, nor the Bavarian state, could carry even a fraction of the costs for the project. Of the RM 15,565,051 in the May 1935 budget, RM 4 million came from Party contributions, RM 8 million came from loans or grants from the German Society for Public Works, RM 3 million from the Reich Institution for Employment Referrals and Unemployment Insurance and the remainder from miscellaneous credit. The amounts of RM 8 million and RM 3 million were directly out of the central government's financial reserves for public works and were part of the political program to ease the severity of the unemployment problem through government spending and, hence, to win support for the NSDAP. The situation changed little in the remaining years with the Reich paying at least 64 per cent of the total costs between 1935 and 1938 and the city of Nuremberg and Bavaria contributing almost exclusively through the donation of land parcels.[15] Yet because of Hitler's support of the project, there was never a severe shortage of funds even if the distribution of financial responsibility remained uneven for the four parties of the ZRPT.

The ability to mobilize funding and increase revenues into the 1940s came as a result of Hitler's constant interest in the project. Hitler's interest, however, ironically limited the capacity of the ZRPT to control the use of those funds. As the ZRPT's function became more and more dominated by accruing government funds to the Party Rally Grounds, the prioritization of the use of those funds came increasingly into the hands of the main architect – Speer – and the head on-site building administrator – Brugmann. Each had achieved their status with Hitler's direct approval. This dynamic followed other sectors of the German economy as the late 1930s introduced a heightened political management of various resources and the war promoted a perceived need by government leaders to centralize the prioritization of key projects. At Nuremberg, this dynamic meant that the prominent architects took control of the funds gathered by the ZRPT.

Hitler indicated his preference for the Party Rally Grounds not only through funding but also by securing the legal position of the ZRPT in relation to other state and Party projects. The administrative authority of the ZRPT was strengthened by the Law for the Redesign of German Cities (*Gesetz zur Neugestaltung deutscher Städte*) issued on 4 October 1937 and including Nuremberg as of 9 April 1938. Berlin had already been covered by the law since 5 November 1937, and Nuremberg (specifically, the Party Rally Grounds) was the second city to be named. The law allowed Nuremberg administrators to draw on resources and materials as needed for this project, often at the expense of other businesses that faced the restrictions of the Four Year Plan after 1936. Furthermore, the law officially declared Hitler's interest in the completion of Nuremberg above other building projects in the Reich.[16]

The formation of the ZRPT, and the legal backing it received, allowed for the centralized planning and financing of buildings and rallies at Nuremberg. But in spite of the ZRPT's charter, Brugmann quickly consolidated all construction tasks under his position as head of the city's Office of Structural Engineering (Hochbauamt). Brugmann oversaw the procurement of materials, contracting firms and the administration of the building sites, reporting his progress and problems to the ZRPT. On paper, Brugmann and his staff ultimately answered both to the administrative control of the ZRPT and to the design authority of Speer and, nominally, Franz Ruff, who controlled the design of the Congress Hall after his father died. In practice, however, Brugmann's tenure as head of construction and of stone procurement allowed him a great deal of independence from the over-sight of the ZRPT as long as he continued to serve the on-site interests of Speer. In this capacity, he pursued the purchase of materials and guaranteed orders during the war for firms including DEST.[17]

Architecturally, the size and importance of the plans (Hitler, unlike Schwerin von Krosigk, saw the architecture at Nuremberg as a top priority) secured Speer and his staff in Berlin a greater role in determining architectural policy on a national level. While the ZRPT approved contracts, obtained financing and administered the building process overall, Speer and his staff had a free hand in design, subject only to Hitler's approval. With the beginning of construction, Speer and Brugmann also received an increase in administrative control over resources and materials allo-cated through the German building economy. Access to the ZRPT in general, as well as Speer's and Brugmann's staffs in particular, became a central concern for firms attempting to secure contracts. DEST was one such firm that strove to maintain its quarrying operations through its connections to Nuremberg administrators and architects.

BUILDING AT NUREMBERG, 1935–9

Following the formation in 1935 of the ZRPT, planning and construction were directed almost exclusively to the two ongoing projects of the Luitpoldhain arena and the rebuilding in stone of the Zeppelin Field tribune.[18] Yet even in the first year, it became clear to the representatives of the ZRPT that the expense and extent of building at Nuremberg would be much greater than they had anticipated. More frequently than not, this was due to Hitler's intervention in the building process and his emphasis on rapid rates of construction. Hitler pressed for completion in record time, adding to the costs and administrative complexity. Until the 1935 Party Rally for example, the ZRPT believed that the Zeppelin Field's massive stone pylons at each end of the stands would be the only part of the project finished by 1936. However, after Hitler visited the site in 1935, he ordered that work be stepped up to have the entire Zeppelin Field – pylons, stands and colonnade – completed by the 1936 Party Rally. The construction staff under Brugmann had to rush the labor on the Luitpoldhain in order to free stone-masons for the much larger complex of the Zeppelin Field. Simultaneously, they organized the significantly larger orders, preparation and placement of stone that the new schedule produced. Expanding the budget thus served to pay for the increase in laborers and work hours as well as the many new stone firms brought on board for the project.[19] All of this occurred because of Hitler's personal involvement in architectural planning that consistently tested the ability of the ZRPT to mobilize Party and state funding to carry out the plans.

In 1936, after completing most of the arena in the Luitpoldhain and the Zeppelin Field stands, the ZRPT turned to the much larger task of working on the Congress Hall. A new focus on the Congress Hall launched another rapid expansion of the construction process at Nuremberg. Hitler laid the cornerstone at the 1935

Party Rally and in the November 1935 meeting of the ZRPT, RM 4 million were appropriated for beginning the foundations in April–August 1936. By August, the stone deliveries to the site were to begin, according to reports by Brugmann submitted to the board of the ZRPT.[20] Brugmann's report is only one sign of the increasing specialization of this administrator on stone-procuring problems for the ZRPT and the importance of that job for the overall construction project.

With over RM 115 million approved for the entire complex by September 1937, more than RM 74 million had been set aside for continued work on the monumental buildings while in excess of RM 47 million had already been used for construction and administration costs. Major spending had gone for the Zeppelin Field, the Congress Hall and the Luitpoldhain. Smaller but significant amounts were given out for the March Field and the paved axis through the complex. By 1937, the construction on the foundations of all of these projects had been either partially completed or begun.[21] Financing for the project steadily improved, due to Hitler's support.

In 1937, Speer also began designs for the last major building added to the plan, the German Stadium (Figures 7, 10). At the 1936 Party Rally, Hitler had announced the building of a new stadium that would be used under the auspices of the SA for the sports spectacles at the rallies. Planning continued throughout 1937, while Hitler officially gave the building its name and laid the cornerstone at the Party Rally of that year. By November 1937, the ZRPT had already approved funds for the initial experiments on the ground conditions, finishing of the model and work for the ground-breaking ceremony.[22]

Because of its size, the stadium posed a greater technical and financial problem for the ZRPT than even the Congress Hall. The German Stadium was to be constructed with a brick and stone core and a granite face, thereby avoiding the use of steel or reinforced concrete. This aesthetic and method of construction served a dual purpose. First, the use of granite and brick picked up on a well-established ideological campaign to promote the use of classical building techniques derived from ancient Greek and Roman sources. As Alex Scobie notes, the German Stadium is a conflation of a horseshoe-shaped Roman circus and the Greek use of a propylaeum placed here at the intersection of the stadium with the main axis of the Nuremberg grounds. (The propylaeum functioned as an honor court and colonnaded hall for regimental standards.) This conflation allowed for the competing and often contradictory claims made about monumental architecture by National Socialist cultural administrators: Greek to emphasize the supposed racial connections between contemporary Germany and its Aryan ancestors, Roman to buttress the claims of Nazi Germany as a new and powerful empire. Further emphasis on the Roman derivation of the building came from the construction of the core out of a series of masonry barrel vaults. This architecture, like other monumental state and Party buildings, helped to support the emphasis on permanence which Hitler associated as early as the writing of *Mein Kampf* (1925) with both specific types of classical public architecture as well as the strength of any legitimate political regime.[23]

Figure 10
ALBERT SPEER, MODEL OF THE
GERMAN STADIUM (detail),
NUREMBERG, 1937
Source: A. Speer, *Neue Deutsche Baukunst*, 1941

Yet the use of granite and brick construction was not simply ideologically significant but also corresponded to the needs of the broader German building economy. The second purpose served by this type of construction was the avoidance of iron and steel, building materials needed for factories and weapons production under the rearmament program established in 1936 by the Four Year Plan. Technically, a building with the scale of the German Stadium could be constructed more quickly and at less labor expense with a structural skeleton of steel and reinforced concrete. But with the demand for steel by the armaments industries as well as Fritz Todt's simultaneous use of massive amounts of steel and concrete on the construction of defenses on Germany's border with France (the

West Wall), these materials became politically regulated by Göring's Office of the Four Year Plan. Hence, it was no coincidence that Speer turned in 1937 to a propaganda strategy emphasizing classical construction techniques (e.g. the use of Roman barrel vaults) to show how the Roman Empire could function as a model for the German Reich. The politicization of sectors of the German building economy required that architects consider alternative materials, a search that was easily justified by the ideological implications associated with masonry construction. While construction would be slowed, the choice of stone and brick for the German Stadium represented the personal aesthetic of Hitler, the ideological claims made for monumental architecture and the conditions of the pre-war German building economy with which Speer had to contend.[24]

Construction and planning took a noticeable step forward in 1938 as the site began to take its final shape with all monumental building projects under way. The ZRPT projected a completion date of September 1943 for most of the complex. By August of 1938, a total of RM 211,019,476 had already been approved for the site, over RM 95 million of which had been appropriated since September of the previous year alone. The budgets for the March Field, the Congress Hall and the German Stadium were raised significantly while the Zeppelin Field and Luitpoldhain (for the most part completed) had only small additions to their budgets. The estimated cost for the entire complex had risen to a more realistic figure (in light of the extent of the work) of RM 600 million.[25]

How far these increased financial resources and the administrative organization of the construction process were part of an augmented ability on the part of Speer and Brugmann to prioritize work on the project is indicated in the protocol from the meeting of the ZRPT board in July 1938. The meeting began with a discussion of the German Stadium. Brugmann described the extent of the work and suggested the formation of two associations (Arbeitsgemeinschaften [Arge]) of building contractors that would be large enough to come together and build the northern and southern halves of the stadium. The board approved his suggestion. Brugmann then requested, at the wish of Speer, funds to pay for a scale model of the German Stadium built to observe the aesthetic effect of the massive structure. Kerrl approved the funds, which served retroactively to cover the financing of the model built in Oberklausen by March 1938. Work began on the foundation of the Nuremberg site in July 1938 and the foundation wall was completed between October 1938 and March 1940.[26]

By this board meeting, city building administrators like Brugmann and architects under Speer dominated the proceedings. After the initial struggles over funding, 1938 marked a decisive break as the control over the project passed from the ZRPT board into the hands of those actively promoting and enacting architectural policy. Speer and Brugmann continued to organize, plan and build while the four parties legally responsible for the ZRPT were reduced to paying the bills.[27] Still, the ZRPT remained an important institution, if only as it was needed by Speer, Brugmann *et al.*, to actualize the architectural plans. This concentration of authority increased Speer's ability to determine architectural priorities in Germany and Nuremberg's position as an extraordinary contract for those stone quarries involved.

The second issue raised at the ZRPT meeting concerned the procurement of the massive quantity of stone required for the German Stadium. Speer's building was to be U-shaped, holding 400,000 people and opening to the east on the side facing the central axis. For the façade of the structure, the planning group of the ZRPT estimated that c. 350,000 cbm of granite would be required. This made the German Stadium the largest single granite commission in Germany, rivaled only by buildings planned for Berlin. (It is worth remembering here that the important commission of the New Reich Chancellery required "only" 5,000 cbm of stone.) As with all of the monumental buildings at the site, Hitler had approved the exact type of reddish-pink granite to be used. At the ZRPT meeting, it was noted that about half of the type of stone approved was Meissen granite, coming from the area around Dresden. The granite works, under the construction schedule, would be required to produce in four years 40 per cent of the granite, or 140,000 cbm. Since Meissen granite works then in operation were producing only 3,000 cbm per year and could only be raised to 6,000 cbm per year, other quarries would have to be opened in the area. To this end, an association was formed of the biggest firms in the Dresden Granite Union and the quarries already operating in Meissen. This association would be large enough to maximize production at existing quarries while utilizing revenues to open new works in the area.[28]

The necessity to mobilize the heretofore unheard of quantities of stone for the stadium building determined the formation of a granite association. Similarly, the contractors' associations consisted of the largest construction firms in Germany when they received their contracts for the German Stadium in August 1938.[29] A firm's size was important to the ZRPT as the project required a unified organization of construction tasks that could not be handled by smaller and mid-size firms. With stone as with construction, the measure of the project naturally favored larger firms or associations of several firms that could pool their resources to fulfill the orders and work at the requested tempo. Construction of the Party Rally Grounds, comparable to other areas of the German economy, tended to be dominated by the largest firms.[30] For the stone and construction industry, state funding directed to monumental projects along with a concomitant demand for expanded productivity influenced the preference for commissioning one firm over another for a project like the German Stadium. DEST's success at garnering a significant share of stone orders from the project depended on its ability to compete with other big firms.

Construction of the German Stadium and the other monumental building projects was well under way by 1939. Specific administrators had been assigned tasks for individual buildings, construction firms had been hired and planning for the procurement of materials had begun. The Labor Ministry also designated the site as "politically important to the state" which enabled the ZRPT to secure needed worker allocations from the offices of the Four Year Plan. This designation was crucial if the construction timetable were to be maintained, especially after the crunch on the labor market that occurred after 1936. The budgets for the German

Stadium, the March Field and the Congress Hall rose over RM 28 million each. Construction continued steadily on the walls of the Congress Hall and on eleven of the twenty-four towers planned for the March Field. The ZRPT also sent out stone orders for all monumental buildings on the site.[31]

On 1 September 1939, war brought an abrupt halt to the speedy construction of the Party Rally Grounds. Except for part of the city building administration under Brugmann and his staff, most of the equipment and labor used by the ZRPT were turned over to the war effort such as armaments production. According to a letter from Mayor Liebel to the Finance Ministry dated 30 September 1939, Speer's staff in Berlin decided what was to be cut and what should remain, undoubtedly with Brugmann's advice. Liebel further added that, to close down the building site by 31 March 1940 as planned, RM 8.7 million would be needed. Yet only RM 1.02 million was used specifically for this purpose while RM 6.9 million was reserved to continue stone orders for the Congress Hall, the March Field, the German Stadium and the great central axis. Liebel backed this petition by invoking Hitler's interest in the project: "Further employment of the stone quarries and stone-processing concerns at least at the prevailing level of productivity . . . has been expressly ordered by the Führer according to information from the Generalbauinspektor Professor Speer."[32] Liebel also requested that, if the war were to last longer than one budget year, RM 170,000 per month be provided for the upkeep of the grounds while RM 15.5 million be provided to continue stone orders through August 1940. With the beginning of war, ZRPT officials confidently believed in the success of the *Blitzkrieg* strategy. As a result, stone procurement would still be a top priority.

The pre-war history of the Reich Party Rally Grounds indicates which conditions of the building process would be favorable to the development of economic function of the SS forced-labor concentration camps. First and foremost was Hitler's direct interest which allowed this site to be privileged and supported Speer's ability (as Hitler's representative) to prioritize specific aspects of the building process. Further, the exponential increase in the cost of the building complex made it the most attractive commission (along with Berlin) in all of Germany. That a good percentage of this cost was devoted to the massive amounts of stone required particularly for the German Stadium would give stone quarries with contracts a substantial and secure income for several years. The size of the complex itself also ensured those firms involved a steady, high-profile assignment. Finally, the speed and extent of construction favored those quarrying and construction firms that, through their control of labor, could focus their resources on production quotas. As an institution with complete control over the punishment of prisoners in concentration camps, the SS filled these requirements particularly well.

BUILDING AT NUREMBERG DURING THE WAR

Accounts of National Socialist architecture frequently mention that building or planning continued through the first few years of the war but discuss this period of activity as the fallacious pursuit of architectural policy in an already failing Germany.[33] This conclusion, however, rests on the hindsight of historians already aware of the fate of the German military drive. Hence, scholars have overlooked the early war years as a period of architectural planning and construction. In these years, National Socialist administrators and architects relied on and believed in a German victory, and they saw the war as a temporary situation that meant a reorientation of their goals and interests for a short period of time. Building on site was blocked for the most part; yet the energy and resources for construction were re-routed to other, no less urgent components of the monumental building economy.

As with other sectors of the economy in the early war years, government administrators clearly focused on the prioritization of particular projects and, in the process, emphasized the production of specific materials in the building economy and the mobilization of labor forces. A description of what types of activities and limits administrators and architects faced during the war appears in a letter of 5 June 1940 from Mayor Liebel again to the Finance Ministry. Aside from the restrictions placed on decreasing the staff and some of the financing of the Party Rally Grounds outlined above, Liebel discussed several choices that could be made concerning the continuation of work at the site based on the seemingly successful progress of the war. Planning was to go forward, even extended, based on Hitler's express wishes for this particular project. Stone contracts and deliveries (including stone masonry) would remain on schedule, though Liebel did hope to limit the amount of funds spent on stone. However, Liebel wanted to reserve the right of the ZRPT to ask for more money if conditions should change. ZRPT administrators would press their interests in completing the site whenever the wartime economic and political situation allowed. Furthermore, Liebel added:

> The increase in need [for materials and labor] can follow from the ending of the state of war but also, during the continuation of the state of war, from the resumption of work at the building site as well as from an augmentation of stone deliveries. I may report confidentially that the Führer recently has issued, via the Generalbauinspektor Professor Speer, the directive to resume the work at the Reich Party Rally Grounds with the use of prisoners of war.[34]

The pursuit of architectural goals during the war included the continuation of planning and the gathering of financial support but privileged in particular the acquiring of resources (above all stone) and the mobilization of labor. That this pursuit included the use of war prisoners to do the hardest construction work indicates to what extremes architects and administrators would go to achieve their goals.[35]

For the most part, the actions taken by the ZRPT corresponded to Liebel's account of what could be done during the first war year. By March 1940, all construction had been stopped on the site and work continued only in planning and stone procurement. Restrictions on non-war building activity compounded by the lack of steel and other materials, and the difficult winter of 1939/40, strongly influenced the general building economy. Nevertheless, even given these circumstances, Todt's GBBau projected that building volume for 1940 would reach 75 per cent of peacetime production. Most building activity focused on projects that had been politically and economically prioritized by the GBBau as of primary or secondary importance.[36] The work at Nuremberg had already been listed in 1939 as "Dringlichkeitstufe 1", i.e. a top priority project.

ZRPT confidence in the progress of building corresponded to the optimistic military advance of the Germans through September 1940. The invasion of Norway in April and the self-appointment of Vidkun Quisling as Prime Minister created a friendly government there and opened opportunities for the procurement of stone (in spite of previous Nazi economic policy that favored a reliance on German firms). With the occupation of Paris and the truce signed with France on 22 June, Hitler rescinded the restriction on construction but only for the so-called Hitler cities: Berlin, Munich, Linz, Hamburg and the Rally Grounds at Nuremberg. The victories sustained the assured tone of administrative correspondence. In July 1940, ZRPT financial officers, in a report on why Hitler had canceled the rally for that year to prepare for the attack on England, made the optimism of the ZRPT clear: "The war could be very quickly concluded, perhaps even in half a year or a year. That England will be destroyed thereby is certain."[37] Procurement of stone and the revival of construction activity emphasized the importance of a preferential architectural policy in a Germany that presumed a quick victory.

It therefore needs to be emphasized that the architectural history of wartime National Socialist Germany is not so much a history of design but rather of production. Most previous art historical accounts have rendered these years insignificant because few new monumental designs were produced. But while design was limited, production continued. Certain high-profile projects such as the buildings at Nuremberg were being realized through the mobilization of resources, materials and labor, and the administration of the construction site. Specifically, acquiring the high-quality stone designated by Hitler for particular projects and facilitating its placement at the building site took priority amongst other steps in the production process. To centralize the orders and deliveries of stone for representational buildings in Nuremberg and Berlin, a new administration was set up in 1940 called the Reich Party Rally Buildings Natural Stone Supplies Association (Arbeitsgemeinschaft Natursteinlieferungen Reichsparteitagsbauten Nürnberg GmbH [Arge Nürnberg]). According to its annual report, deliveries for Nuremberg totaled c. 19,000 cbm (German Stadium: 3,408 cbm). Orders for the pylons of the stadium reached 7,000 cbm of granite while additional orders for rough-cut stone were placed through Swedish and Norwegian firms. Simultaneously, Brugmann's office prepared a technical drawing laying out the necessary rail spurs and locations for the delivery of stone to the German Stadium site (Figure 11). In the drawing, stone deliveries are marked through shaded pylons, particularly on the south side of the building, indicating completion of work through 1940. The orders were arranged through Speer's staff in Berlin, which worked closely with the Arge Nürnberg.[38]

From the beginning of the war to March 1941, the extension of funds for the

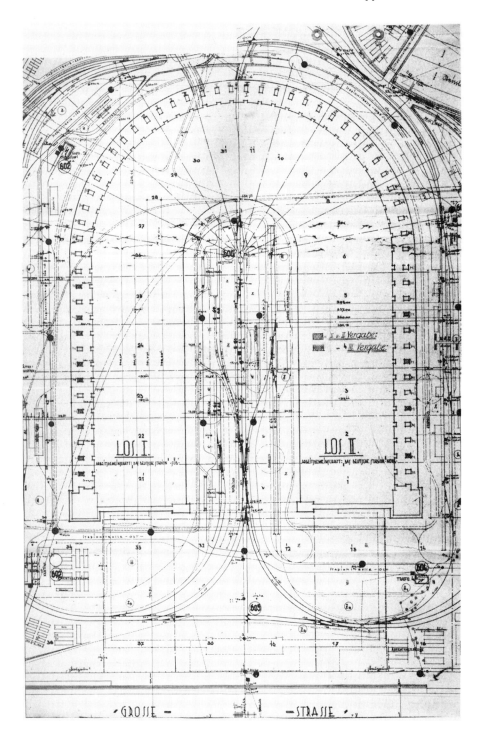

Figure 11
HOCHBAUAMT NÜRNBERG (BRUGMANN), TECHNICAL DRAWING OF THE GERMAN STADIUM
CONSTRUCTION SITE, NUREMBERG, c. 1940
Source: Stadtarchiv Nürnberg

major monuments at Nuremberg supported continued work on the building plans.[39] The resumption of construction activity intensified with the progress made on the Party Rally Grounds throughout the year and focused, again, on labor mobilization and stone procurement. War prisoners, used for the Congress Hall site since October 1940, were forced to work under the auspices of the two contractor Arges on the German Stadium beginning in February 1941. By April, 500 prisoners worked with shovels and machines on excavating the foundation. The orders for stone continued, though at different rates for the various buildings (see Table 2). For example, the Congress Hall placed only 901 cbm of granite orders for the exterior. In this year, workers completed up to the third floor (of four altogether) of the Congress Hall (Figure 12). The building administration for the German Stadium, by comparison, ordered c. 20,000 cbm of granite in Germany and in occupied or friendly territories including Finland, Sweden and Norway, and 2,724 cbm of granite were delivered while work continued on the foundation throughout the year.[40] Thus in terms of stone procurement, Speer's largest project at Nuremberg took precedence during 1941. The SS took advantage of the continued work on the German Stadium by directing several of its stone-quarry operations in this year to the project.

Production and distribution of stone for Hitler's favored projects was further centralized in 1941. The Ministry of Economics ratified a law in June stating that all stone contracts must be registered with the GBBau. This meant that not only did stone production (output) need to be recorded but also stone distribution, guaranteeing that stone reached the key priority projects. Stone distribution now came under the auspices of the Four Year Plan, like other regulated materials such as iron and wood. Further, stone registration with the GBBau was placed under the control of Brugmann, who simultaneously procured stone for the Berlin plans and worked as part of the GBI. By this time, Brugmann had already moved to Berlin as Speer had appointed him in November 1940 to oversee the construction of rebuilding plans in the capital along with his other duties related to Nuremberg.

Table 2: Cubic meters of stone ordered for and shipped to select Nuremberg and Berlin projects, 1940–2

Nuremberg projects	Orders 1940	Shipped 1940	Orders 1941	Shipped 1941	Orders 1942	Shipped 1942
KH	0	6,980	3,501	1,897	1,395	442
MF	(?)	7,423	3,485	5,159	1,834	72
DS	12,000	3,408	20,000	2,724	17,815	68
Berlin project						
SH	41,057	0	28,762	9,972	8,002	7,986

Key: KH: Kongresshalle; MF: Märzfeld; DS: Deutsches Stadion; SH: Soldatenhalle.
Source: Arge Nürnberg Annual Reports, BA, R120/3941d.

With the mobilization of the stone industry centralized in Berlin and his important allies around him, Speer strengthened his ability to pursue building interests in Berlin and Nuremberg simultaneously.[41]

Yet the realities of a protracted war finally affected the Party Rally Grounds in 1942 as resources and state funding were directed towards the military economy. Funds increased from March 1941 to September 1942 but not as dramatically as in previous budgets. Work came to a halt and war prisoners were transferred to armaments industries or other important war-related tasks. The March Field was left with eleven of its twenty-four towers completed, the Congress Hall only finished to the third floor. The German Stadium remained simply a large hole, though some work on the foundation was carried out in the last years of the war.

Figure 12
LUDWIG AND FRANZ RUFF,
CONSTRUCTION OF THE INTERIOR
OF THE CONGRESS HALL,
NUREMBERG, c. 1941
Source: A. Speer, *Neue Deutsche Baukunst*, 1941

Other small tasks throughout the complex were pursued up to the beginning of 1945.[42]

The inability of the ZRPT to pursue its planning and funding efforts depended on the developments of the war and its effect on the German economy. The joining of the United States with the Allies after Germany's declaration of war on 11 December 1941 and the expansion of hostilities deep into Soviet territory provided a significant challenge to the military economy. Fritz Todt died in February 1942 and was replaced by Speer as the Minister of Armaments and Munitions Production and as head of the GBBau. Though Speer and Hitler remained interested in architecture, they were significantly less protective of architectural production. Building at Nuremberg, despite its privileged status, was squeezed by the tasks of the failing German war effort as well as the reprioritization of the building economy and state policy.

Though planning and the procurement of resources continued in Berlin, the ZRPT was not able to maintain its rate of productivity in 1942. Because of the lack of trucks and trains available for non-military industries, only a small amount of stone (584 cbm of granite paving for the central axis) could actually be delivered to the site. The Congress Hall building administration ordered only 155 cbm of granite for the columns on the east façade while less than 2,000 cbm of orders were placed for the March Field support wall (see Table 2). However, orders for the German Stadium remained relatively high with over 17,000 cbm of rough and finished granite. All the while, the ZRPT and Arge Nürnberg continued slowly to lose personnel as they were called up for military service.[43]

By 1943, neither Brugmann nor Speer remained with the ZRPT, a shadow organization with a minimal staff still attempting to maintain the early war optimism and proceed with work on the Party Rally Grounds. Brugmann had already left for the eastern occupied territories to head up an Organization Todt building staff (he died in this service in June 1944) and Speer was busy with his armament tasks. By this time the actual planning and work consisted of minimal design, some construction and ordering of stone controlled mostly by Speer's staff and Nuremberg administrators. Only small quantities of stone were ordered after 1942 for the Congress Hall, the March Field and the German Stadium and few deliveries were made. Stone orders were, however, still being made as late as Spring 1944. Yet by late 1942, the High Command of the Armed Forces (Oberkommando der Wehrmacht [OKW]) had already begun to set up barracks, a canteen and other military facilities on the site.[44] The size of the grounds, its privileged position as a project backed by the local and national governments, important contracting and quarry firms, prominent architects and Hitler himself, did not save the complex from the pressing interests related to the development of the war.

The height of architectural activity at Nuremberg, in 1938–42, occurred during the most optimistic years of National Socialist rule. The pre-war history of the Reich Party Rally Grounds indicates how the design and construction process (particularly in relation to the choice of materials and scale) could lead to other decisions that produced building conditions amenable to the economic function of the SS forced-labor concentration camps. In the war years, the privileging of Nuremberg, the concentration on stone procurement and the need for additional workers led to the use of forced labor on the site and influenced the organization of labor in the quarry camps. Stone procurement for the massive project of the German Stadium came at a time when DEST saw its other potential customers limited by wartime restrictions on building. The prioritization of architectural policy and its implementation at Nuremberg made the Party Rally Grounds a clear target for other institutional, economic and political interests. Through its exploitation of forced labor, the SS attempted to tie key forced-labor facilities to the rising star of Nuremberg and solidify its position in the German building economy.

SS ECONOMIC GOALS AND THE PARTY RALLY GROUNDS

This production history of the building process at Nuremberg is necessary in order to identify the key historical variables that attracted DEST managers to the project and, hence, influenced the policy of oppression in specific forced-labor concentration camps. In this sense, the developing history of the Nuremberg Party Rally Grounds – especially the privileging of the German Stadium in the war years – is part of the explanation of why certain SS administrators made particular decisions at particular times and in individual camps. But it is important to be clear here: Nuremberg architects and administrators did *not* depend on DEST operations, as they searched far and wide for all available quarries that could satisfy their massive material needs. Rather, what the history of building at Nuremberg indicates is that aesthetic choices, the availability of material resources and the evolving wartime political economy of the state all factored into the important preconditions for the SS decision-making process. For while Nuremberg never depended on DEST, SS managers did endeavor to make their forced-labor operations indispensable to the monumental projects of the Party and state by orienting their goals to such projects as the Party Rally Grounds.

By the late 1930s, the SS had focused its plans for expansion of the forced-labor concentration camps not only on the monumental construction project of Berlin but also on the Party Rally Grounds at Nuremberg. The outbreak of hostilities on 1 September 1939 had little initial impact on the continuation of work, especially in the quarries. As noted in the previous chapter, SS quarry concerns along with private quarries were protected from closing and from the transfer of their official SS personnel. Production was sustained not only by the persistence of stone orders and the renewal of construction projects after the 1940 victory in France but also by the influx of political prisoners from throughout Europe. The nature of the concentration camps as institutions designed to punish or kill their inmates perversely guaranteed that the production of building materials would continue. By August 1941, a peak number of 10,613 prisoners was being used in the DEST brickworks and quarries.[45]

Whereas the SS had a specific and immediate interest in the building plans for Berlin from the inception of DEST in 1938, the particular connection of DEST concerns to the Party Rally Grounds came only in this period of military optimism.[46] For example, from May 1939 to March 1943, DEST submitted stone samples from the concentration camps at Flossenbürg, Mauthausen and Natzweiler to be checked by the state materials office. Regulators examined the stones for their resistance to pressure, and DEST sent the results to the ZRPT to be considered for the construction of the German Stadium. The stone samples were all designated good enough to be used at least in the structural support of the building. After these tests, the ZRPT ordered stone for the German Stadium from the quarries at KL Flossenbürg, KL Gross-Rosen (for which no pressure report exists) and KL Natzweiler from 1941 to 1943. In addition, ZRPT administrators indicated as early as May 1940 that DEST works would be one of the few operations that they would use to provide the unusually large stones (averaging 22–6 tons) necessary for certain parts of the stadium. Size, quality and productivity were all factors that linked DEST concerns with the Nuremberg project.[47]

KL Natzweiler was particularly planned in relation to the construction of the German Stadium in Nuremberg, and its development as a stone-quarry forced-labor camp ran parallel to the fortunes of the stadium's construction into the war years. After the victory over France, the SS founded the new camp in Alsace as a forced-labor center and collection point for prisoners captured in occupied western and northern Europe. However, at least until the end of 1941, the camp notably did not serve its purported political purpose in relation to this designated population. That is to say, initially prisoners were coming from other concentration camps and were overwhelmingly of German or eastern European origin. The SS sent the first consignment of prisoners in September 1940 and the quarries were being worked by May 1941. Just as with the chronological development of the stadium construction, the amount of finished stone from Natzweiler for the ZRPT, though small, rose substantially in 1941–2 and then dropped off by 1943.[48]

The increasing supply of political and ideological prisoners sustained the confidence of the SS in expanding its operations and simultaneously provoked few expressions of concern for the deaths decimating the work force especially in the difficult conditions of the quarry camps. Many of the prisoners taken to KL Natzweiler were those suspected of working against the military governments in the northern countries controlled by Germany. Their numbers were enlarged after Hitler's so-called Night and Fog decree of 7 December 1941. The decree meant to halt resistance to the new leaders and was provoked after several attacks led by Communist partisans on the German army in France. Prisoners were not tried in their own country but transferred quietly by the SS to the German penal or concentration camp system. By August 1942, they began to expand the ranks of Natzweiler's inmate population. The total number of NN-prisoners (as they were designated) came to 7,000 of whom 5,000 were from France; attempts were made to centralize some of these prisoners at Natzweiler. By this time, the DEST concern consistently used each month 200–300 of those inmates to quarry stone.[49]

Himmler and Pohl made the decision to direct the quarry at Natzweiler towards the Party Rally Grounds already at the founding of this concentration camp. When the SS resolved to establish two more KL in 1940, Himmler and Pohl went to Speer to inquire about the best places to locate the camps, that is, areas where the stone would be particularly suitable to Speer's plans in Nuremberg and Berlin. KL Gross-Rosen was located in a region of high deposits of blue-gray granite, while KL Natzweiler was on a site that offered a rich and unusual type of red granite suitable for the German Stadium. That Natzweiler was built to produce material specifically for this project was confirmed by a contract for stone signed on 4 September 1941. The contract secured the entire output of red granite at the quarry exclusively for the stadium.[50] With their decision to locate the camp according to Speer's aesthetic material needs, Himmler and Pohl connected the political function of the camp to the privileged position of the German Stadium and its subsequent history.

The quantity and kind of stone the prisoners quarried had a direct effect on the planning and development of the camp. Prisoners forced to work in the harsh climatic and labor conditions of the quarries at Natzweiler were meant eventually to produce at least 25,000 cbm of red granite per year. Because of the slow process by which a hard stone such as granite was quarried in comparison to softer stones, this amount would be impressive for any quarrying enterprise. The 25,000 cbm of granite would contribute to DEST's overall ability to control a large share of the granite production throughout Germany (in pre-war Germany the industry produced c. 80,000 cbm yearly).[51] By focusing on output instead of efficiency, the SS foresaw that the production goals could be reached precisely through driving the prisoners to their deaths in the process.[52] The prioritization of materials by Hitler and Speer led to a similar prioritization of the production process by DEST. Such self-confident aspirations for the SS quarry system depended on the ability of the camps not only to produce large amounts of stone but also to feed that production into the monumental building projects of the Party and state.

It is worth emphasizing at this point that the economic policy governing the expansion of DEST at Natzweiler was by no means the only reason that prisoners were worked hard, even to the point of death. Rather the SS economic policy formed the bond between the political oppression in the camps and the architecture of the Party and state. Death and oppression in the forced-labor camps resulted from multiple causes (including the production of building materials) and were initiated by the agency of different individuals. The commandants, for example, often did not share the production goals of what they saw as a bunch of DEST pencil pushers and viewed their role as simply political, i.e. as punishing the inmates, and had no interest in their labor potential. On the other hand, SS economic administrators often saw the prison labor force only in terms of their productive capacity (as long as they were healthy enough to work). Both groups influenced the day-to-day life and fate of the inmates. Yet, whereas economic and political goals were variably implemented through forced labor, SS administrators and camp commandants agreed that the punishment of the inmates was to be a shared goal.[53]

What this meant for the inmate was that his chances of survival depended on multiple factors. First and foremost were the hygienic conditions and availability of food. Hunger and weakness caused by far the greatest number of deaths. Further, the inmate had to negotiate the potential violence of particular SS officers, guards and Kapos who could physically punish a prisoner on no pretext whatsoever. And, of course, these extreme conditions meant that the inmate had to guard against other inmates who were engaged in the same struggle for survival, fighting for the extra ration of food, the job under a roof in the winter months, or the place in line least likely to be noticed by the particularly brutal guard. In this sense, it is not the case that the economic goal of connecting forced labor to Nuremberg single-handedly dominated the camp life. Rather, the pre-conditions for the decision to use a particular kind of forced labor (quarrying), the experience of the prisoner in the quarries and his health as subject to these labor conditions were all contributing factors that influenced the chances of survival in the already extreme institution of the concentration camp.[54]

With Natzweiler, the relation of camp conditions to the monumental building economy became a reality with the receipt of contracts from the ZRPT in 1941. Because of the size of the German Stadium project, all major German quarries that could produce the reddish-pink granite necessary for the façade had to be mobilized by the ZRPT due to the proposed construction schedule. Throughout 1941, Speer himself visited countries controlled by Germany searching for potential stone quarries and mason shops that could handle the workload created by the projects of Berlin and Nuremberg. Further, K.F. Liebermann, head of the German Stadium building site administration under Brugmann, visited several quarries to check the quality of stone during the year including Natzweiler.[55] The wartime concentration on stone procurement (particularly for the German Stadium) and the favoring of larger supply firms by the ZRPT, provided fertile conditions for DEST opportunities. These conditions continued as long as the military successes allowed.

Stone quarrying, however, was neither the only forced-labor task connected to the monumental building economy in these camps nor the only type of work which influenced the day-to-day life of the prisoners. With the opening of KL Natzweiler and the expansion of the forced-labor concentration camp system between 1939 and 1942, the SS attempted to establish its peacetime role in other important areas of the German monumental building economy. The pursuit of these interests at the height of wartime optimism engendered not only more stone-quarry camps but a diversification of labor at those quarries. Specifically, in late 1940, the SS set up stone-mason workshops at Flossenbürg and planned to establish similar units at the camps at Natzweiler, Gross-Rosen, Mauthausen and Oranienburg II (part of KL Sachsenhausen). Stone masonry was a crucial part of larger quarry firms as it meant that blocks of cut stone could be dressed at least to the general specifications of the intended building projects before shipping, requiring only minimal work at the site itself.[56] The SS used stone-masonry programs set up for such commissions as the German Stadium to integrate into and even dominate parts of the building economy through the exploitation of forced labor.

DEST administrators organized workshops at a time when the stone-mason industry, like other trades, was optimistic about future commissions but remained concerned about the tendencies towards rationalization in the building economy common since 1938. Trade organizations feared rationalization, since it meant a focus on efficiency and productivity, favorable to large firms and threatening to smaller ones. A memorandum of March 1941 on the building trades from the Reich Professional Organization of German Trades (Reichsstand des Deutschen Handwerks) made the situation clear. The authors repeatedly emphasized that the smaller and mid-size firms were unable to compete with the larger firms because of the move from single building sites to larger complexes like the Party Rally Grounds. A dearth of small-scale commissions had resulted from the preference for cooperatives of larger concerns particularly as the war affected small shops more than their bigger competitors. Larger firms had the contracts to do trade work while smaller firms went without or were subsumed under the guidance of larger ones.[57]

The trade association report did not argue against the perceived necessity of rationalizing the building economy, as the trades also acknowledged the need for an even distribution of projects created by the conditions of war or by the expansive demands of peacetime. Yet, concern was expressed with regard to the survival of the smaller shops. With quarry conglomerates like the association of Meissen granite works providing stone for the German Stadium and contractors like the Arge-Süd and -Nord, the tendency towards an oligarchic control of the market was recognized and feared by the building trades. The trade group recommended the rationalization of smaller firms as well, forming cooperative labor pools that could compete effectively with the larger concerns at least on the local level. These cooperatives would allow the smaller firms to raise productivity without large investments of capital typical in the larger firms.[58]

In one of the few available economic pronouncements personally signed by Himmler, the Reichsführer-SS responded to this memorandum from the trade organization with a letter of 13 October 1941 to the Reich Trade Master (Reichshandwerksmeister). This document allows us some insight into SS economic policy and its interest in prioritizing the diversification of work in the quarry camps connected to the monumental building economy. At this point, the SS was not only establishing stone-mason training centers in the concentration camps but also expanding its control over other types of building concerns – cement works, brick-making centers, construction firms – in the occupied eastern territories. Himmler achieved these advances through his appointment as Reich Commissioner for the Consolidation of German Nationhood and institutionalized the new enterprises in the SS East German Building Materials Works.[59] Because of its receipt of contracts from Nuremberg, its development of the concentration camps, the increase in prison populations and expansion in the east, the SS had much to say and hope for in the way of the building trades.

With the addition of stone-mason workshops to the quarry concerns, Himmler could with confidence belittle the fears of the smaller firms and promote instead larger businesses engaging in oligarchic practices, a position which mimics that of the architects and administrators active at Nuremberg. Himmler wrote to Schramm that the trade association's fears concerning competition between small and large firms ran "like a red flag" throughout the report. Himmler saw no contradiction between the smaller firms and the tendency towards a market controlled by businesses engaging in oligarchic practices. As the German building economy would be overwhelmed by building projects after the end of the war, Himmler believed that plenty of opportunities would still exist for the small and medium-size firms. However, Himmler agreed with the trade report in emphasizing the importance of raising performance as a means of lowering costs. To accomplish building tasks in peacetime, he suggested that no wage raises or price wars should impair the building process. Rather, the focus of the trades should be on the quantity of output alone. Productivity, in Himmler's mind and as expressed in the trade association report, could be increased through the careful training of workers and the expansion of apprenticeship programs.[60]

Of course, Himmler's position served the SS's own interests. DEST competed in the building economy as a large firm with an established stone-mason program. At the beginning of the war, 7,805 stone-mason and sculpture (*Bildhauerei*) shops existed in Germany, of which only six employed more than 100 people. As of 1 June 1940, employment stood at 3,781 full stone-masons, 6,080 journeymen and 2,217 apprentices active in private concerns. In order to secure these workers for the building economy, government sources told the trade association in 1942 that soldiers who were stone-masons would be released first from active duty as the military situation allowed. With hostilities supposedly coming to an end, this would increase the number of stone-masons available for monumental projects.[61] The SS wanted to establish a dominant role in this market not to destroy the competition from the trade organizations but in order to establish itself in the anticipated peacetime building economy.

As is evident from its own plans for the concentration camps, DEST was clearly up to the task of charting a path for itself through the stone-mason trades in the German building economy. Already the largest quarrying firm in Germany, DEST foresaw augmenting its powerful position by overwhelming the stone-mason industry as well. The initial impetus for a stone-mason program came from the need to provide masons for the SS's own architectural projects, which were meant to be numerous after the war.[62] SS administrators quickly supplemented this goal with the plan to secure an undisputed position within the private stone-mason industry, competing for monumental building commissions. In a secret memorandum from 5 December 1941 to Heydrich, Richard Glücks (who succeeded Eicke as Inspekteur der KL) and all concentration camp commandants, Himmler made these strong ambitions abundantly clear. Though they now appear to be fantastic (and are often dismissed by scholars as so),[63] they were meant to be immediately acted upon in the camps.

> The building plans of the Schutzstaffel [SS], especially after the war, demand that even
> now far-reaching preparatory measures be taken.
>
> With this belongs first the provision of the necessary building labor force. The
> Schutzstaffel is in the exceptionally favorable position to train and to extract this labor
> force from the prisoners in the concentration camps.
>
> I have therefore commissioned the Chief of the V.- und W.-Hauptamtes [WVHA],
> SS-Gruppenführer Pohl, to train before the peace agreement (for the monumental
> buildings then beginning): (1) at least 5,000 stone-masons, (2) at least 10,000
> bricklayers. If one considers that throughout Germany before the war there were only
> about 4,000 trained stone-masons, the extent of this education task is easy to recognize
> and to survey. But we will use these 5,000 stone-masons, as already now an order from
> the Führer exists for which the Deutsche Erd- und Steinwerke GmbH (as a concern of the
> Schutzstaffel) has to deliver with the beginning of peace yearly at least 100,000 cbm of
> granite for the monumental buildings of the Führer. That is more than all stone quarries
> in the old Reich [pre-1938 Germany] had supplied before the war![64]

Here, the comparison of the number of potential prisoner stone-masons with those
in the private enterprises explicitly indicates that, with the completion of
these plans, Himmler wanted to secure a dominant place for the SS in the building
economy. Himmler attempted to justify the plan in terms of the building economy
as a whole, and his optimism could be sustained at this moment by the German
victories in France and the beginning of the attack on the USSR (before the decisive
battle of Stalingrad in 1942–3). Coupled with the hoped-for production of stone,
Himmler's optimism encouraged DEST's pursuit of linking economic interests to
the monumental building plans of the Party and state. Uniting the policing,
administrative and economic authority of Heydrich, Glücks and Pohl under a
common effort of stone production would further strengthen DEST's chances of
receiving a larger percentage of Nuremberg contracts.

Himmler's letter outlined specific goals for DEST enterprises that would
enable them to compete successfully with private industry and expand his influence
in a peacetime German empire. Such state-supported ventures were not an
anomaly, and, particularly in the war years, large conglomerates operated with the
help of state contracts and political regulation of the market. Similarly, many
private concerns were working with the state and the SS to secure forced labor for
their own work sites.[65] But the point here is not that the SS is unique in turning
to forced labor as an economic tool. Rather, what remained unique about DEST
forced-labor enterprises was the absolute political control over this forced labor
through SS institutional authority. SS political power and Himmler's direct access to
Hitler and Speer significantly strengthened DEST chances of becoming a major
force in the building economy. Though DEST at this time could only point to the
potential output of the quarries, the rapid development of the enterprises and an
already promising amount of quarried and cut stone assured a level of productivity
that must have been attractive to clients like Speer.

Important for Himmler in this letter and elsewhere was meeting production quotas that would guarantee SS goals at Natzweiler and the other quarry camps. As an inducement for increased production in the stone-mason programs, the chosen prisoners were supposed to receive extra rations and clothing. They were also assured through such propaganda as the leaflet "The Way to Freedom" that they would be released. Additional promises were made for separate housing, more free time, better food and increased communication with relatives. The leaflet also maintained that, after the schooling, the prisoner was to be freed, though he must remain in the service of another SS stone quarry where he would be resettled. Such a memo was sent to Natzweiler early in 1942 in preparation for setting up a stone-mason program to process stone for the German Stadium.[66]

Natzweiler had to wait, however, until a significant number of prisoners were trained in the established programs at the larger camps of Flossenbürg and Mauthausen. Oranienburg II at KL Sachsenhausen opened as a center purely for stone-masonry in 1941 while the training program at Gross-Rosen was meant to begin in 1941 but made slow progress throughout its history. Conditions did change slightly for those prisoners who became stone-masons, mostly due to the better working environment of the shop as opposed to the quarry. Prisoners were not released from these concentration camps even after they improved their performance as stone-masons.[67]

With such false promises to the camp population and the commitment of trained personnel and resources, DEST set up the program, though not on the scale originally projected. While preliminary plans were in place for a cutting and polishing shop at KL Mauthausen by May 1940, DEST established its first stone-mason workshop at KL Flossenbürg in October 1940. Initially, some of the prisoners' work went towards cutting the stone needed for the *Autobahn* bridges and some towards the SS's own building ventures, such as troop housing or the construction of the camp itself. Yet, by April 1942, part of the high-quality stone being quarried and cut by the forced labor at Flossenbürg was going as well to fulfill contracts for the German Stadium. In December 1942, 1,200 prisoners were active as apprentices or full-fledged stone-masons at Flossenbürg, a number that, as the monthly report noted, matched the goal set by the central administration. The total number of prisoners being trained in the SS system reached a high of 2,238 by the end of 1942. This number made DEST the largest stone-mason shop in the Germany monumental building economy.[68] Stone-mason workshops provided a means to solidify the connection of the economic concerns to such projects as the Party Rally Grounds.

To train prisoners, DEST managers brought in masters from the private stone industry. The average training period lasted approximately ten weeks and, by 1941, included both a practical and theoretical education in stone cutting. While civilians were used to run the course, a Kapo who had already been trained was appointed to keep the work details in line. At Flossenbürg, premiums (of tobacco, additional food) were only given to prisoners if they improved their productivity, while beatings from the Kapo or (worse) being sent back to the harsh working conditions of the quarry awaited those prisoners who, in the eyes of the SS, failed to advance.

In the early stages of training, the prisoners deemed best suited to the work were most often German men in the camps with criminal records, or Jehovah's Witnesses. Soviet prisoners of war were added by early 1942.[69] These prisoners were chosen based on their ability to meet production quotas.

Yet, even as early as winter 1941, DEST administrators were beginning to question whether the prison population was as easily replaceable as they had believed. Heinz Schwarz, head of the quarry division of the SS economic administration, warned that the end of the war in 1941 would lead to the release precisely of those groups previously favored for stone cutting. This would, of course, threaten the achievement of SS goals and the expansion into the building materials market for the Party Rally Grounds. Schwarz asked in his memorandum of February 1941 that Pohl discuss with Himmler where new labor was to come from in peacetime. But though he, as an economic administrator, worried about the inverse relationship between the severity of punishment and the prisoners' ability to work, Himmler did not share these doubts. Because Himmler had his almost unlimited police authority extended through the development of pre-war and wartime government policy, he had significant room to make the arrest and delivery of prisoners congruent with his economic plans. The receipt of contracts from Nuremberg, one of the few monumental building sites that throughout 1941 did very well in procuring stone, and the need for an extensive police apparatus in the National Socialist state allowed Himmler seemingly to remain confident in pursuing the quarry and stone-mason enterprises in the concentration camps.[70] Such a goal relied on the wartime emphasis on labor productivity, materials and the prioritization of specific projects.

The private stone-mason industry reacted skeptically to DEST when the mobilization of resources and the training of greater numbers of prisoners began. The critique of Gross-Rosen by Naturstein- und Kalkwerke W. Thust, a private quarry firm in the area of the camp, exemplified the problem. In April 1942, DEST received a report from the Reich Trustee of Work (Reichstreuhänder der Arbeit) in Lower Silesia forwarding a complaint from the Thust concern about the stone-mason program at Gross-Rosen. Gross-Rosen at the time had begun to populate a stone-mason trainee program with eligible young men from the occupied eastern territories who were sympathetic to National Socialism. Once the training was completed, they were to apprentice at other concentration camps and then teach prisoners the trade. In this way, DEST attempted to provide its own civilian teaching staff for the mason programs. Thust pointed out, however, that the SS was operating at an unfair advantage in comparison to other quarries and workshops in Silesia. SS wages were higher than those in the private economy, and the private firms were having trouble attracting young people to apprenticeship programs. They could not draw from the entire occupied territory as the SS did. Thust voiced the fear that the apprentices would remain in Silesia and, because of the size of Gross-Rosen and the resources of DEST, would effectively control the market in the area, squeezing out the smaller competition.[71]

DEST administrator Leo Volk wrote the response to the Reichstreuhänder based on consultations with Mummenthey (head of DEST at the time) and

Schwarz. Volk asserted in his letter of 26 May 1942 that the DEST work would not pose a problem for the recruitment of apprentices in the area as the young men were to be drawn from outside of Silesia. Most of the apprentices would also be sent to other DEST concerns after completion of the course, thereby not contributing to a glut in the Silesian market. And, as Volk pointed out, the erection of an apprenticeship quarters and workshop at Gross-Rosen was not only approved by the president of the Silesian work office but personally ordered by Himmler. As this was an SS matter, Volk seemed to imply that the private industry had no say, a position that was strengthened by the political management of the wartime economy.[72] The political function of the camps here was used as a further means of securing DEST's potential peacetime authority.

Thus, in an attempt to establish a large and rationalized quarry and stone-mason industry through the forced labor of the camps, the SS actively pursued its interest, drawing on its own authority to silence the competition. Simultaneous with the high-point of German advances and SS optimism, the central economic administration pressured the concentration camps to increase the output of the prisoners. Prisoners could improve their conditions by volunteering to be trained and thereby escaping the harder labor in the quarries. In the workshops, they were also relatively more valued though apparently driven just as hard. Himmler even voiced frustration that the prisoners were not outperforming their equivalents in the private building economy. In a letter of 23 March 1942 to Pohl, he stated:

> Practically, it must be so that at least the imprisoned unskilled laborer produce more than his free counterpart. One cannot understand why the imprisoned skilled worker should not produce the same as a skilled worker living in freedom. Here hides the greatest reserve in labor power.[73]

Notably, Himmler's frustration is directed at the productivity of the labor force not at improving the labor conditions which might guarantee a more efficient working population. Nevertheless, in a token gesture, Himmler continued by suggesting the establishment of bordellos (staffed with the forced labor of women inmates from other camps) for the best-performing prisoners and a "certain small" pay.[74] With these changes, he believed the programs for training qualified building personnel could not fail. To him, the total control of the punitive function of the camps was precisely that which would secure the increased output necessary for major building commissions.

The creation of stone-mason programs in the camps corresponded to the reinstatement of construction at the Party Rally Grounds and the approval of further funds for stone contracts. DEST had gained German Stadium contracts for all of Natzweiler's production and part of Gross-Rosen's and Flossenbürg's. Stone-mason programs ensured that production could be speeded up at the construction site, thus potentially allowing SS enterprises to participate to a greater degree than quarries that could not provide the same amount of processed stone. That the SS rationalized and expanded its quarry industry system in the same years when privileged architectural projects narrowed to those at Nuremberg and Berlin was no coincidence. Rather, the expansion of the SS system and the continuation of stone orders and construction for the German Stadium in particular were two processes controlled by administrators working together to further their interests.

The increased political management of the German building economy beginning in 1936 made it easier for both the ZRPT and the SS to maneuver: the former had the direct approval of Hitler for its projects; the latter legitimized its economic efforts through the attachment of architectural projects to the oppression of individuals in the forced-labor concentration camps. Before the military changes in 1942, architects and SS administrators focused their concerns on material resources and the productivity of labor to such a degree that these factors became rationalized justifications for the irrational exploitation of the concentration camp inmates. While most SS camp commandants still saw the forced-labor camps as primarily political institutions to incarcerate, punish and even destroy unwanted populations, the majority of SS bureaucrats from Himmler on down saw the practical purposes to which this political oppression could be put. DEST took advantage of its influence on the burgeoning labor population and the prioritized needs of Speer and his architects. SS administrators through the early war years made organizational and administrative decisions for the forced-labor camps which allowed for the uneasy progress of both economic and political goals as each was tied to and legitimized by the monumental building projects. They attempted to achieve these goals by taking advantage of their absolute control over a forced-labor population and access to architectural contracts for projects favored by Hitler and Speer.

The prioritization of architectural policy by the Party and state, the integration of monumental architectural projects into the German building economy and the movement towards an oligarchic market were all factors favoring the SS. Himmler and Pohl attempted to make the political institutions of the concentration camps not only productive but integral to the building economy. To repeat, however, the ZRPT was not dependent on SS economic concerns, as the scale of the project was so massive that Nuremberg architects and administrators mobilized all available quarries that could satisfy their needs, even in wartime. Hence, Nuremberg did not depend on the SS. Nevertheless, the SS attempted to make its forced-labor operations indispensable to such projects as the Party Rally Grounds by a massive expansion of its operations, a differentiation of work at the quarries and its punitive authority over the inmates. Once the initial decision was made to produce specific building materials for Nuremberg with forced labor, the SS geared aspects of its DEST enterprises to particular production quotas and to an extension into the stone-mason industry. In so doing, DEST managers acquired firm contracts from Speer's German Stadium in order to ensure that the camps developed with state architectural policy.

SS policy, however optimistic in the early war years, could not withstand the increasing number of German military defeats beginning in late 1942 with the setback at Stalingrad. The German economy had to mobilize all of its resources for the war effort and Speer, in his role as Minister of Armaments, began to lead the way. This included the use of the forced labor in the concentration camps. New military priorities were set that excluded an architectural or economic focus on the monumental building economy. By May 1943, all the quarries had been closed at Natzweiler and labor turned to armaments duty. Other KL quarries were soon to follow, though minimal quarrying continued at Flossenbürg and Mauthausen late into the war.[75] Even before then, the SS plans were constantly frustrated by the "overall bad human material"[76] that constituted the prison labor force. The SS refused to recognize that it had created these conditions by putting prisoners through the brutal process of arrest, transport and forced labor. From 1939 to 1942 prisoners seemed imminently replaceable and could therefore be treated by the SS as another raw resource, like so much iron. At the time, such a labor practice sustained the optimistic pursuit of connecting SS economic policy to the monumental architectural projects of the Party and state. That the politically driven separation of efficiency and productivity was inherently unstable appears contradictory only in retrospect.

Chapter 4: The Rebuilding of Berlin

The Interdependence of the GBI and the SS

In discussing his early rise to prominence as an architect in 1933–4, Albert Speer stated "I must have had the feeling that it was no affair of mine when I heard the people around me declaring an open season on Jews, Freemasons, Social Democrats, or Jehovah's Witnesses. I thought I was not implicated if I myself did not take part."[1] Speer's limited acknowledgment of his guilt for merely remaining inactive is a consistent theme in both his memoirs and in his account of the SS use of forced labor in *Infiltration* (1981). Much of the art historical literature on Speer has taken up this question of culpability in its attempt to understand the moral implications of Speer's position in the Nazi state or to condemn the architect for intentional obfuscation of his record.[2] But the question of culpability has led scholars to concentrate less on the actions of the architect and his administration and more on his motivations: did he believe in the anti-Semitic ideology that his architecture was used to promote? Was he an ardent National Socialist or a young and inexperienced pawn of Hitler? Should we see his architectural designs as essentially apolitical, as separate from and, hence, unencumbered by the corrupt regime which sponsored them? Should we hold him individually responsible or assume that he is part of the "collective guilt" of the German nation? Guilty or innocent, morally reprehensible or the only truly repentant Nazi? Certainly, these questions are rarely asked for any other architectural period. (Do we ever suggest that Louis Sullivan or Daniel Burnham are "guilty" because their early skyscrapers were built by exploited workers engaging in a prolonged and violently suppressed fight for labor rights?) And yet they permeate the literature on Speer's architecture even while much of the evidence to establish these claims has remained unresearched.

In this chapter, I wish to focus more closely not on judging the motivations of Speer but on analyzing his actions. To examine critically the agency of his staff and their interactions with the SS is to analyze more thoroughly the intersection of SS interests with cultural policy. With the rebuilding of Berlin, not only did DEST administrators adapt the ventures under their control to architectural policy, but architects and administrators working for Speer's office of the Inspector General of Building for the Reich Capital Berlin (GBI) also became involved in and supported the economic interests of the SS. Berlin's status as a pre-eminent architectural project was achieved both through Hitler's direct interest and by the extension of Speer's authority to control architectural policy. The centralization of architectural policy and its prioritization into the war years involved GBI architects in the establishment of specific pre-conditions for DEST enterprises; but it also involved them in the active process of developing forced-labor concerns. Establishing how the GBI increased its authority and the autonomy of its office, and how other administrations (including the SS) aided Speer in this goal helps in clarifying the nature of the architects' agency in the development of DEST.

As with Nuremberg, a discussion of DEST's interests in Berlin requires some attention to the development of the monumental building economy. Quarries and contractors, architects and brick-layers were mobilized by the GBI, making this office the largest single architectural patron in the German building economy. Access to Speer's staff and adaptation to the demands of GBI designs became crucial factors for the success of a firm. This was particularly true for the quarry industry that relied on the privileging of state architectural policy during the war. Analyzing DEST's orientation of specific forced-labor sites to these building conditions further evidences its attempt to become indispensable to the monumental building economy.

Still, in the case of Berlin, it was not just a matter of DEST adapting its concerns to architectural requirements but also the fact that GBI administrators became involved with the quarrying process and, additionally, with the SS policing apparatus. Contrary to Speer's claims of avoiding collusion with the most extreme policies of National Socialism, it is with the support of the GBI that DEST carried out significant aspects of its economic developments. Aesthetic decisions determined the varied stages of the building process including site-clearing operations, administrative organization, funding decisions and, of course, the quantity and kind of building materials. With the GBI and the SS, this process not only promoted economic relations but, increasingly, institutional relations which brought together members of the GBI (Speer, Brugmann, Hettlage, Clahes) with key officials in the SS economic and political administration (Himmler, Pohl, Mummenthey, Schwarz and Heydrich). While these officials never had an easy relationship, their interests converged here in order to enact aspects of their diverse political, economic and architectural goals.[3]

Thus, the interrelatedness of DEST and Berlin architectural policy extended as well to the involvement of Berlin architects with the SS. DEST targeted the Berlin plans for the success of some of its major enterprises, in particular the brickworks and stone-cutting workshops (Oranienburg I and II, respectively) at KL Sachsenhausen and the quarries at KL Flossenbürg. The strengthening of the institutional ties between the GBI and DEST focused on three different developments in the economic enterprises: the initial failure of the Oranienburg brickworks; the close involvement of the GBI in setting up Oranienburg II; and the prominent place of stone contracts with KL Flossenbürg for Wilhelm Kreis' Soldiers Hall (Figure 13), a central monument in Speer's rebuilding plans. But further, the GBI also called on the policing power of the SS to acquire Jewish housing for those displaced by site-clearing operations and, later during the war, to control prisoners of war used in construction work.

The administrative and material contingencies of the building process led to the convergence of a complementary series of policy decisions. This does not, however, indicate a clean and linear narrative, but rather an often episodic and variable involvement of the institutional interests of one administration with the other as they both participated in the developing building economy. An evaluation of this complicated relationship between the SS and the GBI presents not only evidence concerning the ability of the SS to connect its growing political authority to architectural policy through economic ventures. It also shows how GBI architects became involved with SS concentration camps through their willingness to promote architecture not only as an expression of ideology but as a tool of politics.

THE FUNCTION OF NATIONAL SOCIALIST BUILDING IN BERLIN

Berlin was the pre-eminent building site in National Socialist Germany through the late 1930s and into World War II. Its position at the center of state and Party architectural policy was achieved both through Hitler's direct interest in the redesign of the capital and through the centralization and extension of Speer's control over architectural policy as the head of the GBI. The actual plan, announced publicly on 28 January 1938, included a North–South and East–West Axis at the heart of the city, a concentration of subway and train facilities, a redesign of the Königsplatz and a major housing program (see Figure 3). With its numerous monumental neoclassical structures, the North–South Axis became the core of the urban design and was meant to function as the main ceremonial boulevard of the new Berlin.[4] While little of the North–South Axis was ever completed, the construction of particular buildings and the actualization of the site as a whole dominated the activity of construction firms and architects in Berlin. Realization of the plan rested on the ability of the GBI to work with every major political, social and economic institution with interests in the organization of the city.

Even prior to the redesign plan, however, the importance of building in Berlin had been well established in the years before the NSDAP came to power and in the early years of its regime. As with the Party Rally Grounds, building in Berlin was used both as a symbol for specific ideological policies as well as a means of asserting Party (and specifically Hitler's) control over an existing administration. In the late Weimar Republic, NSDAP propaganda effectively characterized Berlin's building administration headed by Martin Wagner as an insidious instrument of Social Democratic policies. Hitler's early pronouncements on architecture and his distrust of the city building administration formed the basis of the ideological and institutional critique of Wagner's administration. Nevertheless, in his first few years in power, Hitler still proposed all construction projects through the existing building

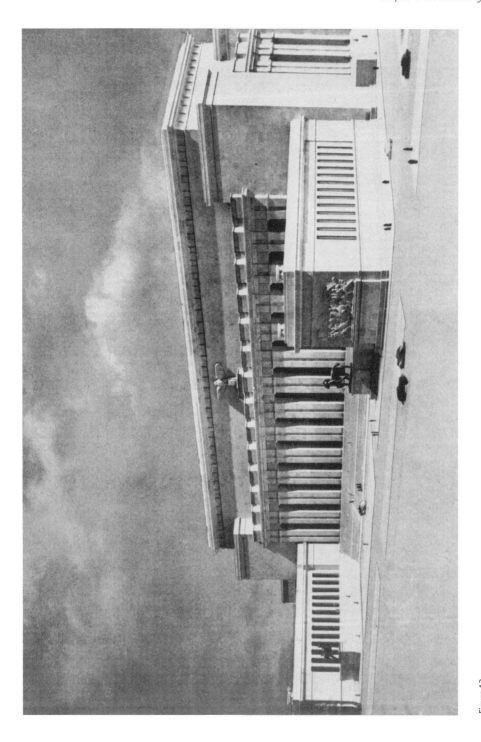

Figure 13
WILHELM KREIS, MODEL FOR THE SOLDIERS' HALL, BERLIN, *c.* 1939
Source: G. Troost, *Bauen im neuen Reich*, 1938

administration for the city. While Jewish members of the architectural admin-istration as well as high-profile Weimar era specialists like Wagner were summarily dismissed or "excused" (*beurlaubt*), Hitler allowed the administration to continue with its duties.[5]

Yet Hitler wanted to have personal control over major architectural projects and increasingly found the Berlin building administration, which was subordinate to the city and state governments, inadequate for carrying out his goals. Both the criticisms of the previous bureaucracy and the priority given to architectural policy by Hitler meant that early on he began to use building in Berlin as a means of controlling projects that would be completed outside of fixed bureaucratic channels. Between 1933 and 1936, Hitler already showed his interest in extend-ing his authority over architecture in the promotion of Troost's plans for the Königsplatz in Munich as well as his involvement with the Party Rally Grounds. In Berlin, Hitler involved himself in the first monumental building completed under his regime, the new Federal Bank project, for which he personally chose the bank's architect Heinrich Wolff over the other five finalists in the competition (including, famously, Mies van der Rohe). Further, Hitler used the special circumstances of the upcoming 1936 Olympics to influence Werner March's design for the stadium as well as additional city planning measures for the layout of the site and the dependent urban infrastructure. In the case of March's design, Hitler indicated his preference for determining building materials by requiring a stone façade to replace March's original plans for concrete and glass. Whereas before 1936 Hitler had no systematic large-scale plans for building in Berlin, his assertion of his own architectural policy and authority over specific projects proved to be an important step towards the creation of the independent bureau of the GBI and the monumental redesign of the city.[6]

In this same period, state policy concerning the unemployment problem was also part of the function of building in Berlin. Directed state funding not only helped to stimulate employment in the city but also increasingly became a means for Hitler to develop his own architectural plans and target his prioritized projects. Throughout the early years of the Third Reich, the issue of funding for building in Berlin remained a perennial problem both because the projects were constantly being changed and the source of funding was never clearly legislated. For example, Hitler stated in a conference with city representatives on 5 July 1934 that he foresaw an immediate need for RM 60 million from the state to be set aside for the rebuilding of Berlin. The city was to add to this fund RM 70 million per year. Hitler alone was to decide on the use of the Reich funds. This kind of executive decision was all well and good for the promotion of architecture and employment, but it left city and state administrators scrambling for where exactly these discretionary funds would come from. By 1937, these moneys were simply set aside by the state and formed the core of what was known as the "Hitler Funds." The control of this credit further consolidated Hitler's executive authority over architectural policy.[7]

Of course, Hitler was not the only one who benefited from his assertion of control. More so than with his work at Nuremberg, Speer's rise to a position of power over architecture in Berlin depended both on his ability to take advantage of projects through his membership in the NSDAP and on his working relationship with Hitler. In early 1936 when the issue of a redesign of the capital first came before the city administration, it was by no means clear who Hitler would select for this effort. Speer had been contracted a year earlier to oversee Nuremberg and had already done specific small-scale projects in Berlin. Through this work, his extensive contacts with Hitler led to the dictator's decision by March 1936 to choose Speer to begin planning the redesign of Berlin. As Wolfgang Schäche points out, the city administration was unaware of the appointment. Only later in the year when the general urban layout was finished did his appointment become public knowledge. Such a history points to the conclusion that Speer's own executive authority over Berlin architectural policy came only after the political consolidation of administrative personnel, the economic stabilization of the building economy and the clear assertion of Hitler's control over building in Berlin. It was only at this moment that this move could be made with minimal administrative opposition and Speer could commence his Hitler-approved plans for the redesign of the city.[8]

THE FORMATION OF THE GBI

On 30 January 1937, Hitler appointed Speer to the post of Inspector General of Building for Berlin. The law establishing the position of the Generalbauinspektor circumscribed the extent of both the architectural and administrative authority of Speer's new job as head of the GBI. Speer's responsibilities centered on the complete design of the Berlin cityscape and a new infrastructure plan for the capital. The function of the GBI was to be essentially limited to the visual environment, focusing on the planning of plazas, streets and buildings. Yet the administrative powers given to the head of the GBI also conferred the authority to formulate architectural and social policy necessary for the enactment of his designs. This aspect of the law was particularly important for Speer's ability to override the city building administration under the control of Mayor Julius Lippert. Though ideally the Generalbauinspektor made decisions in conjunction with other city and state offices, any difference of opinion could be settled by the issuance of an order from the GBI. Finally, the Generalbauinspektor was accountable only to Hitler and thus became an administrative entity separate from both the Party and the state.[9] Speer made good use of his extra-governmental position to carry through his plans by working with (or fighting against) other state administrations.

The timing of the January 1937 GBI law corresponds to the period of the German building economy when political influence on the marketplace came with an attempt to centralize key policy decisions at the state and Party level. For architectural policy, Hitler furthered this goal by gradually extending the authority of the GBI through a series of laws and decrees, beginning with the Law for the Redesign of German Cities from 4 October 1937.[10] As Jost Dülffer points out, the law was not primarily concerned with the formal design of cities but attempted to outline the extent of the government's plans and how those plans were to be enacted. The early jurisdictional battles faced by Speer's administration contributed to the creation of the law that was specifically meant to clarify his authority. For the over forty cities designated by 1940 for redesign, the major significance of the law lay in the ability to create and prepare urban planning administrations outside of the control of local or state governmental institutions. Berlin, as the first city so named on 5 November 1937, was the most successful example of the creation of an independent architectural administration.[11] Its exceptional status and the ability to call on Hitler for support placed the GBI in a strong position to increase its political authority and carry out its architectural plans.

As the redesign law makes evident, the majority of the obstacles facing the newly formed GBI were less design-oriented than they were administrative or organizational. In fact, much of the actual work done by GBI architects and administrators in its first years of operation rested on key administrative decisions preparing for the construction process: financing issues separate from the "Hitler Funds"; acquiring property; procurement of materials; and substitute housing and business sites for those displaced by the urban redevelopment. In concentrating on these aspects of the plan, the GBI instituted policies that often competed with the goals of other administrations. However, the procurement of materials and the acquisition of property for those displaced were also GBI interests that converged with policies of other state and Party offices including the SS police apparatus controlled by Reinhard Heydrich. This dynamic of consensus and conflict with other administrative policies formed a central component of GBI development before the war.

With the interrelated issues of financing and property acquisition, the GBI relied on the legal influence it had achieved through the various laws as well as the practical political support of Hitler. GBI administrators further justified their executive authority by referring in their orders and memoranda to the "wish of the Führer." Based on this political leverage, a financing agreement was reached with the city of Berlin that, as of 1 August 1938, required the city administration to purchase properties designated by the GBI as important sites for the rebuilding projects. All buying and selling of properties and construction on these lands had to be approved by the GBI. Simultaneously, the GBI could direct the city to purchase, sell or build on the lands under its influence. If the property values or properties themselves were damaged due to actions of the GBI, non-Jewish owners had the right to demand compensation for any real or market-value losses.[12] Owners, however, could do nothing to stop the land transactions.[13] The GBI's executive authority as well as access to the "Hitler Funds" allowed it to act without taking into account the established hierarchy of governmental administrations or the claims of property owners.

Mobilization of resources proved to be a more difficult problem for the GBI than funding or property acquisition. Of the building materials needed, the procurement of iron (both as a material for steel frames and for reinforced concrete) was crucial. As noted in Chapter 2, at this time raw materials important for armaments could only be bought directly from the producer with the approval of Göring's Four Year Plan office. Not surprisingly then, Speer began at this time to promote the use of more traditional building materials, particularly stone. Nevertheless, Speer also used his influence with Hitler to obtain iron when other architects could not. The ideological importance placed by Hitler on the Berlin rebuilding allowed for a certain amount of executive privilege in the case of construction materials. Still, a building as important as the New Reich Chancellery (completed in January 1939) used only 2,000 tons of steel, confined to the construction of the roof. The weight of the building was carried by the massive walls, made up of over 20 million bricks and 5,000 cbm of limestone.[14] Thus, though iron was still available in limited quantities, architects relied on other materials for construction, a decision that opened up the opportunity for a working relationship with SS economic concerns.

As with the procurement of materials, Speer's staff relied on their executive authority and their ability to integrate their objectives with the development of other government policies in order to resolve the difficult problem of obtaining substitute housing for those displaced by site clearing on the two axes of the Berlin plan. By 1938, prominent among GBI solutions for acquiring substitute housing was depriving Jews, first, of their tenant rights and then, during the war, their property rights. To achieve this objective, the GBI turned to the policing apparatus of the SS to help enact its administrative goals. Hence, with the help of Heydrich and the Gestapo, Speer's bureau helped administer the concentration of Berlin's Jewish population that eventually led to the deportation of the Jews in the war. Yet, Speer not only helped implement this aspect of anti-Semitic policy but also worked to initiate legal measures against Jewish renter and property rights. Here the executive capacity of the GBI to enact its policies converged with the political and ideological goals of a variety of administrations and, further, brought the GBI in close working contact with SS policing offices that enforced the evictions of the Jews well before Pohl's stone-quarry enterprises began producing for Berlin projects.[15]

While laws enacted against the basic rights of Jewish tenants and property owners remained infrequent until after the pogrom of 9 November 1938, even before this event individual administrations attempted to serve their own interests through developing anti-Semitic housing policy. Throughout 1938, it was not a question of whether to move against Jewish economic rights but how and when. Such decisions were made at the highest level of government, and policy was formulated in this year particularly by Göring, Goebbels and Heydrich. The actual enforcement of policy remained in the hands of the Gestapo.[16] Yet between decision making and enforcement, individual administrations like the GBI put forth policy goals that influenced the timing and enactment of anti-Semitic housing regulations in Berlin.

It is not the conflict between but rather the convergence of administrative interests that is telling about the opportunistic goals achieved by taking advantage of anti-Semitic housing policy. By early September 1938, the GBI had already developed its own internal policy that linked anti-Semitic renters' rights and the construction timetable for specific building plans. Further moves against Jewish tenant rights were noticeably stepped up later in the month by other administrations that held meetings on the subject invariably with representatives of the GBI and the police. One such meeting took place on 22 September in the Justice Ministry and another on 27 September in the Berlin city planning office.[17] Both meetings made specific reference to legitimizing the actions against Jewish renters by the GBI's need for substitute housing. Discussants also referred to the role of the SS in determining the possibility of enacting a new policy through its control of the police and the Gestapo. Under the guise of the GBI's requirements, the registration, separation and concentration of the Berlin Jewish population was to advance with the help of SS policing institutions.[18] Before the 9 November pogrom, SS policing power and the pressure to carry out the rebuilding of Berlin were brought together to advance the eviction of Berlin Jews.

The brutal pogrom of 9 November 1938, however, no longer made it necessary for secret administrative meetings and complicated justifications. The initial interests of the GBI and the Ministry of Justice in denying Jews renter rights were picked up and made into state policy. A high-level meeting called by Göring and involving Goebbels and Heydrich occurred on 12 November 1938 to discuss, among other anti-Semitic policies, the housing question. From this meeting, it was determined that the SS was not yet ready for the problems associated with ghettoization but that restricting Jewish housing rights could go forward. This decision was justified through reference to the needs of the German economy and the preferred goal of forcing Jews to emigrate, a tactic that the SS was already using effectively in Vienna. On 30 April 1939, Hitler signed the new policy which dictated that any Jew could be evicted if the landlord could show that the tenant had replacement housing somewhere else.[19]

Even before this law was enacted, GBI officials had succeeded in making their interests part of the decision-making process. Göring, in a memorandum of 26 November 1938, required that all aryanized dwellings in Berlin be registered with the GBI. He also gave the GBI the exclusive right to decide to whom the property should be rented or leased. In the GBI Enactment Office, a special division on Jews maintained a roster of registered Jewish housing in Berlin, allowing Speer to pinpoint empty housing to which displaced Jews could move. Evictions in Berlin would be handled through GBI officials, who turned to the Gestapo to carry out the task.[20] Throughout this process, the SS had been useful to Speer by agreeing to his authority over Berlin housing and by evicting Jews with its police force. This relationship between Speer and the policing function of the SS would be reinforced and strengthened as wartime conditions accentuated not only the need of the SS for Speer's projects, but the drive by Speer to continue his architectural plans. Here, as elsewhere, the administrative contingencies of architectural policy extended the purview of the GBI by its influence upon and response to seemingly non-artistic state and Party interests.

THE REDESIGN OF BERLIN, 1937–9

All of the administrative policies implemented by the GBI were, of course, directed towards actualizing the design of buildings and urban plans in accordance with Hitler's architectural goals. This design work culminated in the public announcement of the plan on 28 January 1938 although even then the full extent of the building project and the necessary rebuilding of major parts of Berlin were kept secret.[21] But however secret the massive extent of the plan was, newspapers and propaganda articles made very obvious what was meant as the core of Speer's urban design scheme: the North–South Axis. Hitler had suggested the North–South Axis, an avenue that roughly followed other such boulevards proposed for Berlin, well before the Nazi era. Stretching from the turn in the Spree at the Königsplatz in the north to a new central train station in Tempelhof in the south, this axis was to be the key ceremonial boulevard of the new Berlin. The street itself was planned to compete with ancient Rome and the urban design of Haussmann's nineteenth-century Paris. A standardized cornice line as in the large Parisian boulevards was of particular concern to the GBI, and the unity of façades was fixed in June 1939 in relation to the height of the cornice of Peter Behrens' design for the AEG headquarters.[22]

Functionally, the axis was divided into two parts: the northern half, extending from the newly planned Runder Platz (southwest of Potsdamer Platz [Figure 14]), would be primarily made up of government buildings including among others the Great Hall (Grosse Halle), an assembly building Speer designed based on sketches made by Hitler; the southern half had buildings for entertainment, private industry and specific state and Party administrative headquarters. The spatial layout of the Runder Platz facilitated the transition from the purely governmental buildings in the north to the mixed functions of the southern half of the axis. At the southern end of the plan, just beyond a the huge Triumphal Arch (another Speer design adapted from Hitler's architectural drawings), the South Train Station with a gigantic plaza in front of it served as a termination point for this part of the plan.[23]

Speer's design authority as head of the GBI included the overall appearance of the rebuilding as well as drawings for specific structures, notably those mentioned which derived from Hitler's architectural ideas. But Speer farmed out the design of individual high-profile buildings on the axis to other architects, particularly those who had a wide reputation before the NSDAP came to power (such as Behrens) as well as those who were well entrenched in the Nazi state cultural apparatus (such as Herbert Rimpl, designer of the massive state-controlled steel concern of the Hermann-Göring Works). One such architect who relied on GBI patronage was Wilhelm Kreis. Kreis had already established a national and even international reputation with his work on war memorials in Wilhelmine Germany as well as his extensive designs for private and public patrons in the Weimar Republic. His prominent status in the Weimar Republic, however, led to his dismissal from the presidency of the League of German Architects (Bund deutscher Architekten) and the withering away of contracts in National Socialist Germany. His career was rehabilitated, however, when Gerdy Troost promoted him for a Dresden air force building competition in 1935, and then with his participation in the important state-sponsored architectural competition for the Berlin Hochschulstadt

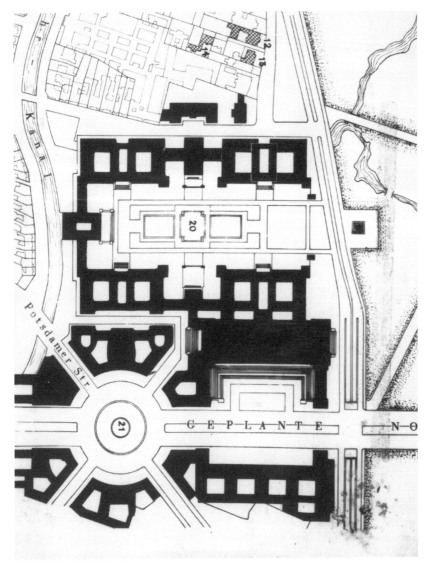

Figure 14
ALBERT SPEER, PLAN OF THE
RUNDER PLATZ AND
HEADQUARTERS OF THE ARMY
HIGH COMMAND (OKH), BERLIN,
c. 1940. The plan shows the
massive bulk of the U-shaped
Soldiers' Hall connected to the
east side of the OKH Headquarters
(20) and lying to the north of the
Runder Platz (21). Note that the
right side of the illustration faces
north
Source: Bundesarchiv

in December 1937. Speer used the Hochschulstadt competition as a kind of try-out
for GBI commissions, involving as it did the planning and design of a large complex
of buildings to be centered on a formal plaza with specific symbolic emphases on
individual administrative structures. The complex was to be built adjacent to the
Olympic stadium and incorporated into the East–West Axis. While Kreis did not win
the competition, it was after this that Speer began to consider him for major Berlin
projects; Kreis responded by becoming an active supporter of National Socialism
and its ideological and racist platform. Gaining the approval of Speer meant
immediate access to Hitler's politically designated projects and an opportunity to
influence architectural developments in Germany.[24]

Kreis' presence legitimated the young Speer's position within the German architectural community and hence it is not surprising that Speer turned to him to design one of the central monuments of the Berlin plan: the Soldiers' Hall (Figures 13, 15, 16). On the North–South Axis, possibly the most intensely planned and continuously worked-on project was the Soldiers' Hall, a building that would become a principal focus of SS economic interests. The Soldiers' Hall formed the monumental front of the massive army headquarters (Oberkommando des Heeres [OKH]) at the intersection of the axis and the Tiergarten. The essential form of the box-like building with its monumental paired column façade and bracketing wings derived from a rough sketch by Hitler. Coming at the moment of intense rearmament, the building functioned ideologically as a reminder of fallen war heroes from the past and as an encouragement for the sacrifice of German men in the potential struggles of the future.[25]

Design work was well under way in 1938, and the contractual agreement between Speer and Kreis for the OKH complex was signed 27 April 1939.[26] Kreis' role as defined by his contract was quite conventional. As head architect, he would complete all plans, submit the technical data necessary for approval by city administrators (*Baupolizei*), complete cost estimates and oversee construction. However, creative control did not rest firmly with him. An explicit clause in the opening paragraph gave the GBI full authority to approve all plans produced by the architect. This confirmed Speer's (or Hitler's) ability to correct the plans at any stage in the process based on considerations not specifically related to the OKH complex. The Berlin project and its leaders overall dominated the individual design and the architect was in effect only one part of the planning team.[27]

The specific design of the Soldiers' Hall as well as the scale of the other buildings planned for the North–South Axis led not only to the administrative maneuvering for substitute housing and financing discussed earlier but also to a particular problem with materials. As with Nuremberg, restrictions on building materials were mostly enforced by Fritz Todt and the GBBau. Yet, the centralization and regulation of building materials did not stop Speer from expanding the plans for Berlin. Speer, because of his influence with Hitler and extra-administrative organization, could contract firms directly and thus obviate Todt's jurisdiction over

Figure 15
WILHELM KREIS, PLAN OF THE
SOLDIERS' HALL, BERLIN, 1940
Source: Bundesarchiv

Figure 16
WILHELM KREIS, SOLDIERS' HALL
(interior), BERLIN, 1939
Source: G. Troost, *Bauen im neuen
Reich*, 1938

Berlin. He was particularly successful in controlling the distribution of stone to serve the GBI's purposes. Although bricks were important to the rebuilding plans, Speer focused considerably more effort on organizing the stone industry in Germany. This put particular pressure on the granite industry as the stone was his (and Hitler's) preferred material. Because stone was never crucial to the expansion of the armaments industry, Speer could control distribution through his office. By the beginning of the war, Speer's administration had divisions for each of the major building sites and an office for stone headed by K.F. Liebermann. The procurement of stone was important enough for the success of the entire operation to require that it alone of all building materials had a separate division in the GBI. The stone industry – including the SS – owed much of its strength, and its survival into the war years, to this preference.[28]

This administrative organization corresponded to Speer's interest in influencing segments of the building economy which would be crucial for the completion of his plans. Speer's decision here rested on the aesthetic preconditions that created the need for specific kinds and quantities of materials determined appropriate by Hitler and his architect. In reference to the Soldiers' Hall, the choice of stone was particularly dictated to Kreis by Hitler via the GBI. Though Kreis had been working on the plans extensively since mid-1938, the decision about the choice of stone for the façade – and thus, the color and general appearance of the building – was made as late as May 1939. Kreis was informed by the GBI that the "Führer deems granite to be the correct material for the Soldiers' Hall."[29] Even if Kreis presented Speer and Hitler with several choices and argued for granite as the correct one, the final decision remained Hitler's. This decision to use the white-speckled granite (such as that available at KL Flossenbürg) indicates how the design process as it was determined by Hitler and Speer produced specific demands on the German monumental building economy.

The choice of white granite was influenced by Speer's overall plans for both Berlin and Nuremberg. Early in May 1939, Speer had encouraged Kreis to take up contract negotiations with quarry firms employed for Nuremberg and even to model his choice of stone on the Nuremberg projects, specifically the Congress Hall. At a meeting later that month (attended by ministerial representatives, army administrators and, from the GBI, Kreis, Speer, Gerhard Fränk and Rudolf Wolters), the choice of granite for the Soldiers' Hall and OKH façades was announced. An unidentified speaker for the GBI (most likely Speer himself) stated that, in the construction of the building, red granite should be avoided at all costs as this color was needed for the German Stadium in Nuremberg. Thus, the stone was to be white, the other color of granite favored by Hitler and Speer.[30] Control over the building process remained in the hands of the GBI and beyond the individual control of the patron (OKH) or the aesthetic choices of the architect.

By mid-1939, construction was under way on several projects such as the House of Tourism, and the entire urban scheme for Berlin had been worked out by the GBI in some detail. The GBI found patrons for all of the buildings on the North–South Axis, finished plans of specific priority projects and began the gigantic task of planning the construction process, from access to labor to accumulation of materials. Further, obtaining substitute Jewish rental housing for non-Jews displaced by site clearing operations at key locations like the Runder Platz was well under way. For the Soldiers' Hall, Kreis' drawings were essentially finished by 1939, complete with the two friezes by Arno Breker on the street-side wings of the building. The accumulation of stone, hiring of contractors, buying of land and clearing of the site began in earnest.[31]

For Kreis' building, the GBI took the first step towards construction by giving the architect the task of estimating the amount of stone necessary for the building and organizing its procurement. Kreis filed a report in May 1939 which outlined the total area of the building, the amount and kind of stone to be used and the price per cubic meter. (The specifications were as follows: total area, 1,575,000 cbm; wall volume, 300,000 cbm; granite facing, 96,000 cbm; marble interior facing, 8,000 cbm.) The total amount of granite needed for the OKH complex Kreis listed as c. 180,000 cbm (including 84,000 cbm for the OKH headquarters), a number that remained as a constant estimate through the war years.[32] The building, thus, required a huge amount of stone, an amount which had to be gathered from all available quarries in Germany and Austria. The placing of stone orders and the organization of their delivery schedules dominated architectural activity at this point in the project.

Once Germany invaded Poland on 1 September 1939, building measures were drastically curtailed. But Speer's administration and authority were linked with the interests of too many other administrative bodies and competing agendas for them simply to have stopped with the outbreak of war. Centralizing control over the Berlin rebuilding effort under Speer's executive authority led to GBI involvement with other politically powerful administrations that were contingent to the construction process. With the *Blitzkrieg* strategy, the magnitude of the plans for Berlin and the organizational and design work they required meant that stopping the relatively few on-site construction efforts for what, at the time, seemed like a short period would do little damage to the project as a whole. Bureaucratic organization of the building process and the political mobilization of sections of the building economy could and did continue as a means of preparing for construction on site. Hence, work was not abated as much as the energy spent on design and construction was transferred to other components of the building process.[33] Though the war closed off the initial phase of optimism, Speer continued to promote the interests of the GBI and, as the war proceeded favorably for Germany, advanced and prioritized these interests to an even greater degree than he had in peacetime. DEST enterprises grew with and profited from the continuation of Berlin building plans during the early war years.

BUILDING IN BERLIN DURING THE WAR

SS and GBI interaction intensified during the war due both to the pursuit of SS economic interests and the successful prioritization of Berlin architectural policy within the monumental building economy. After September 1939, the GBI maintained its planning and design efforts, up to the final proposal for the city dated 1942.[34] As the design process was being completed, various stages of construction were also organized through the GBI Enactment Office. Funding questions were discussed with the appropriate patrons, site supervisors and their staffs appointed and negotiations with contractors started up. The GBI solidified its control of the buying and selling of property while simultaneously acquiring more of the site covered by the North–South and East–West Axes. Some sites were eventually cleared and foundations were begun, indicating that Speer's agenda was not curtailed by the war. Actually, the administrative organization of the building process and the necessary design work produced an increase in activity for the GBI during the initial years of the conflict. The year 1941 proved to be a particularly productive one in which GBI officials focused their energy on specific and privileged aspects of the monumental building economy. This activity could be maintained through the focus on such projects as the Soldiers' Hall and the continued production of materials by firms like DEST.

Speer's letter of 4 October 1939 to Kreis is indicative of how little wartime conditions hindered the building plans for the Soldiers' Hall. In the letter, Speer distinguished the construction from the planning stage, stating that the former must stop but the latter could continue. However, once again, the halting of on-site work had no effect on the crucial component of gathering granite for the interior and façade.

> It is to be expected that a special difficulty in carrying out the planned buildings will be that the necessary stone cannot be procured on time and in large enough amounts. This can be eliminated if the orders for stone – in so far as your planning already allows – are now commissioned, in which storing at the quarry can ensue and, where possible, the stone should also be finally dressed. I ask you, hence, to carry out the necessary [preparations] for your building, especially in view of the fact that the stone-masons and other workers of the stone concerns are protected from unemployment through this action.[35]

It is clear from this letter that Kreis was not ready to begin the actual construction of the building but was still planning and organizing. Hence, the ban on construction was not even an issue for the Soldiers' Hall when the war broke out. Furthermore, Speer, not Kreis, requested that stone orders be continued, and he saw this as a way of avoiding any unemployment in the quarrying industry. This point was crucial for Speer as workers who were unemployed were immediately subject to the draft, reducing any chance that the quarry process could continue. Here as elsewhere Speer was not really worried about unemployment as much as he was concerned that available workers in the stone-quarrying industry could be transferred to the military or armaments tasks. This proved to be a particular problem for the stone industry for, like other labor-intensive sectors of the economy, productive capacity was threatened by any decrease in output affected by the lack of ready laborers during the war. With Hitler's approval, Speer's protection of the stone industry through orders allowed private-sector quarries to continue production and also gave the SS the opportunity to develop its economic enterprises in the concentration camps. The focus of the GBI on the procurement of stone met with great success and, by June 1940, over 180 firms had been given orders for the quarrying of stone for the Soldiers' Hall.[36] This preference for the stone industry also allowed the necessary protection of a significant number of laborers.

By March 1940, an emphasis on the procurement of materials was complemented by GBI progress in effecting the organization necessary before work could actually begin on the site, organization which continued unhindered by the need for wartime recruits. As the next major stage in completing the building, organization of the construction site for the Soldiers' Hall began in February–March 1940. According to GBI accounts, the first phase of the building process was the site clearing, designated to last over a period of seven months. Simultaneous with the site clearing, a tunnel for transporting materials under the Tiergarten and a subway tunnel on the North–South Axis would be excavated, contractors would be hired, and the construction chronology sketched out in detail. Further, foundation work required the removal of c. 250,000 cbm of earth, and technical studies of ground-water levels as well as preparation for sinkage were to be carried out immediately.[37] Rationalizing the building process allowed for a clear prioritization of goals and an ability to focus on what could and could not be done under wartime conditions.

While the drawings were being worked over and the organization of the construction site commenced, stone procurement for the Soldiers' Hall was also decidedly stepped up, particularly after Hitler's June 1940 order (following the defeat of France) to resume work on the rebuilding. Kreis and the GBI handled stone procurement separately from the management of the construction process. As with the Nuremberg buildings, the procurement and delivery of stone was handled through the newly formed Arge Nürnberg. Arge Nürnberg's annual report for 1940 indicates the extension of quarrying for the Soldiers' Hall and the GBI's influence over stone production (through Brugmann, appointed to Arge Nürnberg's governing body and overseeing all stone orders for Berlin and Nuremberg with his position at the GBI by the end of the year). Through such specific projects and the intervention of Speer and Hitler, the quarry industry even increased demand in the first year of the war: the amount of materials ordered exclusively from the German stone industry rose slightly from 1939–40.[38] With Hitler's determined efforts to make architecture central to state policy, and the GBI's control of stone production and distribution through Brugmann, production in the stone industry proceeded unabated in the face of war.

The stone production described in the report shows how the war limited some sectors of the German stone industry and yet how certain politically designated building projects kept granite quarries going. The first war year brought an augmentation of duties for Arge Nürnberg because it took on processing orders for the Soldiers' Hall beginning in early 1940. The workload was large enough to force Arge Nürnberg to erect its own office at the construction site with four engineers to handle the stone orders and specifications. At the same time as receiving a sizable number of stone orders, the quarry industry had to compensate for its first slight reduction in personnel as a result of some workers being pulled into war service. The displacement of the work force and the quantity of stone required for the Berlin site allowed Arge Nürnberg to explain to its members why, in the second half of the year, stone orders for German buildings also went to foreign competitors. While this situation went against the autarchic NSDAP policy of the 1930s, it obviously corresponded to the increasing reliance on an expansionist economic and political strategy with the war.[39] For the Soldiers' Hall, over 19,000 cbm of stone were ordered from German firms while c. 22,000 cbm of unworked stone were also ordered from firms in Sweden and Norway (see Table 2, p. 65). Less than 6,000 cbm were ordered for other Berlin buildings. Within the restrictions of wartime, limitations that influenced the stone industry far less than other non-privileged businesses, the Soldiers' Hall building process was clearly to be continued.

While Germany's campaign in the west succeeded and the eastern campaign against the Soviet Union met with initial success, Hitler never wavered in giving his approval to continue specific building efforts (those controlled by Speer and, nominally, his Munich-based rival, Hermann Giesler). Speer's goal at this point centered on the completion of the planning necessary to begin construction immediately upon the cessation of hostilities, a turn of events that seemed imminent. This became possible with Hitler's consent. Hitler frequently affirmed Speer's efforts personally, as on 29 November 1941 when Speer and Kreis joined him for dinner. "In the course of the conversation, the Führer emphasized to Herr Speer that even during the war he will begin with the building [of the Soldiers' Hall], and that he did not wish to have the realization of his building plans prevented because of the war."[40] Hitler's personal approval and his executive support defined by law allowed Speer to carry out significant components of his architectural plans.

Of the many aspects of GBI activity before 1942–3, the procurement of materials – and above all, granite – received Speer's particular attention in the early war years. Organizing the massive amounts of stone necessary for his projects meant that Speer had to find other suppliers in addition to the private German stone industry. At the zenith of German military advances in 1941, Speer and GBI representatives took an unprecedented number of trips to the newly occupied territories, as well as to neutral and fascist countries, in order to secure the production and delivery of granite to Berlin. In 1941, companies with GBI stone contracts included quarries in Norway, Sweden, Finland, France, Spain and Italy; the GBI also negotiated for stone-mason services from firms in the Netherlands. These contracts – coupled with the quarries already being worked in the former Austria and the Protectorate (Nazi-occupied Bohemia and Moravia) as well as later stone businesses bought by the SS in Poland – show the huge geographic extent of stone procurement and relate the procurement of stone to the geopolitical militarist strategy of domination. Speer and his staff used the gathering of stone as a sure method of promoting their administrative interests and Berlin building plans. Additionally in 1941, the GBI and SS interests became more intertwined in the organization of the German stone industry with the appointment of Mummenthey from DEST to the governing board of the Arge Nürnberg.[41]

Such evidence as the Arge Nürnberg reports also indicates a specific chronology to wartime architectural policy. Specifically, 1941 marked an extension of state policy on many fronts (military, economic, anti-Semitic, etc.) and a corresponding peak in architectural activity.[42] Each of these policy areas was carefully prioritized in relation to the developing wartime conditions. Hence, the organization and centralization of the stone industry in 1941 favored the continuation of orders and deliveries for most of the major Nuremberg and Berlin buildings, particularly for the Soldiers' Hall, above other commissions. Though Arge Nürnberg observed that the war had affected the stone industry in Germany more than the year before, it optimistically reported that sales and orders were down only 10 per cent from the previous year. The annual report also noted that difficulties arose in the stone procurement for the Soldiers' Hall (as well as the OKH complex) not because of the war but due to changes in the design.[43] Nevertheless, over 28,000 cbm of stone were ordered for the project and deliveries totaled 9,972 cbm to the newly opened storage facility on the waterway at Fürstenberg an der Oder–Spree Kanal. This amount was almost the entire quantity of stone delivered for Berlin and outstripped the deliveries made for all of the Nuremberg buildings combined (see Table 2, p. 65).[44] Thus, though the war was encroaching on the independence of the stone industry, the privileged project of the Soldiers' Hall maintained a high quantity of stone orders as well as deliveries and even increased the amount relative to the previous year.

An expansion of the military economy not only encouraged architects to extend their dependence on the production of non-essential materials like stone but also to work on creative ways around wartime restrictions. The new storage facility at Fürstenberg represents an example of how the GBI staff could still manage to find the means of carrying out their building plans. An administrative focus on the transportation of materials including stone was necessary to secure the readiness of the construction process in Berlin. As early as the introduction of the Four Year Plan, the adaptation of industry to the needs of rearmament placed a great deal of stress on the organization of truck and rail transport. The mobilization of troops and machinery for the war increased this infrastructural pressure and left Göring unsympathetic to attempts by Speer and others to elicit approval for their transportation needs.[45] Faced with this situation, the GBI began in mid-1940 to organize its own transportation network for shipping on the extensive canal system through Germany. These efforts led in 1941 to the foundation of a private shipping business called the Transportflotte Speer.

The GBI consistently used the construction of the Soldiers' Hall to justify the creation of the dockyard storage space at Fürstenberg, the initial facility for the shipping organization. The OKH bought the land and the GBI began by mid-1941 to administer the waterway traffic that brought stone for the Soldiers' Hall from quarries, including DEST enterprises. Speer and the GBI formally incorporated the business on 23 August 1941.[46] Though Speer, like the SS before him, did not have the necessary authority as a state agent to set up his own private business, the contingencies of the chaotic situation of truck and train transport meant that the legality of the concern was not challenged by the government. Speer's extension of his administrative authority over all aspects of the building economy might have been impeded by the war but, as in this case, also allowed for manipulating the system when needed.

The victories of 1941 also led Speer to concentrate on labor requirements and to negotiate more intensively for the use of war prisoners to further his building goals. Prisoners of war were significant as Hitler would only allow a continuation of on-site construction activity in Berlin with the use of their labor. Notably, in the GBI report for this year, little distinction is made between the "voluntary" workers from Italy, the war prisoners from France employed in agricultural areas, the not-yet-available ("because of sickness or transportation difficulties") Soviet prisoners and the Czech workers who would be made to come to Berlin under the wartime service draft (*Dienstverpflichtung*). To mobilize the Czechs, Speer also needed the approval of Hitler or Göring; Hitler's approval was received within weeks. Speer's effort to get around the labor shortage proved successful in his willingness to take advantage of any means at his disposal to actualize his plans.[47]

In the meantime, however, the all-important use of Soviet prisoners was being decided outside of Speer's area of influence. Hitler had given Göring the unconditional right to administer the use of all Soviet prisoners of war. Through a secret order, Göring could determine where and to whom Soviet prisoners were to be distributed. The redesign of Berlin, so laments a GBI report, was not taken into account when Göring's authorization was approved. As usual, however, this did not stop Speer from going directly to Hitler to protect his interests: "Herr Speer also made this question [of Soviet prisoners] the object of a discussion with the Führer, whose consent was received to use, for the time being, 30,000 Soviet-Russian prisoners of war for carrying out work in the war program in greater Berlin."[48] The distinction, though, between war work and the redesign efforts remained vague and seemingly at the discretion of Speer and his staff. By the end of December 1941, 55,000 men were working on air force armaments buildings and 10,000 on the Berlin "*Bauprogramm*." To this was added a similar number of foreign workers and prisoners to bring the total work force overseen by Speer's staff to c. 130,000 people.[49]

To acquire prisoners of war and particularly to guard them, Speer had to depend as well on the security wing of the SS under Heydrich. In December 1941, after Heydrich had been named Reichsprotektor for Bohemia and Moravia, Speer talked with him over dinner in Prague. Heydrich wanted to rebuild Prague and to set up a plan that would rival (or perhaps surpass) even Berlin. Speer gave his advice on a number of the buildings that would be part of Heydrich's redesign. In exchange, Heydrich agreed to "send" Speer during the war 15,000 Czech workers and a further 50,000 a year after the conclusion of hostilities. Though Speer's interaction with Heydrich was limited, on this occasion their respective interests in architecture and policing mutually supported one another.[50]

The introduction of prisoners, however, required mobilizing a different set of resources, particularly a watch force that could oversee and control the workers on the various construction sites. For prisoners of war, the GBI needed and turned to the military wing of the SS (the Waffen-SS) to secure the necessary personnel. In June 1941, Speer made one such request for guards from Josef "Sepp" Dietrich who commanded the Leibstandarte-SS Adolf Hitler and the SS regiments in Berlin.

Stressing the importance not of the war program but of the redesign efforts, Speer wrote:

> The construction on the North–South Avenue is to be carried out during the war with prisoners of war. It would be possible for me to increase substantially the number of prisoners of war occupied there if not for the difficulty in obtaining guards. I ask you still once more to see if it is not possible to assign 30–40 men out of the ranks of the general SS . . . to guard the prisoners.[51]

Though a record of Dietrich's reply is not in the Speer files, the significant number of prisoners reported working in the service of the GBI by the end of the year indicates Speer's success in using the Waffen-SS to carry out his plans.

As in the case of war prisoners, Speer's staff also turned to the SS during 1941 to help enact measures to assure GBI control over Jewish-owned housing in Berlin. With the failure of the air assault over England in 1940, the German war command began preparing for a potential counter-attack, raising the need for bomb shelters and substitute housing for those whose dwellings might be destroyed. As a result, Hitler ordered the clearing of 1,000 Jewish houses for the rebuilding efforts with the stipulation that the houses remain free during the war for those left homeless by air attacks. In a letter from the end of 1941, Speer said that Hitler's decision came directly from the architect's own suggestion of how to advance building plans using the wartime regulations depriving Jews of their housing rights. Speer's easy willingness to pursue this policy is also indicated at the bottom of a private memo announcing Hitler's decision to his staff, where Speer typed: "With this necessity [to clear Jews from their housing] the entire site clearing possibly will be justified!"[52]

The GBI immediately increased its participation in the on-going debate concerning actions against the Jews. In the previous housing order from April 1939, only Jews in dwellings owned by a non-Jewish landlord could be legally evicted. The GBI, however, now began to support the work of the Reich Labor Ministry to devise a law that would include Jewish tenants in Jewish-owned housing as well. Through the concerted efforts of the Labor Ministry, the office of the Deputy to the Führer, the Justice Ministry, the Interior Ministry and the GBI, the law was swiftly finished and published by April 1941. Under the new law, all Berlin housing units that became free, including those in Jewish-owned properties, had to be registered with the GBI (or Giesler's office in Munich) and could not be re-rented without the approval of the architectural administrators. This meant effectively that Speer had the right to control evictions and the dispersal of inhabitants of the large and already tightly "crammed" Jewish communities in Berlin.[53] Speer now was able not only to oversee the concentration of the Jews but also to extend his authority by ordering the evacuations of Jewish tenants from thousands of dwellings in Berlin.

Architectural policy was joined to the wartime fears concerning the potential bombardment of German cities in order to further the campaign against the Jews.[54] While Speer himself was less directly involved than in 1938 due to the amount of effort he was putting into a variety of architectural tasks, his staff (particularly Karl Maria Hettlage and Dietrich Clahes) redefined GBI anti-Semitic policy and actively pursued its implementation by working with the converging ideas of a variety of administrations. So, for example, Hettlage chaired a meeting on 28 January 1941 in which Party and state officials (including representatives from Heydrich's RSHA) were given GBI directives on how many Jewish houses would be needed immediately for both "Aryan" homes destroyed through bombing raids and construction work related to the Berlin redesign. All designated Jewish houses were defined by their relative importance to the redesign efforts, including notably the Tiergarten site where the Soldiers' Hall was to be built. At this gathering, the original order from Hitler to procure 1,000 Jewish houses was worked out and coordinated under the auspices of the GBI.[55] GBI representatives confidently formulated the agenda while other institutions like the SS were called on to implement the policy. Once again, architectural interests and state policy intersected at this optimistic juncture in the development of wartime Germany. GBI administrators had the assurance that, in terms of enacting Jewish housing policy in Berlin, they could direct the SS effectively as an extension of their own institutional authority.

In the summer of 1941, Speer issued the orders for the clearing of over 5,000 Jewish apartments. A further 4,500 were cleared from 18 October to 2 November of that year, 1,000 of which were made exclusively available to the GBI. The power of Speer in this field was dramatic, as exemplified by his letter to the influential Martin Bormann at the end of 1941 in which he explicitly reprimanded Bormann for attempting to appropriate Jewish housing for his own purposes. Speer based his authority to control Jewish housing on architectural and wartime policy:

> About two years ago, the Führer had placed Berlin Jewish housing at my disposal for my "demolition tenants" and around August of last year ordered on my recommendation that housing blocks which were designated to be cleared [for the rebuilding] should be cleared already during the war. The use of the available Jewish dwellings and empty housing then should be kept ready for families rendered temporarily homeless through bomb damage [to their houses].[56]

When Speer was writing this letter to Bormann at the end of 1941 it was no longer a case of moving Jews into new housing but, as of 18 October 1941 (the date of the first transport), the "evacuation" of Jews to their certain death in the East.[57] To the extent that the GBI's involvement with Berlin anti-Semitic policy can be documented, architectural policy functioned well with the wartime political and ideological goals of the state. The year 1941 proved to be an exceptionally active one for the GBI, involving as it did the pursuit of clearly identified aspects of the building process as well as an attempt to merge several of its key policies with the wartime building economy and other state and Party interests including anti-Semitic policy.

Through such means as the transportation of stone by ship, the use of prisoners of war and the expropriation of Jewish housing, the GBI managed to continue significant architectural activity well into 1942, particularly for the

Soldiers' Hall. Planning on the Soldiers' Hall proceeded, as did the drawing up of stone specifications for the quarries. Stone orders were again fewer than the previous year, but they nevertheless continued at a not insubstantial rate (see Table 2, p. 65). The orders were broken down to detail the division of materials needed for various parts of the plan, such as the pedestals for the columns in the inner hall. Other building projects were not far enough advanced in their planning to place such specific orders. Of all the buildings in the Berlin plan, only the OKH complex managed to have stone delivered in 1942, "not least through switching the deliveries to the waterway," as the Arge Nürnberg annual report indicates.[58]

However, by 1943, GBI plans were increasingly curtailed by the reprioritization of labor allocations and resources for the war effort. Wolters reported to Speer in February that all architectural activity (including planning) had been replaced by war work. He further stated that the order to switch to war-important duties did not affect Kreis' bureau as most of his staff had already been transferred to the GBBau. By this point, Speer was involved almost exclusively in armament production. As a result of the loss of government support, the stone-quarrying industry finally lost its exemption status through an order of the Reich Representatives for Stone and Earth (Reichsbeauftragten für Steine und Erden) from 3 March 1944.[59] Contact between the GBI and the stone-quarrying enterprises reduced itself for the most part to the negotiation of payments for the storing and protection of stone that could not be delivered to a GBI storage facility.

Yet, even under these conditions, exceptions were made. According to the last Arge Nürnberg report, written in September 1944, the order from the Reich Representatives for Stone and Earth made quarrying for Berlin and Nuremberg allowable "only as compensatory work in relation to war-important provisions and for the employment of apprentices and of labor unsuitable for wartime tasks."[60] With this, under-age youths could still be trained in stone cutting and "unsuitable labor," a category covering certain concentration camp prisoners, could continue to quarry. Thus, from the 180 firms recorded in June 1940, DEST was listed as one of seventeen remaining firms from which the GBI placed stone orders in February 1944.[61]

Concerning the Soldiers' Hall, perhaps the most descriptive and characteristic document of the last phase of activity is a letter of 9 February 1944 from the current head of the OKH Building Administration (a certain Herr Doblin) to the GBI. This document describes the history of the building process, indicates the importance of stone to wartime planning and declares the optimism that the war might yet be won.

> The OKH Building Administration . . . had been set the task in 1939 to carry out the new building of the OKH and the Soldiers' Hall which were planned in the course of the redesign of the Reich capital and designed by Herr Generalbaurat Prof. Dr. Wilhelm Kreis. To this end, extensive measures of various sorts were taken (especially the procurement of stone necessary for these buildings) with the result that, currently, already c. 44,300 cbm of granite and c. 6,200 cbm of limestone are finished. . . . The production

continues, if also only to a humble extent. The turnover currently amounts to
c. RM 100,000 per month.[62]

Not only was roughly 25 per cent of the stone necessary for the OKH complex quarried in the period 1940–4 but, though limited, production continued even as late as this letter. Doblin's optimism and the ability to press on with stone orders remained as an after-effect of the mid-war strength of the quarrying industry. The perseverance of the administrators behind the OKH complex lasted until the termination of the Building Administration's stone division on 21 December 1944.[63]

Stone procurement dominated budgetary considerations and allowed for a continuity between pre-war and wartime GBI activity. That the Soldiers' Hall was privileged above other projects in respect to stone, indicates as well its place at the heart of wartime building in Berlin.[64] The procurement of stone was the driving force of the construction process in the early war years and became the focus of the last major project to be worked on in Speer's plan for rebuilding Berlin. This policy was compatible with other demands on the early wartime German economy. The GBI pursued all available avenues to perpetuate its importance and carry out its plans: the approval of Hitler, the agreement of Göring and Todt, the maneuvering of Speer and the oppression of the Berlin Jews. With this pursuit of architectural interests, the SS had little trouble in adapting its own economic goals to suit the massive organization of resources by the GBI. The prominence of architectural policy and the economic and military conditions at the beginning of the war ensured that the co-existing interests of the GBI and the SS economic office could converge to achieve the brutal juncture of architecture and political oppression. In this process, GBI administrators were not simply passive technocrats responding to demands from above but rather active agents in pursuing their own policies and influencing those of other administrations including that of the SS.

SS ECONOMIC CONCERNS AND SPEER'S PLANS FOR BERLIN

Prioritizing stone quarrying, as we have seen, depended on several factors: an initial aesthetic decision, a determination of quantitative needs, a large amount of labor, some trained stone-masonry personnel and transportation from quarry to site. What with the SS control over forced labor as well as its access to Speer and Hitler, the stone needs for the Berlin rebuilding plans could easily be incorporated into the development of the forced-labor building material concerns. With both stone quarrying and brick making, DEST economic activity focused on Speer's projects with the knowledge that contracts would continue unabated due to Speer's increased authority and the readiness of the GBI to adapt to wartime restrictions. Given that the two administrations had already worked together to make use of prisoners of war and against Jewish housing rights, their further amenable interaction seemed secure. Hence, DEST adapted several of its major building materials enterprises to the demands of the rebuilding of Berlin. That the relationship between DEST and the GBI shifted regularly from cordial to hostile, and produced variable and often disastrous results, never deterred DEST administrators from remaining optimistic about their economic enterprises. And further: volatile relations did not prevent GBI administrators from continuing to engage in the development of forced-labor concerns.

Forging a stable forced-labor economy partly based on Berlin contracts proved to be difficult in practice. The failure of the brickworks at KL Sachsenhausen exemplifies the problems the SS faced both in its orientation to Speer's Berlin plans and its institutional relationship to the National Socialist bureaucracy. Yet, the SS failure did not imply a retreat from economic policy, limiting the camps to a strictly punitive function. The failure of the brickworks led Pohl to increase the professionalization of DEST managers, to apply more modern management techniques and, as a planned result, to further the ideological and economic goals of the SS by strengthening its position within the monumental building economy.[65] Hence, the brickworks' inefficiency led to an increased level of innovation in pursuing multiple avenues of economic growth contingent on the production of building materials.

A significant part of the problem the SS had with the construction of the Oranienburg Brickworks (begun 1938) at KL Sachsenhausen was administrative. Similar to many government administrations that attempted to replace civil servants with loyal Party followers, the SS appointed its own administrators – either economists close to the SS or SS members themselves – to organize the plant and facilitate its production and market growth.[66] SS-Obersturmbannführer Arthur Ahrens was chosen to organize the brickworks. Ahrens had been important earlier in negotiating the purchase of the quarry site at Mauthausen and proved to be influential in choosing the most up-to-date technology for the brickworks at Sachsenhausen. However, his lack of business expertise, compensated for only by his Party zeal, quickly revealed itself as, from the start, the brickworks ran into major technical problems. This in turn led the GBI to doubt the skills of Ahrens and the efficiency of the SS as a reliable source of building materials. The GBI required more from DEST than politically committed personnel; its focus on output necessitated as well an administrative emphasis on productivity, an emphasis that intensified with the pressures of the wartime economy.[67]

DEST began the construction of the site in August 1938 and planned to build here the world's largest brickworks. The funding for the work came from an agreement of 1 July 1938 in which DEST promised the production of 120 million bricks a year, for ten years, in exchange for pre-payments from the GBI.[68] These bricks were specifically designated for the rebuilding of Berlin, as the size of the architectural project and the lack of iron allotments required alternative structural materials. Fascinated by modern machinery, Ahrens chose the most modern technology, utilizing the new dry-press process instead of the accepted wet-press method. These press techniques were distinguished by their differing response to the content of water in the clay. A wet-press technique uses clay with a higher water content, while a dry-press required relatively less moisture in the raw material. The advantage of the latter was that the firm spent less time in curing molds for firing.

As Michael Allen points out, this system might very well save time (and, hence, expense) but necessitated a close and professional attention to the composition of the clay. It was a relatively high-skilled operation, even if it preserved the digging of clay as a labor-intensive job that the camp commandants would approve of. With twenty-four tunnel ovens and thirty-six presses producing bricks through full automation, labor was thus reduced to clay digging, overseeing production and loading the finished product, all in an effort to increase (theoretically) productivity.[69]

However, because of Ahrens' inexperience at industrial management and the uncritical SS enthusiasm for new technology, the factory (which began operation as early as February 1939) immediately ran into problems. The technical direction of the plant had been given over to the Spengler Firm under Ahrens' supervision. Without worrying about initial test runs, the firm built the factory which later proved to be flawed in its technical details, particularly the ovens: the clay dug from the neighboring pits (by forced labor) was unsuitable for the specific dry-press technology. Thus, the brickworks had to be completely reconstructed around the established wet-press technique after the extent of the problem had been discovered by mid-1939.[70]

Coming at the height of German military optimism and the enlargement of the forced-labor populations, the setback proved disastrous to SS economic plans. Pohl summarily dismissed Ahrens from the management of DEST, forbade any business communication between Ahrens and DEST administrators and deprived him of his SS membership. Ahrens was replaced by the engineer and brick specialist Erduin Schondorff who, ironically, had been one of the main patent sources for the method used by the Spengler Firm. This effort signaled Pohl's intent to establish not only an ideologically committed but also professionally trained administrative staff in order to guarantee high rates of productivity. By the time the contract with Spengler was dissolved on 1 March 1940, and the plant rebuilt, the financial loss for DEST totaled at least RM 4.65 million. Pohl himself inaugurated the new factory (with the wet-press technique) on 24 October 1940.[71]

It was subsequent to this reorganization that Speer and his staff took a more active role in influencing DEST operations and in becoming involved in the development of the concerns. The inefficiency of the Oranienburg brickworks produced immediate funding problems as the enterprise remained dependent on GBI payments for bricks delivered. In a letter of 17 January 1942, Speer admonished Pohl over the brickworks' constant need for capital in order to recover from its losses. Speer complained that, if Pohl had listened to his advice initially and built the brickworks near a better source of clay, Pohl would not be facing financial difficulties, particularly as the use of forced labor was supposed to lower production costs substantially. Not only did Speer see the DEST concern as dependent on his patronage but he also felt that it was within his purview to suggest changes that would avoid the difficulties of new financing. Speer advised taking Oranienburg I out of DEST and making the GBI the main partner of the brickworks. Though Speer was "reluctant" to take this on with his many other concerns, "it would be however the only way one could avoid the prolonged negotiations with the Finance Ministry and the Chief of the Reich Chancery."[72] Thus even with this setback, the orientation of the DEST enterprise to the Berlin plans and Speer's interest in having a major brickworks at his disposal resulted in an SS and GBI attempt to advance their mutual goals. Speer concluded in his letter: "You can be sure, however, that I, together with my co-workers, will consider all possible ways that could help you and the Oranienburg work."[73] Though Pohl rejected Speer's plan, the willingness to work together, as in this instance, marks the ability of DEST to further its economic concerns through its orientation to Speer's goals.

After the failure of the Oranienburg brickworks, Pohl consistently appointed specialists in DEST enterprises and further relied on amicable relations with the GBI to continue a successful expansion into the building economy. These relations not only concerned funding of the works and a client for their output but, in specific cases, GBI technical and administrative input on the organization of camp labor and operations. The example of the other concern at KL Sachsenhausen – Oranienburg II – indicates both the ability of DEST to adapt its program to the Berlin plans and the willingness of the GBI to be actively involved in the productivity of the forced-labor camps. Oranienburg II, a stone-processing center where prisoners cut stone delivered for specific Berlin building projects, proved this flexibility of the SS and the viability of its architectural policy. In catering to the client and relying on GBI advice, DEST operations here as at Nuremberg attempted to make themselves indispensable.

From the very beginning of planning for Oranienburg II, DEST and the GBI worked closely together to ensure the success and productivity of the enterprise. Administratively, Salpeter, DEST's business manager, represented the SS, while Brugmann represented the stone-production interests of the GBI. In a discussion about the opening of the stone-processing center held at GBI offices on 15 August 1940, the mutual relationship between the two administrations was clarified:

> To the gentlemen present, Herr Professor Brugmann reports on the necessity of erecting a storage facility as well as a new [stone-] processing workshop. It appears effective to re-educate for this work the prisoners found in the camp [KL Sachsenhausen].
>
> Herr Dr Salpeter from the Reichsführung SS declares himself fundamentally ready to construct this work and facility on behalf of the GBI. The necessary work force is amply available. The construction can take place immediately.[74]

As in previous DEST enterprises, the justification for the work rested on the supposed re-education of the prison population who, in the process, would contribute to the construction of Hitler's monumental building projects. By 1940, that construction rested on the prioritized GBI activity of stone procurement. Unlike previous proposals, however, the protocol indicates that the GBI played an active role in going to the SS (as opposed to a private firm) for its needs. Whereas it is unclear which party actually first suggested the new facility, here as elsewhere in the correspondence the GBI claimed the initiative in the organization. Plans were worked out and refined by the GBI which also supervised the construction team, while the SS provided assistance with the "practical arrangement" of the camp.

This last responsibility included the particular policing structures required for the camp.

The appeal from the GBI was yet another opportunity for the SS to expand its economic activity through the construction of a new stone center based on the punishment and exploitation of its captive prison population. By mid-1941, the SS had prepared a final draft of the contract between DEST and the GBI in which the GBI was given the following tasks: paying for the concern (RM 6 million in anticipated payment for future stone processing, to be drawn on by DEST only as necessary); procuring necessary stone; assuring that "despite the war" the work will continue as part of the war building program; and providing technical data for all machines and equipment. In return, DEST would: run the camp under the direction of the GBI; consult the GBI for all intended changes; and guarantee all production for the use of the GBI or other architectural projects named by the GBI. The enterprise itself was the property of DEST alone.[75] Thus, to avoid the problems that arose with the Oranienburg brickworks, DEST gave more administrative control to GBI specialists and oriented the workshops completely to the goals of the Berlin rebuilding. In the process, DEST could assume the advantages that came with having the GBI as sole client. Providing a market for SS economic expansion during the war justified the continued use of forced labor in the building materials industry (rather than in armaments) and concentrated work on specific preferred facilities.

Though DEST kept the terms of the drafted contract by submitting detailed accounts of funds used throughout 1941–2, the workshops were still having problems due to wartime conditions and mismanagement. While contract negotiations continued through the end of 1941 (the GBI resisted some of the terms), DEST nevertheless began work and drew funds from the GBI in the fall of that year. Oranienburg II was to be a large complex with modern machinery, linked to Berlin and stone suppliers by canal traffic and justified by the plans for the redesign efforts. By March of 1942, DEST had ordered new equipment and building materials which were to be brought to the site by water transport.[76] However, after paying RM 2 million in 1941, the GBI held up the release of more funds, as the architects feared the money was being mishandled. This led DEST to plead its case in a letter of April 1942 explaining its needs and how the money had been spent in the interests of the Berlin plans.[77] GBI reluctance indicated in the contract negotiations and funding concerns perhaps slowed the economic development of the workshops but did not prevent their eventual use for the Berlin building program. The mistrust between administrations and the internal questioning of who initiated the facility did not get in the way of a convergence of Speer's and Himmler's interests here as elsewhere in the monumental wartime building economy.

But a War Building Program put forth by the SS on 23 May 1942 and agreed to by the GBI on 3 October 1942 ended both the contract negotiations and the questions of funding. The program included the erection of the basic infrastructural elements of Oranienburg II that would enable prisoners to work on armaments tasks during the war and cut stone at the conclusion of hostilities.

Several stone-mason halls and barracks had already been finished by 1942. The new program called for the additional construction of the train line from the canal to the Oranienburg train station, the canal bridge, the heavy cranes and other elements of the plan. Even in this proposal and its attendant contract, the project was still justified by the re-education of prisoners and the processing of stone for the GBI. As a result of the program the SS continued to build and the GBI continued to pay, reaching the total sum of RM 3,873,703 by 24 March 1944.[78]

During the war, in order to have an economic use for the forced labor from KL Sachsenhausen, the SS needed to adapt to the needs of the GBI as one of the few major builders still active in Germany. This happened to varying degrees in the administrative and physical changes made after the failure of the Oranienburg brickworks and in the construction of Oranienburg II. The authority of Speer and the GBI staff and their willingness to continue to carry out architectural policy would have been hard to match in terms of finding another patron suitable to the size of DEST operations. By October 1941, the first stone had been delivered to Oranienburg II although, beginning in 1942, the entire work was slowly transformed to the recycling of raw materials for the armaments efforts. In these years of transformation, 1,000 prisoners were employed by July 1942 in both stone processing and recycling and, in 1943, the number rose to over 2,000, the vast majority of whom came directly from KL Sachsenhausen.[79] The stone-processing center allowed DEST to link the economic enterprise closely to the plans and even the authority of the GBI. This link extended once again the connection between the political function of the concentration camps and the government's monumental architectural policy as prioritized by the architects of the GBI.

THE SOLDIERS' HALL AND KL FLOSSENBÜRG

While the GBI began to help fund and organize the SS brickworks and workshops, DEST also expanded its efforts to attract GBI stone contracts in order to exploit economically its control over the large numbers of new wartime prisoners. As related in the history of building in Berlin during the war, stone procurement became the dominant focus of GBI activities up to 1943. By having planned the original forced-labor concentration camps around granite quarries, in line with Hitler's and Speer's requirements, DEST could also prioritize the work in the forced-labor camps in order to take advantage of the extension of stone procurement in these years. It did so in the quarries of KL Flossenbürg through contracts for Kreis' Soldiers' Hall. In this instance, as in Nuremberg, the agency of the architects is less active than in the Oranienburg stone-processing center but nevertheless is present in their aesthetic decisions and the stone contracts that became key conditions for the focus on productivity evidenced at Flossenbürg.

The DEST work at Flossenbürg received its largest and most regular granite orders for the Soldiers' Hall, orders which commenced in 1940 coinciding with the full-scale operation of the camp.[80] Yet given the SS goal of establishing a position within the German monumental building economy, did the project succeed or fail at the stone quarries of Flossenbürg? To answer this question, it is worth analyzing the camp's production statistics and qualitative output for the early war years. From the opening of the camp in July 1938 to January 1940, work by the prisoners consisted of building up the compound and preparing the quarry. Of the limited sales recorded in these early years, 85 per cent came from architectural stone in 1939, and 40 per cent in 1940. In the latter year, the sale of materials for the construction of roads rose as part of total sales; or, in other words, at the moment when Flossenbürg began to take on contracts from Berlin, its qualitative output had been diversified. This was less of a planned diversification than it was a result of the normal development of a quarry: once a quarry is in full operation, its stone can be cut for specific contracts but, in the process, increasing amounts of stone remnants are produced suitable, e.g., for road building. Such a productive process not only represented the material conditions of the stone in the quarries but also a recognition of the pragmatic pressures of the wartime building economy.[81] A focus on Soldiers' Hall contracts led to an increase in other kinds of usable but (to DEST) secondary building materials.

Hence, the varied output of the quarry did not dominate DEST considerations in the early war years as more and more of Flossenbürg's stone was guaranteed for the high-profile designs of the Soldiers' Hall. Though Flossenbürg entered into production four months after Mauthausen, through its contracts with Berlin it quickly came to dominate DEST's granite sales (see Table 1, p. 41). For 1940 (the first year in which non-SS clients received stone from the camps), the work at Flossenbürg produced over half of all stone sales with an output of over 2,800 cbm. Flossenbürg and Mauthausen evened out in 1941 when Flossenbürg produced 2,848 cbm and Mauthausen 2,635 cbm. Exact statistics for granite do not exist for the camps between January and May of 1942; however, between June and July, when, in the previous year, around 60 per cent of the stone was quarried, the rate of production at Flossenbürg remained stable (from 1,690 cbm in 1941 to 1,646 cbm) while Mauthausen's rate steadily increased (from 1,111 cbm to 1,539 cbm).[82] Though in comparison to Himmler's dream of producing 100,000 cbm per year these results were modest, the DEST works at Flossenbürg and Mauthausen in particular were slowly fulfilling the goals set by the SS. These statistics indicate a consistent increase in productivity through 1942. That, for Flossenbürg, this increase resulted from the reliance on the patronage of Speer and his staff was a factor of central importance to DEST and its efforts to further the economic expansion of the SS through the sale of stone.

KL Flossenbürg retained a strong profile in the overall economic organization of DEST because of its high output of architectural stone. As noted, production went up at Flossenbürg after 1939, allowing DEST to capture the largest single share of the German granite market. Of course, its ability to enhance its rate of productivity depended on the abuse of the camp labor force, an abuse that focused on the labor-intensive and physically exhausting process of quarrying and cutting stone. Through the economic expansion of the quarry enterprise and its ability to increase output, the punishment of prisoners was linked to the building materials market and contracts for Speer's plans for Berlin. By 1940, approximately 10 per cent of the production of the DEST work went to the Soldiers' Hall alone; with the optimism of 1941, DEST managers expected this percentage to rise with the extension of the quarry system.[83]

Nevertheless, in practice, the wartime political and economic conditions that fostered an emphasis on maximizing labor potential and output forced DEST administrators to re-evaluate their expectations if not their policy goals. In an inter-office memo of 20 February 1941, Heinz Schwarz, manager of DEST's quarry oper-ations, took seriously Himmler's goal to extend production at the camp. He described the existing work at KL Flossenbürg and how it needed to be changed if Himmler's goals were to be met and Soldiers' Hall contracts increased. Schwarz identified four problems which needed to be solved: the "people problem;" the need for raw materials; the need for credit to build up the site; and accessibility to transportation to bring the stone from the site. Since new investment needs amounted only to c. RM 400,000, Schwarz wrote that obtaining credit should not be "all that difficult." The required approval for raw materials and machines was proceeding with relative ease while partial support had already been received and orders placed for cranes, compressors, wood for the stone-mason halls and other machines. The transportation situation, Schwarz acknowledged, was bad and would probably become worse with the coming demobilization. This, however, should not stop the SS from energetically moving ahead with its plans.[84]

But the "people problem" – i.e. access to a forced-labor population in a volatile military situation and an already tight labor market – presented the SS with particular difficulties in 1941 because of the general expectation of the end to the war. The SS faced both political questions, in terms of the post-war availability of prisoners, and economic ones, as to whether the numbers would be sufficient to continue the extended development of a stable position for DEST within the (peacetime) monumental building economy. Much of Schwarz's memorandum thus discussed both the need to clarify exactly what quantity of prisoners they could expect and how many the concern needed in order to obtain the desired production results. Schwarz expounded on the situation as follows:

> Anyway, before production and investment can be spoken about, the people problem (the availability of prisoners) must *first* be clarified for the long term. For this, it is necessary that the head of the main office, SS-Gruppenführer Pohl, ascertains from the Reichsführer-SS [Himmler] in what degree prisoners after the end of the war are to be placed at our disposal. The experience has arisen that recently many discharges have taken place, principally of Poles. It is to be assumed that after the war a general amnesty will be implemented. It is then easily possible that, e.g., criminals who have served their sentence will be released. In addition it is easily possible that also the Jehovah's Witnesses will be set free. Just these elements were up till now for us the workers best suited for the training to be stone-masons and other specialized workers. In order to carry out a plan in the long term at all, clarity must be achieved as to how much suitable labor power is available to us especially also after the war.[85]

Political questions as to the "availability" of forced laborers were as significant here as they had been crucial for justifying the foundation of the forced-labor camps in the first place. Yet although Schwarz found it necessary that Pohl discuss the matter with Himmler, he expressed little doubt in the memorandum that planning could or would continue. While the problem of gathering enough prisoners for the forced-labor work force needed to be addressed, implicit in Schwarz's memorandum and the SS economic administration as a whole was not the need to shift to private wage-earning workers or maximize worker efficiency but simply to find a new source of people to arrest and press into service. In the confident position of KL Flossenbürg as producer for one of the most high-profile Berlin buildings, the question was not whether a prison force could be accumulated but how and who would make up that force. The political function of the SS as the Reich's policing authority was a given for Schwarz whereas the changing numbers and social make-up of the prison population were seen as potentially compromising for economic planning.[86]

Labor, and who would make up that labor force, were key to the economic viability of the Flossenbürg work if the political function of the camps and the continuity of stone contracts were to be assured. Later in the memorandum, Schwarz addressed exactly the sort of work needed to achieve the goal set by the HAVW of 12,000–15,000 cbm per year. Schwarz estimated, based on the performance so far, that four prisoners could do the work of one civilian laborer (omitting from his report any consideration as to why such a disparity between the two forms of labor might exist). With this statistic, he assumed that the concern at Flossenbürg would need 2,200 men (1,000 workers, 1,200 stone-masons). Given the relatively tight labor market for stone-masons in Germany, Schwarz suggested that after the war perhaps the SS could employ foreigners in the concern. However, in the end, he rejected this idea on the grounds that the necessary housing would not be available and suggested another possible labor source instead. Striking what appears to him as a solution to the release of prisoners and the SS refusal to use civilian labor, Schwarz argued for the mobilization of war prisoners who could remain just outside the KL grounds guarded by armed forces personnel. As with the GBI contracts, the particular economic opportunities brought about through the occupation of territories and police rule were a spur to the development of DEST forced-labor policy.

Schwarz's memorandum thus offers the opportunity to address some of the fundamental economic principles of the SS. Clearly, the SS wanted to realize its goals through forced labor, which was reified as a static resource to be accumulated and used up for its productivity. The separation of efficiency from output allows Schwarz, as a representative voice of DEST, to combine his analysis of forced labor with comparisons to the private economic sphere. The SS economic division treated its concern at Flossenbürg as a quarry among other German quarries, setting its production goals and even the rate of production by its forced laborers against those in the private sector. Since all quarries were being influenced by the politically driven emphasis on monumental architecture and its prioritization during the war, DEST administrators (like others) could focus on those two important variables to the contemporary building economy: access to labor and acquisition of contracts. Of course, such an administrative policy avoided the exceptional basis of DEST enterprises in the political function of the concentration camps. Or rather more specifically: it was the special status of the SS as a political institution that determined the ability of DEST personnel to formulate a plan based on productivity and on a working relationship with GBI architects.

Returning to the Soldiers' Hall production statistics, DEST was most successful in exactly that part of its enterprise that was an exception, i.e. the nexus of political and economic policy in the use of forced labor to quarry the stone. Because of the punitive function of the camps, Flossenbürg had little problem in maintaining adequate numbers of prisoners and, while Speer via Hitler could still make architectural policy a priority, procuring necessary stone contracts. Having set a goal of 2,200 men for Flossenbürg, by the end of 1942 DEST was using almost 2,000 laborers, 1,108 of whom were apprentices being trained to cut stone. Wanting to increase production to 5,000 cbm in 1941 and again in 1942, however, they succeeded only in approximately sustaining the 1940 rate of production (2,848 cbm). Yet the DEST work at Flossenbürg continued to receive credit and, above all, to obtain regular orders for the Soldiers' Hall until Quarry II closed in the fall of 1943.[87]

While productivity goals were not met, Schwarz's prediction that the Soldiers' Hall would use more and more of the granite quarried proved to be accurate. Of the c. 44,300 cbm actually produced for the entire OKH complex, 25,875 cbm remained stored at the quarry sites at the end of the war; this sum, broken down by firm, shows that J. Steininger of Nuremberg had produced the largest proportion of the remaining stock (2,164 cbm) but DEST had produced the second highest amount (1,824 cbm). These quantities by far exceeded those of the numerous other firms listed, only one of which (Widy's Söhne, Schrems) produced more than 1,000 cbm. Though other firms might have had holdings at the Fürstenberg facility which would not have shown up on this post-war 1945 list, the large quantity of stone from DEST indicates the importance of the OKH complex to its work.[88]

Among the concentration camp enterprises, Flossenbürg had the highest percentage of granite in the DEST total. As Schwarz's memorandum indicated, DEST administrators directed the concern at KL Flossenbürg (just as with Natzweiler and the German Stadium) towards the project of the Soldiers' Hall. Of the 1,824 cbm of DEST stone on the 1945 list, 1,382 cbm came from KL Flossenbürg, the remainder split between Gross-Rosen, Mauthausen, Natzweiler and preparation that took place at Oranienburg II. If the 1,382 cbm is related to the productivity of Flossenbürg between 1940 and 1942 (Table 1, p. 41), we see that the stone amount stored at the camp comes not to 10 per cent but 16 per cent of the c. 8,570 cbm total produced in these years. Since Schwarz's estimate of 10 per cent covers only 1940, it becomes clear that the percentage of granite production for the Soldiers' Hall at KL Flossenbürg rose significantly throughout the development of the enterprise. DEST had succeeded in increasing the output of its

Flossenbürg work and directing that production towards GBI contracts for the rebuilding of Berlin.

KL Flossenbürg maintained a reasonable rate of production during the war years through its emphasis on a particular kind of architectural quality granite, the availability of stone contracts and the abuse of a labor population working under extremely strenuous conditions. The forced-labor KL system – with its use of punitive measures to increase production and the belief in an unlimited and thus disposable labor supply – encouraged and enabled the productivity of the camp and its continued development during the war. With the Soldiers' Hall contract and the majority of KL Flossenbürg's production being architectural stone, the SS economic division confidently built up the forced-labor enterprise. The orientation of the camp, from its inception, towards the monumental projects of the state, and then its later specific orientation towards production for the Soldiers' Hall, provided the means by which the political ends of oppression were carried out. As an attempt to balance the strenuous conditions that drove prisoners to their deaths and the demands of production quotas, the DEST work satisfied the punitive goals of the SS and the requirements of its architectural patrons.

When Speer officially took over the redesign of Berlin in 1937 his extra-administrative authority was limited to the task of carrying out the urban plan. The changing circumstances of the late 1930s and early war years – the focus of architectural policy on Berlin, Nuremberg and Munich; the stepped-up actions against the Jews; the occupation of foreign territory; the use of war prisoners as laborers – favored the intensification of the interaction between the GBI and DEST. With these two agencies, it was not a case of mutual interest; rather, it was a matter of diverse interests that nevertheless converged. Subject to the initial military victories and the priorities of the wartime economy, both administrations maneuvered to secure their authority and architectural or economic goals. Only with the coming of repeated military setbacks and the administrative and economic reorganization of the National Socialist state in late 1942–3 would each of these institutions give up on their peacetime projects. After this point in time, Himmler and Speer found a new common ground in the use of forced labor for the production of armaments. But while the conditions of war allowed, Speer's plans for Berlin required increasing amounts of quality stone and bricks that the forced-labor concentration camps under Himmler, with their enlarged prison populations, could help to provide. That architectural decisions at times played an active part in the organization and development of these forced-labor camps is also a part of the historical record.

Chapter 5: The Political Function of SS Architecture

At a time when German military advances in the east had been highly successful, Himmler published an article that recommended a particular architectural tradition to the readers of the SS magazine, *Das Schwarze Korps* (January 1941). Entitled "German Castles in the East," the article introduced a photo essay on supposedly Germanic fortified castles from the medieval period. Himmler optimistically emphasized the contemporary military successes by comparing the triumph of past rulers claimed as Germanic to the present National Socialist occupation of eastern territories which would continue the military and architectural traditions.

> When people are silent, the stones speak. By means of the stone, great epochs speak to the present so that fellow citizens (already of the first generation) are able to uplift themselves through the beauty of self-made buildings. Proud and self-assured, they should be able to look upon these works erected by their own community. . . .
>
> Through seven centuries, the castles of Allenstein, Heilsberg, Marienwerder and Neidenburg were just as much witnesses of well-fought conquest and most tenacious defense as they were symbols of higher German culture for all generations of the old "Ordensland" of East Prussian – of this germ cell of the Prussian-German state. . . .
>
> The stones have not spoken in vain . . . the fields are German again.
>
> Buildings are always erected by people. People are children of their blood, are members of their race. As the blood speaks, so the people build.[1]

Himmler drew on the defensive medieval monuments to legitimize the military victories in the East as the inevitable return to the soil of an older German dynastic culture. He emphasized for the reader the connection between the "race" of a people and its architectural achievement. Architectural greatness and military prowess were presented as complementary components in the destiny of the German people. In the pages of the SS journal, these bombastic claims came from and legitimized the expanding political authority of the SS at the highpoint of the German military drive.

That Himmler should choose as his subject medieval defensive structures in the East was not simply fortuitous. In contrast to Hitler's pronounced interest in classical societies, Himmler repeatedly turned to the Ottonian Empire established by Henry I in the tenth century, a dynasty founded on incursions into the eastern territories of the Slavs and on defense against the Hungarians. To the SS, he held up the Ottonians as examples of noble German knight-warriors. This ideological projection influenced the education, military training and institutional identity of SS members as a new caste of German knights.[2] Himmler's fascination with the history particularly of Henry I and the Ottonian Empire actuated the purchase of historically important sites, pronouncements on the revival of a German elite in SS publications and even the architecture of specific forced-labor camps. Modern industrial warfare and the institution of the concentration camps were not seen as coming into conflict with a comparison to the feudal order of Henry I. That the SS developed from a very different technological, social, economic and political basis than existed in medieval Germany, did not hinder Himmler from promoting their apparent connectedness.

Of course, Himmler's vague and distorted notion of the Germanic past was not the only guiding beacon for SS ideology. But his faith in the relationship between ideological goals and political power, each of which could be expressed and enacted architecturally, defines as well a key component of his interest in the quick extension of DEST enterprises in the early war years. Hence, his article and his interest in Henry I raise a crucial issue for the exploration of the architectural policy of the SS: the ideological, architectural and political concerns that had conditioned the economic interest of DEST in Nuremberg and Berlin building also had specific effects on the institutional architecture of the SS itself.

But turning to an analysis of SS institutional architecture in this chapter means more than adding an anecdotal pseudo-medievalist coda to our account of DEST and the monumental building economy. Rather, in this book I have been arguing for an interpretation of Nazi architecture that takes its cues from what the participants in the production process considered important, not from the standpoint of a post-war (or even pre-war) art historical assessment of what was publicly considered aesthetically significant form. Specifically, the involvement of the SS in the building economy depended on which architectural projects it considered pre-eminent based on its own economic and institutional criteria. These projects included the high-profile projects of the Party and state but also involved the massive public facilities the SS constructed for its own use and, finally, the structures at the forced-labor camps themselves. Taking SS architecture seriously entails extending our art historical use of political history to include not only how specific forms served SS institutional interests but also how formal decisions were functionally instrumentalized for other, seemingly non-artistic goals. It also entails understanding that a broad range of architectural types were fundamentally related to the oppressive policies of the Nazi state.[3]

To get at this history requires paying attention to the chronological development of SS architectural interests. Before 1939, the function of SS architecture served multiple purposes including the individual power-political

interests of Himmler, the practical interest of building sites for forced-labor operations and the promotion of a public institutional identity. With the developments
of the war, these functions were adjusted to include the expanded role of the SS
as a pan-European policing force as well as Himmler and Pohl's own plans for a
massive extension of post-war SS facilities. These plans relied on the increase in
camp prisoner populations as well as on the production of building materials in the
forced-labor sites of DEST. An augmentation of SS goals also determined a more
aggressive construction program for the work camps as permanent and productive
institutions.

In this period of military optimism, the redesign and expansion of the architecture of KL Flossenbürg and KL Mauthausen exemplifies the projection of
an authoritative institutional identity as well as the perceived need to punish and
exploit the enlarged labor force. Both the SS central administrative offices in Berlin
under Pohl and the on-site building administrations in the camp made decisions
about the facilities to be erected. Construction of the watch towers at Flossenbürg,
for example, resulted from such an exchange between Berlin and the camp architects. The determination of the decision-making process at Flossenbürg exposes
Berlin's control over aesthetic considerations in camp architecture and elements
of the plan that SS architects considered important. Furthermore, through the
forced-labor construction process, these plans were connected to the destruction
of specific groups designated as enemies of the National Socialist state. A history of
the construction of the walls at Mauthausen exhibits the brutal effectiveness of the
building details and the contradictions inherent in establishing an SS economic
empire through the decimation of its own labor force. Aesthetic policy and punishment, available materials and forced labor – these were the interrelated factors that
are exposed in an examination of the SS institutional architecture and the camps of
Flossenbürg and Mauthausen.

Himmler's pronouncements in his article provide an example of how form, as
it is tied to ideological interests, can be pushed to a grotesque extreme based on
contemporaneous conditions. Yet, to limit ourselves to an analysis of design
and reception plays into a mystification of the criminal basis of SS architectural
interests, interests that were justified in the SS press but also functioned (as
at Nuremberg and Berlin) to carry out specific political and economic goals that
furthered the extension of SS power over millions of individuals in Germany and
occupied Europe. While the transparency of the SS's projection of meaning onto
architecture goes far to explain many design decisions, the institutional significance
of architecture to the SS must be extended beyond how the buildings were used
to promote a public identity for this policing institution. Certainly, institutional
architecture for the SS was about asserting ideological goals; but it was also related
to a strategic policy of accumulating power in the course of the volatile internal
struggles of National Socialist Germany in the face of broader structural
developments leading up to and including the early years of World War II.

THE FUNCTION OF ARCHITECTURE FOR THE SS

As in the case of monumental building projects, SS architecture served a number of different functions. In addition to the institutional requirements for space and facilities, SS leaders and administrators adapted their architectural plans to the internal political dynamics of the Nazi state as well as the development of the building economy and, with the beginning of war, militarist expansion. These adaptations helped promote policies aimed at projecting an ideologically cohesive institutional identity as well as an external assertion of permanence. After the outbreak of World War II, SS architectural goals were further extended to plan for and advance the importance of the SS in a dreamed-of post-war German-dominated world order. A development of such fantastic claims depended on a step-by-step expansion of SS political authority and a measured increase in the productivity of forced-labor operations which could be adapted to the new internal institutional demands for building materials. Hence, the involvement of SS personnel in aesthetic and planning decisions for their own buildings necessitated taking into account the social, political and economic function of architecture in the expansion of the "Hitler State."

The design and construction history of the SS Barracks (SS-Kaserne [Figures 17, 18]) in Nuremberg indicates the level of SS participation in the building process as well as the initial use of architecture by SS personnel to promote ideological and political goals. Here, both Himmler and Pohl participated in making comments on or influencing the project, though with different results. Himmler's interest remained focused on the political dynamics of the polycratic Nazi state while Pohl concerned himself, as was his purview, with the administrative infighting of the building process. As one of the largest and most public SS buildings constructed, the brick and stone structure became a kind of shadow sixth building for the Party Rally Grounds, and its construction between 1936 and 1939 allowed the SS administrators involved to manipulate architectural policy for the implementation of personal and institutional goals.

In 1936, the same year Himmler was named head of the German police, the SS strove to consolidate its power throughout the National Socialist state. Part of Himmler's drive to give the SS a more prominent official profile included his involvement with public architectural facilities for the SS, drawing support from the architectural decisions already made by Hitler and Speer. In this regard it is not surprising, then, that the SS would turn to the most active and high-profile monumental architectural site in Germany, the Reich Party Rally Grounds. As early as May 1936, Pohl had informed the local SS administration that suitable land in Nuremberg should be found, land that gave SS participants in the party rallies a place to stay and access to the grounds; this request was forwarded to the city building administration and Mayor Liebel. By September, a site had been chosen on the Frankenstrasse very near the Luitpoldhain Arena. Pohl had already become well involved with the project and carefully listed all of the different functions and needs that would be required for the building. Walter Brugmann received Pohl's request

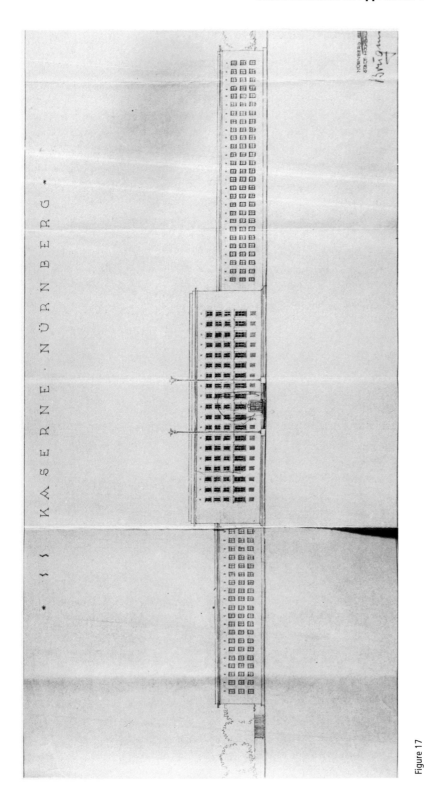

Figure 17
WALTER BRUGMANN, ORIGINAL DESIGN FOR THE SS BARRACKS, NUREMBERG, 1936
Source: Stadtarchiv Nürnberg

Figure 18
FRANZ RUFF, SS BARRACKS
(central section, as built), 1939
Source: Stadtarchiv Nürnberg

and began working on the design. In these early dealings over property, functional spaces and design, Himmler played no role. His one appeal to Pohl was to have the designs finished and on his desk by the end of September.[4]

But while Pohl consolidated the administrative organization of the site and Brugmann took over the aesthetic design, when the plans arrived at Himmler's office in September the Reichsführer used the experience to establish a cultural tie to Hitler, a strategy that had become typical for Nazi leaders vying for Hitler's approval.[5] Brugmann's plans showed two three-story wings set back from a central six-story monumental entrance with square doors and windows marked with stone surrounds. With this in hand, Himmler received Speer's approval and the promise that Speer would show the design to Hitler. Himmler's perspicacity paid off: Hitler became actively involved by the beginning of December 1936, and had made specific suggestions on the design and layout of the site. Pohl also jumped on Hitler's participation, citing his involvement in memos and noting his desire to have the construction tempo speeded up. Further, Himmler apparently decided that Brugmann and the building administration did not have the appropriate prestige for the given project and thus named Franz Ruff to take over the design work. It was thought that, for such a project, an architect who was already involved in the Party Rally Grounds would be more appropriate for the monumental SS Barracks. (Ruff was already commissioned by the ZRPT to complete the Congress Hall.) In this choice, as in others, Himmler appeared to have no particular architectural opinions of his own, but took his cues from Hitler, Speer and other Party officials who had strong views on how to build.[6] Himmler acted to push the prestige of the SS by securing a Hitler-approved architect as well as solidifying his social position in the state political hierarchy through the pursuit of a project that attracted Hitler's personal interest.

In late 1936, Himmler visited the proposed site with Mayor Liebel, Brugmann, Speer and Ruff, the most influential representatives of the Party Rally Grounds architectural administration. Himmler made comments concerning the functional aspects of the building (e.g. the need for underground garages) but left the aesthetic considerations up to Ruff. Throughout 1937, Ruff's designs went through several phases, all of which were approved or changed based on Speer's or Hitler's wishes. It was probably at this stage that Brugmann's central section was altered with the introduction of a large arch, giving the entrance the character of a stripped-down Roman Imperial triumphal arch. Such an alteration was of course consistent with the ideologically loaded classical references of the Party Rally Grounds themselves. Further changes focused less on design details and more on the choice of materials. Ruff originally suggested that the façade should be in stone, but Speer decided to face the building with plaster. Then Hitler ordered stone but changed his mind to make the building half stone and half plaster walls. Ultimately, the central section as well as some detailing were completed in stone while the walls of the wings were finished in exposed brick. The design was finalized by 20 September 1937 as per Hitler's suggestions and the building was ready for SS personnel by the 1939 Party Rally.[7] The building corresponded to the propagandistic function of projecting a monumental role for the SS at the important Nuremberg site as well as establishing Hitler's interest in Himmler and SS cultural policy.

Meanwhile, Brugmann and the city building administration disengaged themselves as much as possible from the project. This not only had to do with the hiring of Ruff as a prestige architect (who did not get along with city administrators) but also with Pohl's use of the site as an attempt to prove the administrative effectiveness of the SS in its own building projects. Pohl took charge of the construction timetable and pushed the on-site building administration to meet the deadlines set by Hitler. Further, he coordinated the purchase of land, negotiated payments for property and work done, and dealt with conflicts between the architect and the city administration over jurisdictional questions. But, for all of Pohl's efforts, one reason that the city administration withdrew from the project was a clear sense by 1937 that the SS local administrators were generally incompetent and unprofessional. Further, Brugmann feared that the SS would force all costs for the building onto the city if given the chance. The Nuremberg barracks provided an important administrative experience for Pohl and his staff but not necessarily one that turned out in the way they had planned: the June 1939 opening of the facility was a year behind the originally worked-out schedule.[8]

Not surprisingly, the propagandistic value of the Nuremberg barracks guaranteed that the top SS administrators would be drawn to the project. With less obvious sites, Pohl was nevertheless equally involved. Unlike Himmler, Pohl, as leader of the SS-Verwaltungsamt and then in 1939 the SS Central Budget and Building Office (Hauptamt Haushalt und Bauten [HAHuB]), actively participated in design decisions made for buildings under his jurisdiction. In August 1938, for example, Pohl requested, and received for his approval, plans for the layout of the grounds of KL Flossenbürg and the SS housing estate next to the camp. Furthermore, he wanted to promote buildings at Flossenbürg and other SS complexes in an exhibition of "artistically" rendered drawings of the structures in July 1939, though no record exists as to whether the exhibition actually opened.[9] At this stage in the rapid expansion and construction of the forced-labor quarry and brick-making enterprises, Pohl interested himself in promoting and influencing the design of the new camps.

While he did not promote a particular historicist aesthetic, Pohl did use his authority to guarantee that SS structures projected a unified and monumental presence. Such a strategy exemplifies the actions of SS administrators in the late 1930s as they attempted to consolidate and assert the importance of their institution in a peacetime German state. With this goal in mind, Pohl made suggestions on formal elements in the design process that led to specific changes in the architecture of the new camps planned after 1936.

For example, at KL Buchenwald, Pohl ignored the general layout of facilities while focusing his attention instead on the entrance building (Figure 19). As at other camps, the entrance building became the key and often the only building designed to have any symbolic effect on the SS guards and the prisoners. Entrance buildings were considered monumental architecture (permanent structures made from brick and plaster or with some stone structural or aesthetic elements) and often were the first part of the camp the prisoners saw. Nevertheless, most SS correspondence rarely strayed beyond a description of the arrangement of rooms, offices and materials to be used. In a typical letter of 7 September 1937, the SS building office at Buchenwald described the function of the interior of its planned entrance building:

Figure 19
ENTRANCE BUILDING, KL
BUCHENWALD, c. 1938 (present
condition)
Source: Author

With a total length of 63 m, the Entrance Building will be built on the axis of the camp. The one-story building with a centrally arranged tower will be constructed out of brick and be given an entrance gate in the middle.

The left wing includes: 26 arrest cells; a watch, wash and lavatory room; a reception and examination room; and a machine room as well as a 1.5 m wide corridor running throughout. On the right side is the stairwell (accessible from the outside) that leads to the watch tower. In the right wing, left of the first entrance corridor, lies the service room of the Block Leader from the Camp Office, and, straight on, the orderly room. From the second entrance corridor, one reaches the office of the Camp Manager (left), the Report Manager (straight on) and the office of the Camp Architect (right). In the second corridor, a lavatory with washing facilities will be built. The third entrance leads to the building office, with connection to a storeroom and lavatory with sinks.[10]

The analysis of the interior is practical, describing little of how the rooms will be designed, only their function and arrangement. Yet the report does mention two key elements which would be designed carefully: the central tower that allowed the guards to see both sides of the camp, and the entrance gate, which often contained an inscription in the grillwork such as the infamous "Work Makes One Free" (*Arbeit Macht Frei*) at KL Dachau (at Buchenwald, it was "To Each his Own" [*Jedem das Sein*]). Individual camps varied the design, but the basic functional elements remained the same.[11]

Pohl, however, was concerned with more than just a practical design, and he took a particular interest in influencing the construction of the entrance building at Buchenwald. The original plan finished in September 1937 foresaw a one-story half-timbered building with a central brick tower, aligned with the axis of the camp. Pohl approved funds for the construction but sent the designs back to the camp to be reworked because the middle section did not conform to his sense of architectural proportion.

The middle portion of the planned building does not correspond to the demands that I must make regarding the architectural form. It appears impossible to me to build this roof construction [of the tower] in the form planned, as it stands in no relation to its substructure. Therefore I ask that the design of the middle portion once again undergo a thorough reworking. In case the rooms in the tower construction are required to this extent and in this height, I ask [you] to handle the entire middle portion as a separate two-story building mass and to connect on the sides the building's wings with the remaining rooms.[12]

Pohl left the specific function and arrangement of the entrance building rooms up to the camp administrators while interesting himself in the formal conception of the structure. For Buchenwald, his criteria were not specifically symbolic, rather he focused on assuring a monumental unified structure that would correspond to the importance of the SS and the concentration camp as institutions. The plan was changed by the end of September, corresponding to Pohl's demands.

Of course, the push to build more monumental and permanent structures was conditioned by this moment in SS development, the period of the late 1930s when it was expanding both the political and economic function of the concentration camps. Such optimism for the future expansion of the SS and Germany in general translated as well into the broad architectural claims made in the official periodical for the SS, *Das Schwarze Korps* (1937–45). In this periodical, discussions of architecture were used to give SS administrators and architects design ideas from projects approved by the central office in Berlin and also to solidify an institutional identity through the promotion of particular architectural styles and examples. Articles were neither consistent nor accurate in their reference to monuments and epochs but were meant to inspire the SS membership and be used as a model for institutional architects. Most often authors cited classical architecture (particularly that of the Roman Empire), but they also discussed ancient Greece, Egypt and medieval German architecture as paradigms of previous architectural traditions. While relying on semi-accurate historical accounts or superficial formal comparisons, the buildings illustrated were invariably explained with the thesis that powerful dynasties will build the best architecture. This thesis would be repeated in multiple articles. SS authors described architecture not merely as the result of political, military or "racial" dominance, but as expressing and actively perpetuating power. When speaking of the eighteenth and nineteenth centuries, for example, an anonymous author claimed:

> Exactly as the "Prussian Style" fundamentally signified nothing less than a revelation of Nordic thought, so the master sensibility (which, at that time, was especially strengthened politically) of the Germanic ruling class in England and Scandinavia used as well classical forms. This sensibility never acquired, significantly speaking, the usual slavish copying of the antique typical particularly in France, but rather stubbornly persevered to the spatial sentiment specific to our race.[13]

Yet the interest of the SS in using ideological pronouncements on architecture to promote a continuity between previous powerful epochs and its own present strength went beyond pronouncements in its magazine and the construction of the various institutional structures under its control. Pohl's economic administration was also responsible for the managing of specific historical sites that the SS purchased or leased from the state, sites that supported the belief in a pseudo-scientific racist ideology of the superiority of Germanic peoples. The SS had framed its image as an elitist racial institution from its inception as Hitler's personal guard unit, and after 1933 it became more concerned with stringent physical and social requirements for new volunteers. Himmler often personally approved marriages for SS men, and new members had to prove their "Aryan" heritage back to 1750 for officers or 1800 for enlisted men. Members were to consider themselves as a social elite, and, as such, the SS aligned itself with older traditions of aristocratic service, particularly that of medieval knights under Henry I of Saxony. In 1936, Himmler even observed the thousandth anniversary of Henry I's death at the tomb site in the cathedral of Quedlinburg. The belief in the SS as an elite contributed to the acquisition and administration of important architectural and archaeological sites including Ehrenbreitstein, a fortress over-looking the Rhine near Koblenz; the cathedral at Quedlinburg, in Thuringia; and the seventeenth-century castle of Wewelsburg outside of Paderborn.[14]

The castle of Wewelsburg (Figure 20) in particular was meant to foster the projection of the SS as a superior institution that resurrected the Germanic past by supposedly continuing the Teutonic traditions of rulers like Henry I, and its history indicates how that ideological goal and architectural plans varied with the changing political conditions of the state. Himmler bought the castle in 1934 to serve as the center of a new training school for SS officers and, in accordance with this function, he ordered the remodeling of the building from 1934 to 1942. Though the castle actually used by the SS was begun in 1604 by the bishop-prince Theodor von Fürstenberg, it was built on a site where many previous fortified structures had stood. An archaeological dig in 1924 discovered the existence of a Saxon fortification on the bluff where the castle was later built. Though the evidence proved to be thin and speculative, the SS claimed the site as part of the empire of Henry I around the time of his campaign against the Hungarians c. 930. After visiting several other possible sites in the area, Himmler decided that this would be the location of the officers' training school.[15]

Herman Bartels, an SS architect who had previously done restoration work in the area, managed the project. The three-sided castle was constructed with towers at each corner, the most prominent of which was at the northern tip of the triangular building. The structure was built out of limestone with a steeply pitched roof. Bartels set about redesigning the rooms and planned a large space for the most important SS ceremonies in the north tower. A crypt in the basement level of the north tower reconstruction was meant for solemn rituals and the laying in state of

Figure 20
CASTLE AT WEWELSBURG,
seventeenth century
Source: Bundesarchiv

SS leaders when they died. The Columned Hall above the crypt served for receptions, while the upper floor of the tower, the Gruppenführer Room, was never completed.[16]

For the rebuilding of the castle, the SS used not only state resources but also the forced labor of prisoners and materials from DEST enterprises. The construction of the north tower was carried out between 1940 and 1942 with prisoners from a subsidiary camp of KL Sachsenhausen established at the site in 1939. In 1941, this compound was made into an independent concentration camp, the smallest in the SS system, and renamed KL Niederhagen. At least 1,285 prisoners were killed through the forced labor and unhygienic conditions in the concentration camp. Stone was procured from DEST enterprises including KL Flossenbürg whose 1941 and 1942 balance reports noted stone supplied to the SS complex. As the economic enterprises were based on the increasing political authority of the SS, the procurement of materials and the labor of prisoners was relatively easy. Backed by Speer's approval even in late 1942 after he had become the Minister of Armaments and Munitions, the SS had the ability to pursue the Wewelsburg project.[17]

In these early militarily successful war years, the construction of the north tower with forced labor corresponded not only to the growing political authority of the SS. An alteration of the plan at this time also projected the SS as the center of a presumed post-war universal German world order. Under Bartels' plan, Wewelsburg was to be the hub of a vast administration and housing complex arranged in concentric circles emanating from the castle. The core of this circle was the north tower, where the symbolic and official functions of the highest SS officers were to be conducted. This carefully worked-out complex emphasized the centrality of the SS to the (German) world and asserted the elitist and powerful base of the organization. Such elitism, stemming from vague notions of the continuation of medieval traditions (including the establishment of coats of arms for all higher SS officials, a museum of Germanic culture and even the interior decorations acquired by Himmler that included tapestries and wrought iron fixtures), promoted the self-designated role of the SS as a knightly order on the medieval model.[18]

Wewelsburg was by no means the only site at which the SS contemplated medievalist structures to communicate its continuity with previous Germanic regimes and its dominant presence in a Germanized Europe. In the eastern occupied territories, Himmler worked to "repatriate" settlers of German descent from the USSR and other parts of Eastern Europe by calling for a massive plan for farm and small-settlement communities. As with the SS Barracks in Nuremberg, SS attempts to control the planning and establishment of German communities in the East was partly meant to assert its authority against the administrations of Frank (head of the Generalgouvernement in Poland) as well as Rosenberg (as Reich Minister for the Eastern Occupied Territory). But this political power play was also based on SS ideological goals of establishing a Germanic East. As part of this process, Himmler proposed the establishment of agricultural settlements, and plans were drawn up for ideal small villages modeled after pre-modern Germanic sites.[19] In this sense, the historicist pretensions of Wewelsburg and its connection to a belief in the German domination of Europe were contiguous with the presumed function of other SS projects put forth in these optimistic war years and corresponded to the developing political function of the SS within the German state.

BUILDING AT KL FLOSSENBÜRG

These grandiose schemes, political power plays and ideological projections depended on the ability of the SS to expand its policing authority and architectural projects. But while this process has clear implications for the public facilities of the SS, what effect, if any, did developing SS policy have on the construction of the con-centration camps? Was that effect only functional in that the expansion of the camps, the development of forced-labor operations and, finally, the gruesome transformation of eastern sites into the death camps all depended on different kinds of architectural facilities? Did the architectural goals of the SS go beyond the kind of generic monumentality Pohl demanded of the entrance building at Buchenwald? As with Nuremberg and Berlin, the answers to these questions involve exploring the integration of aesthetic decisions with political and economic policy. In turning to the concentration camps, the convergence of these issues marks the brutal extreme of the effectiveness of architectural policy, political oppression and the production of building materials in DEST enterprises.

Before the war, camp architecture consisted mostly of standardized watch towers of brick and plaster, as well as a few permanent structures housing admin-istration, facilities (kitchen, washroom), a place for executions (often a basement) and a crematorium. Only the arrangement of these buildings differed from camp to camp although all shared some variation of the traditional pavilion plan so prevalent in modern institutional architecture.[20] KL Sachsenhausen, for example, was a triangular camp with barracks emanating out from the entrance building and roll-call plaza while Dachau had the camp administrative buildings lined up on one side of the central plaza, the prisoner barracks on the other. The forced-labor brickworks and, later, the death camps in the conquered eastern territories were constructed with functionality and economy of materials in mind and bore few signs of the kinds of aesthetic and ideological considerations prevalent in the more public SS structures.

The stone-quarry camps of KL Flossenbürg and KL Mauthausen were exceptions to these standardized designs. Though these compounds were also arranged with the institutional barracks form (including a central axis with a roll-call plaza [Figure 21]), the entrance building and guard towers significantly differed from the other forced-labor and death camps. In the case of Flossenbürg, the massive watch towers, supporting walls and the entrance building were made of stone with some amount of detail work. Mauthausen, also with stone watch towers, was designed with a monumental walled façade connected to the SS garages and the administrative headquarters. This architecture depended, of course, on the stone-quarry operations of the camp and the forced labor of the prisoners. As a result, these monumental stone architectural projects functioned

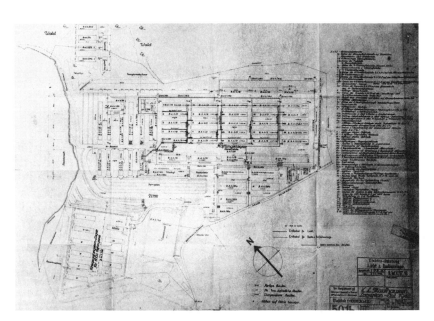

Figure 21
PLAN OF KL MAUTHAUSEN, 1942
Source: Öffentliches Denkmal und
Museum Mauthausen

not only as symbolic expressions of the permanence of the SS but as the means (in combination with the quarries) of destroying as many prisoners as possible at the high point of SS optimism between 1939 and 1942.

Construction at KL Flossenbürg exemplifies how the SS economic administrators, on-site camp building personnel and DEST officials worked together to promote aesthetic decisions that went beyond the functional needs of the camp. As with other camps, the buildings used by the prisoners were flimsy structures and, in the case of the barracks, purchased from private firms. But the SS acquired better materials and organized a careful process of design for the camp administrative buildings, walls and watch towers.[21] An assessment of the building of the watch towers at Flossenbürg (Figures 4, 22, 23) elucidates the direct connection between SS architectural plans and the concentration camp system which buttressed its institutional authority.

By 1939, all approval of building design, distribution of funds and ordering of materials for the construction of the concentration camps was managed by the SS HAHuB, Hauptabteilung II C. However, the Hauptabteilung II C constantly struggled with mismanagement, and Pohl appointed in June 1941 the efficient and experienced Hans Kammler to professionalize and rationalize operations. Kammler retained this position throughout the war. (Kammler had been a councillor [Baurat] of the Berlin building administration who entered the SS in May 1933.)[22]

Both the central offices in Berlin as well as the on-site administration participated in organizing the building process. The HAHuB produced the initial plan of the camp compounds and often provided rough sketches for the buildings considered to be significant. These plans would then be sent to the building administration at the camp, worked out in detail, and, after 1941, returned to the

Figure 22
WATCH TOWER, KL
FLOSSENBÜRG, c. 1940 (present
condition)
Source: Author

HAHuB office for Kammler's personal approval (and, sometimes, that of Pohl as well). The organization of construction – ordering of supplies and machinery, use of prisoners – was conducted at the camp but subject, as with budgets, to the approval of Hauptabteilung II C. By 1940, plans also had to be sanctioned on their

Figure 23
WATCH TOWER, KL FLOSSENBÜRG
(detail), *c.* 1940 (present
condition)
Source: Author

aesthetic merit by Fritz Blaschek, a Czech architect who ran the artistic division (*künstlerische Fachgebiete*) within the HAHuB for all SS building. The construction itself would be managed by the camp building administrators and overseen by the commandant. Prisoners were used for the actual labor.[23]

While the administrative organization and reorganization gives us a sense of the hierarchy of the building process, specific decisions about camp buildings were made in relation to particular geographies, functions, available forced labor and materials. KL Flossenbürg was initially laid out in September 1938 after a visit to the site by Salpeter (the head of DEST at the time), Commandant Weiseborn, Government Building Inspector Eckstein (a HAHuB representative), and Georg Mayrl, head of the camp building administration. These representatives fixed the preliminary camp boundaries as well as the site for the SS housing settlement bordering the camp. The plans of these two compounds were based on traditional institutional and housing types. Camp barracks and buildings were set at regular intervals in parallel rows; the housing estate, on the other hand, borrowed from established residential patterns by including units built at an angle to two curving roads that wound through the complex. HAHuB administrators in Berlin approved and corrected the designs for the SS officers' houses that were made with half-timbered walls, a low gabled roof typical of the region and a granite foundation and basement story. Housing was completed from 1938 to 1940 with all stone coming from the DEST work and the use of prison labor.[24]

Other than the SS housing estate, the permanent structures of the complex were all completed after the approval in November 1940 of the camp's expansion. This was precisely the period when the SS was most optimistic about the success of its economic ventures because of the increased number of prisoners of war. Some structures such as two of the watch towers and the first entrance building were already under construction in 1940. After the HAHuB made the decision to extend the camp, however, a new plan became necessary. This plan required that one of the watch towers and the entrance building be torn down and rebuilt at new sites. A certain Untersturmführer Kuiper, an architect with Hauptabteilung II C, designed the new plan that included an extension of the prisoner compound, a monumental stone entrance building aligned on a new central axis, seven stone watch towers and other smaller structures, all to be built with forced labor. The building administration in the camp completed the working drawings for construction.[25] As at Wewelsburg, the progress of war victories and the political extension of SS authority led to the construction of more monumental structures. At Flossenbürg, however, these structures were needed not only for the ideological claims of the SS but also for the expansion of its role as a policing force and as the provider of building materials for Berlin through the DEST quarries.

Building began in 1940–1 and, after the plans were finalized, Kammler retroactively approved funding and construction. The entrance building design changed slightly after the first version was torn down to allow an alignment of the structure with the axis of the camp; how it was changed is unclear, however, as the original plans do not exist. Construction began in July 1941 and 80 per cent of the building was finished by October 1942 with completion by December 1943. The seven watch towers were designed by July 1940 at which point materials were ordered and construction began, though changes in the plan also seemed to have been made after this point. Six of the seven towers were completed by August 1942. HAHuB correspondence designated both of these structures as monumental building to distinguish them in terms of size and the permanence of the materials used.[26]

With its muddy and rocky forest ground, Flossenbürg required deep foundations for the monumental buildings. This was especially true for the watch towers, built on the steep pitch of the hill on the north side of the camp and on a sharp drop in the shallow valley on the south side. As in other camps, the watch towers were above all functional buildings set up to allow the guards to see the entire camp and identify or shoot any prisoner who walked too close to the electric fence. Yet, in spite of the use of readily accessible materials of stone and wood, several aspects of the completed structure indicate that the towers were more than just functional. Great care was taken in cutting the stone for the shallow arch of the door frame, the window surrounds and, especially, the quoining on the corners of the battered structure. Berlin administrators singled out the trapped windows that allowed the guards to shoot into the camp and the placement of stone at the corners as the two features of the towers where the design was to be more elaborate than elsewhere. According to a report from Mayrl on 17 April 1941, these were also the elements of the structure that caused it to be more expensive than previously assumed by the SS. However, costs were not cut to make the building simpler, but rather further funds were allocated to pay for the stone and windows.[27]

The design process also indicates that SS architects and administrators found aesthetic considerations important for the watch towers at Flossenbürg. The

HAHuB had ordered the use of facing stone and quoining by May 1940, that is, before all plans were finalized. In August of that year, an exchange of letters and drawings took place between the HAHuB and the Bauleitung Flossenbürg as to the exact specifications and placement of the stone. After Rottenführer Hauser, an engineer from the HAHuB, visited the camp in July, he expressly ordered that in all drawings, only the corner and frame stonework should be indicated while the façade stone was to be placed by craftsmen at the site. The reason behind this decision seemed to be one of efficiency as it was significantly easier to allow the setting of the stone facing at the site than to dictate such specifications beforehand. Yet an aesthetic element was also involved as the specifications for the cornerstones were fixed (not less than 25 cm high) and the parallel layering of the façade stones was to follow the careful guidelines outlined by Hauser. All joints were to be as thin and even as possible, the stones were all to be wider than they were tall and the whole façade should have "a playfully crafted order" as stated in a letter from the HAHuB to the building administration. Hauser, who visited the site to check the work on the walls already begun by 20 August 1940, kept the handling of the stone consistent for all of the towers but requested that each tower have a different form. He ordered the Bauleitung to prepare variations of the basic tower design and send the drawings to Berlin.[28]

Of course, the towers made use of the speckled blue-gray granite available through the forced labor of the DEST stone quarry at the camp. Whereas other materials such as brick and steel were regulated through centralized government agencies of the Four Year Plan, the camp Bauleitung often acquired the stone purchased from DEST through orders over the phone. The total cost of the specially cut stone for the corners, windows and doors of the watch towers amounted to RM 2,716 per tower. Stone was delivered to the site either by truck or, most often, taken from the quarries on carts by prisoners. The SS economic administration in Berlin stringently enforced DEST's monopoly on stone work and contracts to the point where it chastised the KL Flossenbürg Bauleitung for using stone-masons without going through DEST.[29] Thus the use of forced labor to construct the camp and to quarry the stone was administratively linked.

While all camps had access to forced labor, only the DEST camps had access to their own supply of building materials. This allowed for different architectural considerations that could include the placement and cutting of stone, considerations that allowed for more aesthetic interpretations of the massive permanent structures. At Auschwitz, for example, certainly the size of the camp and its imposing administrative buildings (including the infamous entrance gate) projected the institutional authority of the SS. But these buildings were mostly brick and plaster structures designed with functionality as the brutal criteria of the design process.[30] With Flossenbürg's towers, the buildings were designed to be no less imposing or efficient, but to these functions was added the ability to adapt the designs to the interest in monumental stone architecture. The varying appearance of each institution stems from organizational decisions that determined location as well as type of forced labor. Further, architectural choices stemmed from the chronological development of the camp system which progressed from the forced-labor concerns to the later extreme of the death camps.

At Flossenbürg, forced labor was not limited to the hard labor in the quarries and at the construction site but was also used in the building administration itself. With the war drawing civilian workers and even SS members into other important industries, the SS increasingly turned to prisoners for alleviating the scarcity of labor. Prisoners preferred administrative jobs to other labor details largely because they were inside, avoiding the harsh weather that was a constant threat to their survival. As early as the fall of 1939, the Flossenbürg DEST work had a Communist prisoner sent from Dachau to do technical drawings for the wiring of the camp and buildings. When this prisoner was sent back to Dachau, the DEST administration asked Mayrl to find a replacement prisoner amongst those at Flossenbürg.[31]

Architects and draftsmen were also needed by the building administrations, as SS officials in Berlin recognized by early 1942. Blaschek, at that time, was looking for architects in the prison populations suitable for pressing work at Dachau. Of all the camps, he decided to visit Flossenbürg and Mauthausen to evaluate the prisoners used in their building administrations. These trained prisoners, however, were often also needed in the armaments industries. They were being released (according to the complaints of building administrators) by the SS-RSHA at a greater rate than they could be replaced. Thus, though not significantly better off, it appears that architecturally trained prisoners were at a premium in the camps at the height of the war, a situation that often at least prompted extra rations and a job indoors.[32]

The towers at KL Flossenbürg indicate which projects SS administrators in Berlin considered important and also the coordination of SS economic concerns with the construction of the camps. The care with which the buildings were planned and constructed involved aesthetic decisions in the development of the political and economic functions of the camp. Such an involvement came at the height of SS optimism and confidence in a German military victory. SS administrators evidenced their assurance in expanding the concentration camp system and their economic enterprises. At specific camps like Flossenbürg, such assurance was also manifested in the monumental stone architecture of the institution itself.

BUILDING AT KL MAUTHAUSEN

Yet the massive construction sites of Flossenbürg and Mauthausen were also used as work details for physically abusing and even destroying specific camp populations. Hence, the architecture of the camps of Flossenbürg and Mauthausen offered another means by which the SS could carry out the punitive function of the camp. While Berlin administrators and on-site construction managers discussed the aesthetic merits of the plans, actually building these stone structures often meant certain death for those prisoners forced to carry out the task. Hence, in their confidence in building structures and asserting their institutional interests, SS administrators took up the role assigned to such individuals by Walter Benjamin:

"Whoever has emerged victorious participates to this day in the triumphal procession in which the present rulers step over those who are lying prostrate."[33] Even though the SS triumph was short-lived, it would prove devastating for the inmate population.

As at Flossenbürg, the SS used the construction of the Mauthausen concentration camp both to project the permanence of the institution (to themselves, the town and the prisoners) and to destroy the most unwanted enemies of National Socialism in the process. The prisoners forced to build the entrance gate, the SS garages and the great wall half surrounding the complex did so at minimal expense to the SS and maximum distress to themselves (Figures 5, 24). The building site became second only to the quarry as the worst possible commando to which a prisoner could be assigned. Architectural choices made by the SS in the construction of Mauthausen effectively served the political function of the camp as an institution which Heydrich had already determined no one should ever be allowed to leave.[34]

Construction can be divided into two phases. These phases, as at KL Flossenbürg, correspond to the initial development of the forced-labor camps and their subsequent expansion with the early German war victories. Construction began with the erection of a functional preliminary camp (1938–9) and then, with the increased optimism of the SS, the building of permanent and symbolic structures (1939–42). Site clearing, building of the wooden barracks and the erection of the electrified barbed-wire fence around the complex were completed in 1938–9. The SS built these functional structures with the use of the first group of Austrian prisoners who were sent to the camp beginning in August 1938.[35] Construction activity on the permanent buildings at Mauthausen took place between 1939 and 1942, though some work was continued up through 1944.

Several architectural elements indicate that the permanent buildings of the

Figure 24
INMATES CONSTRUCTING THE
WALLS AT KL MAUTHAUSEN (SS
photo), *c.* 1941–2
Source: Main Commission for the
Investigation of Nazi War Crimes
in Poland (Courtesy of the US
Holocaust Memorial Museum
Source Archive)

camp – the wall, the gate, the administration building and SS garages – were meant to be symbolic as well as functional in design. The site itself suggests such motivations. The camp was located at the top of a low hill in a potato and oat field where the soil was particularly unstable but from which the façade could be seen clearly by townspeople or travelers.[36] The permanent structures were built contiguously in a complex that ran the entire length of the south- and northwest sides of the camp. Only these two sides of the camp – the faces exposed to the public eye – were permanent constructions while the south- and northeast sides of the camp were bordered by electrified barbed-wire fences.

The southwest wall faced the access road leading up from the Danube valley forming the first impression for those who entered or approached the camp. The wall, as with all the permanent structures, was built out of the blue-gray flecked granite from the camp stone quarry Wienergraben. A tall structure, the wall was punctuated with evenly spaced turrets and sight holes at alternating heights (Figures 25, 26). The turrets were accessible by guards who patrolled the front of the camp but unnecessary from a functional perspective as the view from the top of the wall was not blocked by any interceding structures. The sight holes, modeled on medieval defensive structures, appeared from the outside to be positions from which the SS could protect the camp against some imaginary attack but were even less functional than the turrets. The holes, alternating but regularly spaced, did not correspond to any internal purpose. They opened into the SS garage and were not associated with any possible use for defense or even access for sight as many of them were too far above the ground to be employed for observation. The turrets, the sight holes and the stone walls themselves indicate the interest of the SS in massive construction that projected a loose ideological relation to the defensive structures of the Middle Ages. As discussed in relation to Wewelsburg, the SS

Figure 25
SS GARAGES AND WALL
COMPLEX, KL MAUTHAUSEN, c.
1942 (present condition)
Source: Author

Figure 26
OUTER WALL (seen from inside
the SS Garages), KL
MAUTHAUSEN, *c.* 1942 (present
condition)
Source: Author

administration consistently referred to this period as a model.[37] Cheaper materials, simpler construction and a more amenable site could have been chosen, as had been the case at other camps. But, at the height of war victories, the SS at KL Mauthausen built instead using a particular technique and with materials that strengthened its claims to be considered the successor of the knights of Henry I.[38]

Of course, unlike the castles of Henry I, SS concentration camps were designed not to keep attackers out but prisoners in. As with the DEST quarries at the site and the labor camp at Wewelsburg, the construction of the permanent structures between the summer of 1939 and 1942 served the punitive goals of the SS through the conditions prisoners faced in working on the massive stone complex. In this period, the total number of prisoners rose from 1,475 in May 1939 to *c.* 7,400 by December 1941 and then fell to 6,727 in December 1942. The known registered dead in the camp from 1939 to February 1942, at which point more exact records stopped, totaled 6,025 (though even these numbers, collected from SS records, represent only an incomplete count that, for example, does not include prisoners executed immediately upon entering the camp). Prisoners were most often initially assigned work in the quarry or, in particular cases like that of the Spanish Republicans, work on the construction of the permanent structures. These were the two most strenuous work details that would wear the prisoners down through the combination of hard labor, exposure to the elements, arbitrary abuse from Kapos and guards, and purposeful killing.[39]

Hence, during the period of greatest building activity, SS punitive policy was connected to architectural policy through both the economic enterprises and the SS's own construction requirements. The stone quarry formed the link between government monumental building projects and the construction plans of the SS (Figure 27). Almost every former inmate testimony focuses on this commando, equated with death by the prisoners.[40] The quarry was the beginning of the construction process for the permanent structures, and most of the stone for building came from the deposit next to the camp, the Wienergraben. Conditions were bad from the opening of the camp and even after 1943 when the DEST enterprise was less important to the SS than the armaments concerns.

In the construction process, work details were prioritized in terms of the kind and severity of punishment, a practice that continued as long as the wartime victories allowed for a belief in a seemingly endless supply of forced labor. It is important to note here that punishment at the labor camps was often

Figure 27
VIEW OF PRISONERS CARRYING STONES ON THE STEPS OF THE QUARRY (SS Photo), KL MAUTHAUSEN, c. 1942
Source: Rijksinstituut voor Oorlogsdocumentatie (Courtesy of the US Holocaust Memorial Museum Source Archive)

differentiated based on the political, social or national affiliation of the prisoner. That is to say, while the aesthetic choices based on particular kinds of high-quality granite provided the pre-conditions for the location and forced labor at the camps for most inmates, they formed the pre-condition only for punishment of specific designated populations like the Jewish inmates as well as some other exceptions such as the Spanish Communists. Whereas many fewer Jews were deported to the forced-labor camps than, obviously, to the even more extreme death camps in the eastern occupied territories, nevertheless those that did end up in Mauthausen were often murdered at the quarrying sites that were constructed as a result of the SS interest in the monumental building economy. The artistic pre-conditions for killing at Mauthausen indicated a radicalization and prioritization of anti-Semitic policy which crystallized by the end of 1941 in the institutionalization of destruction at the death camps.[41]

While the SS on-site personnel "selected" many groups such as Jews for hazardous work in the quarries, the Spanish Republicans in particular were assigned to the difficult work on the wall and garage construction during these years. Spanish transports began arriving in 1940 after Germany had overrun France and those Republicans who had escaped from Franco's Spain were caught by the occupying forces. Between 1940 and 1942, approximately 7,500 Spanish Republicans or members of the International Brigade who had fought against Franco were interned at Mauthausen. Though they represented the political spectrum from liberal to left, the majority of these prisoners were Communist Party members or anarchists. The Spanish were the first large group of non-German or Austrian prisoners to be sent to Mauthausen. Most probably because of their training and ability to survive the conditions of the civil war in Spain, they also had a higher survival rate than other national groups when given equal treatment. However, because of their virulent anti-fascism and leftist commitments, the Spanish were given almost exclusively the most brutal tasks. Their numbers were greatly depleted through abuse in the stone quarries and, particularly, in building the walls of Mauthausen.[42]

Sebastián Mena summarized the work of the Spaniards at Mauthausen in his testimonial:

> Our work consisted, as for all the Spanish, in carrying the stones from the quarry to the camp in order to pave the intervals between the blocks and to construct the surrounding wall and the other buildings. We were in a special company, with the worst Kapos who, with no matter which pretext, could kill us – what to them merited the felicitations of the SS. Thus we were continually suspended between life and death, from the quarry to the camp. This distance was approximately one kilometer; one performed it daily from ten to twelve times, and as it was necessary each time to ascend or descend the stairs of the quarry . . . one is able to say that our calvary required twenty-four times 186 steps. For the Nazis, a block of granite had more value than a human life.[43]

The 186 steps of the quarry formed the site of multiple abuses, abuses heaped particularly on the special labor details (Sonderkommando) with the Spanish prisoners. The physical effects of such work were evident to the inmates.

> The first Spanish that we met [reports Manuel Razola] had legs covered with sores, their faces resembled a skull; nothing remained of them but the bones, and their voices as well were just as extinguished. If they fell, they no longer succeeded in raising themselves; these men continued to work nevertheless, and certain ones among them who were at the point of death – because they died with all their lucidity – let themselves fall in a corner.[44]

The Spaniards worked in order to survive and continued to operate under the conditions created by the SS in the attempt to live through the experience.

The massive wall, garage and administrative complex, as mentioned by Mena, was the last stage of the building process for the Spanish forced labor, after the quarrying and carrying of the stone. That the Spanish also experienced the construction of the wall as deadly as the quarrying of stone is the basis of another prisoner, Navarro's, testimony:

> After that it was the work – for certain, the quarry; for another: the labor detail "Garage Building," for which the Kapos were reputed for their barbarity and known for their taste for blood. They got intoxicated in seeing the blood flowing from the wounds that they brought on. Their names must be cited: Franks, the Kapo, Otto, the aspiring Kapo. The Czechoslovakians worked with us. Every morning we would leave the camp and return at night, bruised by the blows and united in the pain, and holding each other by the hand (to the great rage of the Kapos who never understood our solidarity). This labor detail was considered as the one for those condemned to death and every evening there were victims to bring to the crematorium.[45]

Hence, the construction of the permanent complex not only provided the SS with a means of projecting its own identity related to medieval fortifications and of continuing the work at the DEST enterprise. It also fulfilled the political goals of the state in eliminating oppositional groups, a necessary component of the architectural policy of the SS.

The monumental walls of Mauthausen came about through the accessibility of forced labor and DEST materials, the latter being a key condition which differentiates the stone-quarry camps from other equally brutal concentration camp institutions. As in the case of the Party Rally Grounds, the rebuilding of Berlin, the SS Barracks in Nuremberg or the reconstruction of Wewelsburg, the choice of materials played a crucial role in promoting architectural goals. The use of stone allowed for a varied projection of historicist associations – from Greek, to Roman, to German medieval. But, of course, it also buttressed the hoped-for success of DEST enterprises in the monumental German building economy. In this sense, whether it was Kreis' Soldiers' Hall or the walls of Mauthausen, the orientation of specific forced-labor camps to the building economy meant that the development and implementation of oppressive policies would be inextricable from architectural concerns. The grotesque success of such a nexus of political, economic and architectural goals is evidenced by the destructive construction process of the walls at Mauthausen.

At the beginning of the Ottonian Empire, Henry I built a series of forti-fications to keep the Hungarians from attacking his realm. Labor on the sites was carried out by serfs and subjects, who, in case of an invasion, would themselves be protected by the walls of the castle.[46] SS administrators, in imitation of the Ottonians, described themselves as social heirs to German medieval society and established some of their institutional architecture with vague reference to this period. Yet the massive towers of Flossenbürg and the walls of Mauthausen relied on social and political structures radically different from those of their supposed antecedents. Though certainly intimidating to any potential enemy, Flossenbürg and Mauthausen were not, of course, defensive institutions. Rather they were used offensively both to assert the identity of the SS and against the individuals forced to quarry stone for DEST and construct the camp itself. Ultimately, SS punitive practices in the camps were economically and institutionally self-destructive, for the economic policy and the institution itself depended on the labor being destroyed. The SS was in this respect, as in many others, quite different from any precedent.

Chapter 6: Conclusion

In the early morning of 29 April 1945, Hitler committed suicide in his Berlin bunker. The advancing US Army had already succeeded in liberating KL Flossenbürg on 23 April and would arrive at KL Mauthausen on 5 May. In this moment of collapse, as the Allied and Red Army offensives from the west and east sealed the fate of National Socialist Germany in the last struggles of World War II, the short-lived Dönitz government attempted to establish a transitional German cabinet. One of the appointed ministers, Albert Speer, wrote the following to acting Foreign Minister Lutz Schwerin von Krosigk:

> It is necessary concerning this [the bringing together of a cabinet, in which Speer would be the Minister of Economics and Production] to choose, then, executive leaders for the individual ministries who in reference to their political past are suited to be recognized by the Allies. – I do not believe that this can apply to myself.
>
> Besides, furthermore I am also not in the position in my technical knowledge to carry out the duties of the Reich Minister of Economics, which at the present moment must deal to a large degree with the problems of the economy of finance, credit and currency.
>
> I am an architect. And it is exactly as unthinkable an undertaking to engage an artist to do debt repayment as – in the past – to assign a champagne dealer [Joachim von Ribbentrop] the Reich Foreign Ministry.[1]

It is at this time that Speer began to emphasize the distinction between his qualifications as Hitler's favored architect before 1942 and his political and administrative skill as head of the Ministry of Armaments and Munitions after 1942. His trial at Nuremberg followed this exclusive emphasis on his technocratic role in organizing the armaments industry.[2] In analyzing Speer, art historical and historical scholarship has generally respected this split between his artistic and political concerns. As a result, scholars have ignored the essential political interests served by his actions as the most powerful architect in National Socialist Germany.

This split in the analysis of Albert Speer's career in Nazi Germany points to the key historical problem addressed here. The history of National Socialist architecture has largely been represented as separate from a comprehensive and chrono-logically specific analysis of its political history. That is, art historians have avoided a thorough investigation of the function of building for Party and state policy. Today, decades after the fall of the Third Reich, scholars continue to promote a caesura between architecture and politics, between architecture as an expression of ideo-logical and aesthetic goals and the integration of architectural policy with non-artistic state and Party objectives. Given this prevailing methodological practice, it is not surprising that the interest of the SS in architecture and the monumental building economy has so far merited little more than a footnote in the art history of the period.

This book has been devoted to reasserting the material conditions of archi-tectural policy and practice, and has supported this assertion by analyzing the development of SS economic concerns in relation to architectural and political goals. The SS established its architectural policy when it aligned the political goals of the camps with an economic expansion that depended on the punishment and destruction of prisoners through labor. An analysis of the architectural projects of Nuremberg, Berlin and, ultimately, of the towers and walls of Flossenbürg and Mauthausen indicates that the most criminal component of the political history of art in National Socialist Germany can be unequivocally located in the forced-labor concentration camps of the SS.

At stake in this history have been several recurring and overlapping issues. The formulation of a specific economic policy for DEST, the need to adapt to the particular development of the building economy, the issue of the prioritization of projects within wartime Germany and the effect of such conditions and decisions on the abuse of labor in the camps are all relevant factors in assessing the interests of the SS in the monumental building economy. DEST administrators proved them-selves increasingly able to adjust to short-term power struggles in order to continue promoting their long-term economic interests. These administrators were not unlike the staff of the GBI and the numerous other officials in National Socialist Germany who competed within ever expanding spheres of authority. DEST was, however, in the unique position of pursuing its economic interests in the building materials market through its extensive abuse of the camp labor force. Little interest was shown in maximizing that labor potential, and even less in making individual workers efficient by acknowledging their most basic needs. Rather, DEST considered the work force as a whole, its members no more than a mass of numbers showing up in a budget report. Particularly in the early war years, DEST reports focused on the rising production statistics in which the deaths of individual laborers did not appear. An impossible rate of production was needed for the scheduled completion of the monumental architectural projects, and DEST did its best to take advantage of this condition by making quantitative output its overriding concern. Put more directly, the forced-labor camps were organized to be economically successful through the inmates' ability to produce, an ability that simultaneously served economic, political and architectural goals. Even though the "economic success" of the labor camps was never achieved – or rather, SS administrators mismanaged their concerns and never recognized the inefficiency of the political suppression of labor – we should not be blinded to the fact that there were devastating consequences from this attempt to integrate architecture with state and Party policy.

Whether in relation to Berlin and Nuremberg or the institutional architecture of the SS itself, the decision-making process for DEST depended on the aesthetic choices of the architects and the government policies influencing the development of the building economy. The agency of Speer, Brugmann, SS architects and Hitler brought the design process in direct contact with punitive camp policy. Himmler, Pohl and their staff of economic managers responded in kind, all the while keeping in mind the particular self-promoting interests of the SS. Such competition and cooperation between individuals and administrations conditioned the triangulation of architectural policy, the building economy and SS goals. An uneven nexus of the emphasis on labor productivity, the need for specific building materials and the practice of oppression in the forced-labor camps is highlighted through the systematic analysis of the actions of architects and the function of the SS economic concerns.

The fact that such a history has been relatively ignored for more than fifty years can be explained with the prevailing assumption, generally held in the discipline of art history, that Nazi culture is, at worst, a *reflection* of oppressive practices and, more commonly, a culture duped by non-artistic concerns.[3] However, as we have seen, a functional understanding of the relationship between cultural agents and government policy gives us a very different view of the connection of art and politics during the period. Such a connection has not only been avoided in art history but also formed the presupposition of the prosecution and the defense at the Nuremberg Tribunals, both in the trials of Speer and then later in the case against Pohl, Mummenthey (representing DEST) and the other economic managers of the SS. The testimony evidences the view that architecture was ideologically misguided but essentially a neutral or even benevolent factor in the policy decisions of the accused.

Speer's trial boiled down to his use of forced labor as Minister of Armaments and Munitions after 1942. Looking at the testimony from the point of view of his architectural interests, we can see again and again how Speer and his defense lawyer, Hans Flächsner, emphasized 1942 as a clear division between two types of activity, one artistic, the other technocratic. This year was crucial, of course, as it freed Speer from counts one and two of the tribunal: he could not have planned an aggressive war or conspired in the planning stages as the war had already been under way when Speer took office.[4] Called to the stand on 19 June 1946, Speer and his lawyer began with a short biography that emphasized his early training as an architect carrying on the family tradition (both his father and grandfather were architects). In turning to his activity as head of the GBI, Speer made it clear that the economic and the psychological effect of his pursuit of building even during the war was antithetical to German war aims. This break between the neutral, even anti-war activities of an architect and the crimes laid at the feet of the National Socialist administration received further emphasis in the famous claim of responsibility made by Speer in the following day of testimony:

> [It] is my unquestionable duty to assume my share of responsibility for this misfortune before the German people. This is all the more my obligation, all the more my responsibility since the head of the late government has evaded responsibility before the German people and before the world. I, as an important member of the leadership of the Reich, therefore share in the total responsibility, beginning with 1942.[5]

Establishing the importance of 1942 as a turning point would occur again in Flächsner's closing statement for the defendant. Here, too, architecture played a subtle role. Speer's pre-1942 defense, according to Flächsner, rested on his lack of involvement in any activity having to do with the planning or conduct of the war. He was an architect. So, Flächsner commented:

> Naturally it was from purely artistic reasons that the Party took over responsibility for building. It strove to give its buildings a uniformly representative character. Considering the peculiar nature of the architectural demands, it was natural that each architect should follow his own line in solving the problems put to him. The activity of the defendant as Commissioner for Construction was therefore relatively restricted and of minor importance, since he did not even have an office of his own [!] at his disposal. It would be erroneous to try to deduce therefrom any participation by the defendant in any crimes against the peace. The same is true of the defendant's other functions prior to and during the war, up to his assumption of office as minister.[6]

Like a chorus, Speer's entire testimony was punctuated with the refrain of his neutral artistic endeavors, while his post-1942 use of forced labor as a government minister was marked as separate from his "minor" architectural concerns.

At Nuremberg, reports on the full involvement of GBI architects with state and Party policy would probably not have led to Speer's condemnation, but they would have made the judges, prosecution and defense take seriously the cultural activity of architecture as a component of broader National Socialist political goals (certainly as seriously as they took, for example, the ideological training of German youth under Speer's co-defendant, Baldur von Schirach). In fact, as most historians report, Speer's background as an educated architect and the assumptions about architecture as an aesthetic pursuit actually played a favorable role in his defense. These assumptions, based on class favoritism and the belief that cultural production is more or less neutral, led to remarks that could be construed as sympathetic by judges including the Americans Francis Biddle and John Parker. As Bradley Smith has documented, Speer was even respected by Robert Jackson, the US prosecutor, who thought that Speer must, after all, be a "decent fellow."[7] In regard to the evidence presented here, it should be seen as one of Speer's achievements in his defense that he succeeded in splitting his career into two halves, and that his architectural activity could rely on a court biased to his cultivated self-presentation and naive about the extreme political function of architecture in National Socialist Germany.

But what of the SS administrators? Speer had been tried as one of the twenty-two major war criminals in front of an international Allied tribunal; in contrast, the WVHA staff was tried from January 1947 to May 1949 by the US Military Tribunal in what was known as "The Pohl Case." The general strategy of the WVHA administrators in their Nuremberg testimony was to depict themselves as technocrats who worked to solve economic problems and follow orders, i.e. as firmly outside of any decision-making processes related to oppression in the camps and conditions for forced laborers. Here, too, the economic function of architecture as a condition for the seemingly rational production of building materials was raised by the defendants as justification not for their prosecution but for their acquittal.

Pohl's defense testimony made evident the attempt to define himself as a technocrat, a position which he and other WVHA members promoted. Typical was his vague and convoluted response to a question concerning his involvement with concentration camps prior to the spring of 1942 (when the WVHA was formed and directed towards forced-labor armaments tasks):

> Until the taking over of the economic enterprises in 1938–39 I dealt [administratively] with these workshops of the concentration camps; as chief of the WVHA I did not have anything more to do with the concentration camps as such, the same with all the other units of the Waffen SS. Now, in particular, all budget matters were dealt with in our organization. As such there were no other activities apart from these matters.[8]

The key issue which Pohl sought to avoid here was his influence over the allocation or abuse of forced labor before 1942. His defense carefully built upon his background as a "passive civil servant type of man" who handled budgets and management but had nothing to do with the labor conditions of the camps.[9] To no avail, however; he was convicted and hanged in 1951.

Other WVHA administrators also emphasized a similar managerial neutrality. In defense of his technocratic role, Karl Mummenthey, head of DEST, stated that Speer went to Himmler to request the use of forced labor for building materials (i.e. that the SS played no active part) and, further, stressed that the economic interests of DEST actually worked against the politically repressive measures of RSHA and the camp commandants. According to Mummenthey, production of building materials was based on *preserving* not destroying the individual laborers. Marking the separation between a supposedly legitimate use of labor and punishment, he stated:

> As an economic enterprise the DEST was vitally interested in obtaining and preserving skilled workers and other workers whereas the RSHA and its subordinate departments, particularly the commandants of the concentration camps, were in all cases quite obviously interested in the security angle. Therefore, the obvious natural interest of the DEST on the basis of the regulations issued by the Reich Ministry of Justice contradicted the practices of the RSHA.[10]

Well, yes and no. As we have seen, a conflict between productivity and exploitation was the clear result of the attempt to make the camps both economically useful and politically oppressive. But DEST officials did not see this as a contradiction at the time; like the commandants, they were committed to the use of concentration camps as centers for "re-educating" those considered to be enemies of the state. By describing DEST as a business like any other, Mummenthey attempted to separate the abuse of forced labor from the management considerations of DEST administrators. His projection of the conflict between economic and political interests is belied by the administrative consensus that reigned in crucial phases of the development of forced-labor operations, particularly in their adaptation to monumental architectural goals.[11]

These testimonials are brought up here to clarify the rhetorical post-war depoliticization of architecture evident in Speer's deposition as well as in the technocratic definition of DEST managerial tasks. Such an attitude also dominated in the appointment of architects and the actual architectural practice of rebuilding Germany after the war. Certainly, architectural debates about the ideological significance of built forms did continue, mainly because supposedly "fascist" forms were seen as functionally dissonant with the democratizing interests in the western zone. But, even though such debates have continued into our own time, attempts to point out the political role played by architects in the Nazi era or to critique the dominant political and economic interests architectural practice served, remained as cries in the wilderness, falling on deaf ears among the western occupying forces as well as the architects who maintained a strong hold on the rebuilding efforts.[12] Debating the meaning of a particular aesthetic was tolerated as long as the practical work of rebuilding bomb-damaged cities could move forward.

It is clearly not surprising that post-war occupying forces turned to the members of the GBI to begin reconstruction efforts. Speer himself had set up a staff for the reconstruction of bomb-damaged cities in the later years of the war. These architects were well trained and had already begun thinking about the issues faced by city administrations that wished to rebuild, issues such as whether to maintain historic cores, how to use destruction as a means of modernizing transportation routes and what balance to strike between housing and governmental building efforts. Because these architects had also worked on projects intimately related to Speer's use of forced labor and his dealings with the SS, many of them came to doubt their potential usefulness in the post-war period. Konstanty Gutschow, for example, maintained that the most he could do was serve in an advisory role after 1945, since his past as head of the redesign of Hamburg and his intimate work with Speer compromised him politically; in fact, he considered himself as so compromised that his future success as an architect was out of the question.[13] The experience of rebuilding, however, would prove that even the architects underestimated the degree to which their past actions would be stripped of political significance in the post-war era. Architectural pasts were safely emptied of their political content and debate raged on the rhetorical ground of stylistic interpretation.

The fears of Speer's staff architects were assuaged, at least in part, with the appointment in 1947 of Friedrich Tamms to head the rebuilding of Düsseldorf, a move approved by the British occupying forces. As Werner Durth documents, Tamms not only continued to construct a large-scale architectural and infra-structural plan for the city as he had done for Lübeck as part of Speer's staff; he also actively gathered together many of the ex-GBI architects to work on the plan and to design specific buildings. Soon, a number of architects and administrators, including Wolters, Gutschow and others from the GBI, were safely ensconced in Düsseldorf rebuilding work. By the summer of 1949, these architects and admin-istrators had finished the plans and openly displayed them to the public in the largest architectural exhibition of the occupation period. As icing on the cake, Karl Maria Hettlage, a key financial advisor to Speer's staff and involved in the thick of GBI attempts to work with the SS on anti-Semitic housing policy, was called upon in October 1949 to convince the public that the rebuilding plan was economically sound.[14]

But, with the exhibition of the Düsseldorf plan and Tamms' control of rebuilding, the National Socialist past of Speer's staff had not been totally for-gotten. A consortium of architects, calling themselves the Architektenring Düsseldorf, quickly raised a protest about the plan and about Tamms' heavy-handed control over architectural reconstruction.[15] Their criticisms centered on the formal simi-larities between the new city plan and such Nazi plans as that proposed for Berlin. They questioned as well the anti-democratic actions, past and present, of Tamms and his staff. In a debate that raged until 1952 and attracted the attention of the national press – involving the participation of such prominent exiled architects as Martin Wagner and Walter Gropius – the Architektenring targeted as remnants of the Nazi past the monumental scale of the plans, the use of ceremonial boulevards and the conservative "Germanic" aesthetic of the new Rathaus. (This building, designed by Julius Schulte-Frohlinde, the leading architect for Robert Ley's Deutsche Arbeitsfront, allowed modernist and liberal architects to lambast Tamms for bringing in the prominent anti-Semitic architect.) Conflict reached a head after a volatile November 1951 meeting between Tamms' group and the members of the Architektenring when the meeting ended in an uproar, allowing an Architektenring representative to steal a plan of the Rathaus and make it available to the press.[16]

In their argument, the critical architects showed an awareness of the connection of architecture to government and economic policy. Further, they proclaimed that Tamms and his staff had attempted to obscure these connections from the Nazi period. However, the Architektenring made these criticisms to no avail. Precisely because of the political ties of Tamms, Wolters *et al.*, combined with the desperate need to rebuild bomb-damaged cities, the architectural debate raged violently in the press and the studio but not in the halls of government or industry. The British occupying forces were silent on the debate, as well as on the scandal that broke out over Schulte-Frohlinde's Rathaus design, and Tamms' bureau was backed up tacitly by the city and state governments which responded with indifference to the Ring attacks.[17] This indifference rested on a refusal to take seriously the political function of architecture, insisting instead on a culturally normative view: that architecture was practical (rebuilding) and perhaps aesthetically controversial, but not integral to the broader political process. Such an attitude not only covered the practice of Speer's staff in the National Socialist period but also the continued activities of his architects in the post-war period. Dominant economic and political interests, while most often quite different from their Nazi predecessors, continued to be served.

Certainly, their past activity with the GBI was not a question of life-and-death as it had been in Speer's trial. Yet the architects around Tamms relied on an apolitical attitude towards architecture that guaranteed them steady work – actually, the most prestigious work – in the post-war period. Many of these architects had freely acknowledged and supported the interests of the SS and the National Socialist state, particularly when such interests converged with their own. It had been the personal concern of these architects to plan the built environment of Nazi Germany using every means available. After the war, however, these architects could count on the attitude that prevailed at the Nuremberg Tribunals to absolve them of any suspicions concerning culpability in their architectural activity. In the immediate post-war years, the structural relationship between architecture and politics under National Socialism did not arise as a subject for scholarly treatment, let alone judicial review. Past political activity was overlooked in Düsseldorf as elsewhere as long as it had been subordinated to architectural planning. While these architects endured a level of ideological critique of their National Socialist buildings, these criticisms increasingly focused on the forms of particular buildings, not on particular architects (excepting Speer), especially as those same architects easily slid into the steel and glass modernism accepted by western patrons during the Cold War.

Art historians – like their journalistic, governmental and industry counterparts – respected this focus on the interpretation of particular Nazi buildings and Speer's architectural career. In this way, scholars of art history have remained outside historical debates concerning the economic development of the SS. And yet, if a political history of art is to have any critical value, such a limited focus must be jettisoned in favor of a more expansive, a more materialist and, hence, a more historical understanding of cultural production. As has been argued in relation to the development of DEST, architectural goals were one means by which the structural adaptation of the German political economy was turned towards the enactment of fascist objectives. As with other societies and other moments in history, state policy decisions meant to affect some element of a society's organization (a crucial part, after all, of a definition of "politics") were sometimes influenced by and often determined architectural production and urban planning. In this sense, the SS is not so much an absolute exception in the history of art. Rather it exemplifies the radical extreme of architecture's potential involvement with oppressive political practices. Understanding the functional relationship between SS economic goals, architectural production and oppressive state practices clarifies the dynamic process by which cultural decisions are made, affecting what appear to be non-artistic social, political and economic policies.

Notes

Chapter 1: INTRODUCTION

1   See, for example, the collections of essays in D. Ades *et al.* (eds), *Kunst und Macht*, London, Hayward Gallery, 1996; W. Nerdinger and E. Mai (eds), *Wilhelm Kreis. Architekt zwischen Kaiserreich und Demokratie 1873–1955*, Munich, Klinkhardt und Biermann, 1994.

2   I am referring here to such work as the analysis of Nazi architecture and Hitler's "desire" in A. Balfour, *Berlin. The Politics of Order 1737–1989*, New York, Rizzoli International Publications Inc., 1990.

3   The first comprehensive attempt to analyze the development of SS forced-labor economic ventures was E. Georg, *Die wirtschaftlichen Unternehmungen der SS*, Stuttgart, Deutsche Verlags-Anstalt, 1963. Drawing from the Nuremberg Tribunal documents, Georg lays out the organization of the SS economic administration and the variety of businesses controlled by the SS. He also provides statistics on the production of building materials in the quarry and brick-making concerns. Yet, while he mentions that some materials were being produced for monumental building projects, he does not explore the relationship between specific forced-labor operations and state architectural policy. When discussing the quarry camps in particular, historians have followed Georg's analysis. For a useful overview of SS literature (up to 1992), see R. Gellately, "Situating the 'SS-State' in a Social-Historical Context," *Journal of Modern History*, 1992, vol. 64, pp. 338–65.

4   See, for example, the analysis of SS brickworks in H. Kaienburg, *"Vernichtung durch Arbeit". Der Fall Neuengamme*, Bonn, Verlag J.H.W. Dietz, 1990.

5   My analysis here follows a modified functionalism that includes an understanding of the importance of agency and moments of consensus as well as conflict in the developing structural conditions of the Third Reich. This materialist position works away from the by-now undynamic intentionalist/functionalist debate in historical scholarship. Briefly stated, the "functionalist" position developed in response to an "intentionalist" focus on Hitler and his ideology as the key to explaining Nazi Germany. Functionalists, alternatively, argued that the structural conditions and

institutions of the Nazi state resulted in a more or less unplanned "cumulative radicalization" of policies. For the parameters and limitations of the so-called intentionalist/functionalist debates, see C. Browning, "Beyond 'Intentionalism' and 'Functionalism': A Reassessment of Nazi Jewish Policy from 1939 to 1941," in T. Childers and J. Caplan (eds), *Reevaluating the Third Reich*, New York, Holmes and Meier, 1993, pp. 211–33.

6   In their desire to maintain a close connection to Hitler, the social relations between leaders of the Third Reich were fraught with competition and intrigue. For an assessment of this situation as analyzed through the art collecting practices of the Nazi elite, see J. Petropoulos, *Art as Politics in the Third Reich*, Chapel Hill, University of North Carolina Press, 1996.

7   A recent notable exception to this limited focus is D. Dwork and R. Jan van Pelt, *Auschwitz. 1270 to the Present*, New York, W.W. Norton and Company, 1996.

8   For the most recent discussion of the relationship between SS ideological goals and camp punitive practices, see M.T. Allen, "The Banality of Evil Reconsidered: SS Mid-Level Managers of Extermination through Work," *Central European History*, 1998, vol. 30, pp. 253–94.

9   D. Neumann, "'The Century's Triumph in Lighting': The Luxfer Prism Companies and their Contribution to Early Modern Architecture," *Journal of the Society of Architectural Historians*, 1995, vol. 54, p. 47.

10 Barbara Miller Lane's important early work on the variable and at times contra-dictory ideological motivations for National Socialist architecture called for just such a differentiated account of art and politics. Nevertheless, this call has rarely been taken up by art historians of the period who continue to focus on formulating a monolithic notion of Nazi ideology as dominating architectural policy. See, for example, K. Backes, *Hitler und die bildenden Künste: Kulturverständnis und Kunstpolitik im Dritten Reich*, Cologne, DuMont Buchverlag, 1988; cf. B. Miller Lane, *Architecture and Politics in Germany 1918–1945*, Cambridge, Massachusetts, Harvard University Press, 1968.

11 Georg, *Die wirtschaftlichen Unternehmungen*; Kaienburg, "Vernichtung durch Arbeit." See also Kaienburg's edited volume of essays on the concentration camps and the German war economy (H. Kaienburg [ed.], *Konzentrationslager und deutsche Wirtschaft 1939–1945*, Opladen, Leske + Budrich, 1996). His contribution to this volume is a good summary of arguments developed in his earlier book.

12 Allen, "SS Mid-Level Managers;" U. Herbert, "Labour and Extermination: Economic Interest and the Primacy of *Weltanschauung* in National Socialism," *Past & Present*, 1993, no. 138, pp. 144–95.

13 Notable in this regard is Herbert's argument that, before 1941, concentration camp forced labor was geared emphatically to the punishment of the inmates, and not to the enactment of any real SS economic goals. In his otherwise significant analysis, here he relies on the standard literature which in turn relies predominantly on Georg (*Die wirtschaftlichen Unternehmungen*).

14 In reference to Nazi Germany, the political function of architecture was first

thematized in J. Thies, *Architekt der Weltherrschaft: Die "Endziele" Hitlers*, Düsseldorf, Droste Verlag, 1976.

15 For a synthetic and succinct overview of political economy and history, see C. Maier, *In Search of Stability: Explorations in Historical Political Economy*, Cambridge, Cambridge University Press, 1987, pp. 1–16.

16 For a well-argued example of this tendency, see K. Hoffmann-Curtius, "Die Frau in ihrem Element. Adolf Zieglers Triptychon der 'Naturgesetzlichkeit'," in B. Hinz (ed.), *NS-Kunst: 50 Jahre danach*, Marburg, Jonas Verlag, 1989, pp. 9–34. A systematic comparative analysis of Italian and German fascist ideology in relation to architecture can be found in A. Scobie, *Hitler's State Architecture. The Impact of Classical Antiquity*, University Park, Pennsylvania State University Press, 1990, pp. 9–36.

17 See also the discussion of the problems surrounding the debates concerning Nazi ideology in I. Kershaw, "Ideology, Propaganda, and the Rise of the Nazi Party," in P. Stachura (ed.), *The Nazi Machtergreifung*, London, George Allen and Unwin, 1983, pp. 162–81.

18 Here, I am following the extraordinary work of Tim Mason. See, in particular, Mason's summary of his ideas as a response to his critics reprinted in T. Mason, *Nazism, Fascism and the Working Class*, Cambridge, Cambridge University Press, 1995, pp. 295–322. See also the comparative analysis of Italian and German fascist economies in Maier, *In Search of Stability*, pp. 70–120.

19 My point here stems from Mason's concept of the "primacy of politics," first developed in a 1966 essay in which he argued that a radicalization of political initiatives stemmed from the economic domestic crises of the late 1930s and into the war. See (translated and reprinted) Mason, *Nazism*, pp. 53–76.

20 More recently, Allen has argued that the polycratic definition of National Socialist Germany emphasizes only the contradictions and conflicts between ministries rather than the ideological consensus which also reigned. He would substitute "polysemous" for "polycratic" to emphasize the multiplicity of relations between bureaucracies (Allen, "SS Mid-Level Managers," pp. 258–9). However, it seems to me that a polycratic characterization of the administration does not preclude an assessment of those moments when individual or political consensus was also reached. It is precisely in these moments that the contradictory nature of the Nazi state is indicated. Hence, I maintain the term "polycratic" in this account. Cf. F. Neumann, *Behemoth: The Structure and Practice of National Socialism*, London, Victor Gollancz Ltd, 1943.

21 Mason, *Nazism*, p. 325. (Emphasis in the original.)

22 L. Krier (ed.), *Albert Speer: Architecture 1932–1942*, Brussels, Archives d'Architecture Moderne, 1985.

Chapter 2: THE INTEREST OF THE SS IN THE MONUMENTAL BUILDING ECONOMY

1 A. Speer, *Infiltration: How Heinrich Himmler Schemed to Build an SS Industrial Empire*, J. Neugroschel (trans.), New York, Macmillan Publishing Co. Inc., 1981.

2 "Opportunism" is used here to describe SS actions, not intentions or long-term

goals. Overy makes this distinction clear in his analysis of the similar situation that existed for Göring in his efforts to militarize the German economy. See R. Overy, *Goering, the Iron Man*, Boston, Routledge and Kegan Paul, 1984, pp. 50ff.

3   H. Kaienburg, *"Vernichtung durch Arbeit". Der Fall Neuengamme*, Bonn, Verlag J.H.W. Dietz, 1990, pp. 28–30; F. Pingel, *Häftlinge unter SS-Herrschaft. Widerstand, Selbstbehauptung und Vernichtung im Konzentrationslager*, Hamburg, Hoffmann und Campe, 1978, pp. 23–30.

4   H. Buchheim, "Die SS – das Herrschaftsinstrument," in *Anatomie des SS-Staates*, vol. 1, Munich, Deutscher Taschenbuch Verlag, 1979, pp. 35–45; R. Koehl, *The Black Corps: The Structure and Power Struggles of the Nazi SS*, Madison, University of Wisconsin Press, 1983, pp. 3–35.

5   M.T. Allen, "The Banality of Evil Reconsidered: SS Mid-Level Managers of Extermination through Work," *Central European History*, 1998, vol. 30, pp. 260–8; J. Tuchel, *Konzentrationslager. Organisationsgeschichte und Funktion der "Inspektion der Konzentrationslager" 1934–1938*, Boppard am Rhein, Harald Boldt Verlag, 1991, pp. 159–204. Eicke held his post until November 1939 at which point he headed a front division of SS soldiers. See also the history of Columbiahaus, the commercial building designed by Erich Mendelsohn for the Potsdamer Platz and later taken over as an SS detention center, in A. Balfour, *Berlin. The Politics of Order 1737–1989*, New York, Rizzoli International Publications Inc., 1990, pp. 118–52.

6   E. Georg, *Die wirtschaftlichen Unternehmungen der SS*, Stuttgart, Deutsche Verlags-Anstalt, 1963, pp. 12–14; Pingel, *Häftlinge unter SS-Herrschaft*, pp. 35–9.

7   Georg, *Die wirtschaftlichen Unternehmungen*, 14–24. For an art historical assessment of Allach, see G. Huber, *Die Porzellan-Manufaktur Allach-München GmbH*, Marburg, Jonas Verlag, 1992. For an analysis of the SS mineral water enterprise, see J. Henke, "Von den Grenzen der SS-Macht. Eine Fallstudie zur Tätigkeit des SS-Wirtschafts-Verwaltungshauptamtes," in D. Rebentisch (ed.), *Verwaltung contra Menschenführung im Staat Hitlers*, Göttingen, Vandenhoeck & Ruprecht, 1986, pp. 255–77.

8   For Pohl's appointment as Verwaltungschef and the duties of the newly created Verwaltungsamt, see BA, NS3/564, pp. 48–59. See also Pohl's biography in his file at the Berlin Document Center. The best discussion of the overall development of the SS administration under Pohl remains the PhD dissertation of Michael Allen. For the 1935–6 changes, see M.T. Allen, "Engineers and Modern Managers in the SS: The Business Administration Main Office (*Wirtschaftsverwaltungshauptamt*)," PhD diss., University of Pennsylvania, 1995, pp. 30–60.

9   See the discussion of the Bavarian situation and voter patterns before and after 1933 in I. Kershaw, *Popular Opinion and Political Dissent in the Third Reich*, Oxford, Clarendon Press, 1983, pp. 10–110. Although due to the usual slow-down in the winter months as well as the general unemployment problem, one report from January 1932 produced by the building trades for the government listed the rate of unemployment in their industry at 88.6 per cent. See the report on the "Beschäftigungsgrad im Baugewerbe" in BA, R13/VIII, p. 27.

10 R. Overy, *The Nazi Economic Recovery, 1932–1938*, second edition, revised, Cambridge, Cambridge University Press, 1996, p. 46. This revised edition of Overy's 1982 work provides significantly more discussion of whether there was or was not a particular "fascist economy" in the early recovery period.

11 Overy, *Economic Recovery*, 1996, pp. 36–51. See also D. Silverman, *Hitler's Economy. Nazi Work Creation Programs, 1933–1936*, Cambridge, Massachusetts, Harvard University Press, 1998.

12 F. Seidler, *Fritz Todt: Baumeister des Dritten Reiches*, Munich, F.A. Herbig Verlagsbuchhandlung, 1986, pp. 97–159.

13 See the Schwarz memorandum of 19 July 1939, in BA, NS3/436, p. 30. See also other orders by Schwarz sent to the SS-HAVW from 1939 to 1941 in this file.

14 Mason discusses this period in detail in his analysis of how the multiple domestic crises of the pre-war years influenced the Nazi rush to war in 1939. See T. Mason, *Nazism, Fascism and the Working Class*, Cambridge, Cambridge University Press, 1995, pp. 53–76.

15 H.-E. Volkmann, "Die NS-Wirtschaft in Vorbereitung des Krieges," in W. Deist *et al.* (eds), *Ursachen und Voraussetzungen des Zweiten Weltkrieges*, Frankfurt am Main, Fischer Taschenbuch Verlag GmbH, 1989, pp. 329–52. For the nature of this managed economy, see Overy, *Economic Recovery*, 1996, pp. 36–51, 66–7. See also the interpretation of the significance for the building economy of the first six orders from Göring's office in "Vierjahresplan und Bauwesen," *Beilage zum "Baumeister,"* 1937, vol. 1, p. B14.

16 For the construction of the West Wall and the role of the GBBau, see Seidler, *Fritz Todt*, pp. 163–70, 203–6. See the letter from Göring to Todt of 9 December 1938 outlining his tasks as head of GBBau, in BA, R43II/1012, pp. 110–11. The struggles over iron and the attempt to increase domestic production and consumption are detailed in Overy, *Goering*, pp. 62ff.

17 K. Backes, *Hitler und die bildenden Künste*, Cologne, DuMont Buchverlag, 1988, pp. 126–7, 153–9. See the survey of different building types, in B. Miller Lane, *Architecture and Politics in Germany 1918–1945*, Cambridge, Massachusetts, Harvard University Press, 1968, pp. 185–216. For the most complete account of the ideological significance of neo-classicism and stone, see A. Scobie, *Hitler's State Architecture. The Impact of Classical Antiquity*, University Park, Pennsylvania State University Press, 1990.

18 NSDAP administration letter, in BA, R2/27174, p. 138. See Scobie's discussion of the relevance of stone to Hitler and the theory of "ruin value" (Scobie, *Hitler's State Architecture*, pp. 93–6). For specific examples of the influence of Speer and Hitler on aesthetic decisions concerning the choice of stone see Chapter 3 (Nuremberg) and Chapter 4 (Berlin), this volume.

19 G. Steinlein, "Vorkommen, Eigenschaften und Verwendungsarten deutscher natürlicher Gesteine," *Beilage zum "Baumeister,"* 1936, no. 5, pp. B91–3. See also Overy's (1996) discussion of the attempt to cut down on foreign financing and production in the German economy.

20 Stone industry personnel and architects recognized these political limitations. See,

for example, "Die Lenkung des Baumarktes," *Beilage zum "Baumeister"*, 1937, no. 6, pp. B132–3; "Wirtschafftliche Dienstpflicht," *Beilage zum "Baumeister*," 1938, no. 8, p. B222.

21 M. Broszat, "Nationalsozialistische Konzentrationslager 1933–1945," in *Anatomie des SS-Staates*, vol. 2, Munich, Deutscher Taschenbuch Verlag, 1967, pp. 46–74. For a comprehensive institutional analysis of the role of Eicke and the Inspekteur der KL, see Tuchel, *Konzentrationslager*.

22 *Konzentrationslager Buchenwald*, Buchenwald, Nationale Mahn- und Gedenkstätte Buchenwald, 1990, pp. 14–16; Tuchel, *Konzentrationslager*, pp. 2, 6–8. Tuchel cites a speech given by Himmler in November 1937 to SS-Gruppenführer where he mentions the need for larger facilities and "in case of a war" the construction of perhaps even bigger camps.

23 Broszat, "Konzentrationslager 1933–1945," pp. 66–74; R. Gellately, *The Gestapo and German Society. Enforcing Racial Policy 1933–1945*, Oxford, Clarendon Press, 1990, pp. 68–72; Pingel, *Häftlinge unter SS-Herrschaft*, pp. 33–77. For Himmler's successful attempts to increase the authority of the SS in 1935–6, see Tuchel, *Konzentrationslager*, pp. 307–17.

24 Broszat, "Konzentrationslager 1933–1945," pp. 68–76; Pingel, *Häftlinge unter SS-Herrschaft*, p. 74. Broszat discusses several orders Himmler used to fill Buchenwald at this time.

25 Note that the majority of historical literature on the pre-war phase of the concentration camps does not deal with the issue of productivity in the quarry and brick-making concerns. This literature assumes that, prior to the SS involvement in the armaments industry, the political suppression of inmates was the only real goal. (See, e.g., U. Herbert, "Labour and Extermination: Economic Interest and the Primacy of *Weltanschauung* in National Socialism," *Past & Present*, 1993, no. 138, pp. 164–5.) For an overview of the early development of forced labor, see K. Drobisch, "Hinter der Torinschrift 'Arbeit macht frei'," in H. Kaienburg (ed.), *Konzentrationslager und deutsche Wirtschaft 1939–1945*, Opladen, Leske + Budrich, 1996, pp. 17–27.

26 Cited in *Konzentrationslager Buchenwald*, p. 16.

27 For Pohl's statements to Schwarz that support this dating, see BA, NS1/547, p. 4. As Kaienburg points out, who initially suggested the use of prisoners for the production of building materials is unclear. Speer named Himmler as initiator (A. Speer, *Inside the Third Reich*, New York, Macmillan Company, 1970, p. 144) while Mummenthey named Speer in the Nuremberg Tribunals (*Trials of War Criminals before the Nuernberg Military Tribunals*, "The Pohl Case," vol. 5, Washington, DC, United States Government Printing Office, 1950, p. 567). The SS referred to Hitler's orders in its correspondence. Cf. Kaienburg, *"Vernichtung durch Arbeit,"* p. 74, n. 19.

28 Though many historians mention DEST, few texts have dealt directly with this aspect of SS economic policy. Four exceptions should be mentioned: Allen, "Engineers and Modern Managers"; Georg, *Die wirtschaftlichen Unternehmungen*; M. Kárný, "Das SS-Wirtschafts-Verwaltungshauptamt. Verwalter der

KZ-Häftlingsarbeitskräfte und Zentrale des SS-Wirtschaftskonzerns," in Hamburger Stiftung zur Förderung von Wissenschaft und Kultur (ed.), *"Deutsche Wirtschaft." Zwangsarbeit von KZ-Häftlingen für Industrie und Behörden,* Hamburg: VSA-Verlag, 1991, pp. 153–69; and Kaienburg, *"Vernichtung durch Arbeit."* Note, however, that because all of these authors are concerned with productivity and abusive forced labor used after 1942 for armaments concerns that they under-analyze or underestimate the effect of DEST on this phase of concentration camp development. Further, these authors have not systematically analyzed the connection between the KL and specific monumental state and Party architectural sites. In terms of the general administrative and managerial development of the SS, Allen is the best source.

29 The term *"Naturstein"* denotes not only natural stone but particularly stone chosen for aesthetic (as opposed to structural) reasons such as granite, marble, limestone, etc.

30 See Mummenthey's report, in BA, NS3/1343, p. 255. For the *Gesellschaftsvertrag,* see IMT Document, NO-1032. Georg, *Die wirtschaftlichen Unternehmungen,* p. 43. Kaienburg stresses that the SS consistently hid its involvement with an economic venture, most blatantly through the creation of DEST as a GmbH (limited liability company). However, the documents show that the situation was more complex. That is, the SS defined its role depending on its audience as either a private concern or a Party affiliate.

31 Memorandum to Schwarz, in BA, NS1/547, pp. 4–6. Note that profit appears never to have been either an officially proclaimed or actual motivation in SS policy, as Michael Allen makes clear. See also the discussion of the legality of SS business operations in Allen, "Engineers and Modern Managers," pp. 128–40.

32 J. Billig, *Les Camps de concentration dans l'économie du Reich Hitlérien*, Paris, Presses Universitaires de France, 1973, pp. 138–45; Georg, *Die wirtschaftlichen Unternehmungen,* pp. 25–41. See the memo from Pohl of 20 April 1939 giving the new breakdown of offices and the Himmler order of the same day giving Pohl responsibility in both the RFSS and the Ministry of the Interior, in BA, NS3/436, pp. 1–2.

33 Allen, "Engineers and Modern Managers," pp. 115–28; 141–8. For more on the early mismanagement of some of DEST's earlier projects, see Chapter 4, this volume.

34 For the organizational structure of the HAVW before 1941, see BA, NS3/1470, pp. 74–6. The HAVW was reorganized in September 1941, at which point DEST became part of Amt W I along with the SS porcelain works. For the organization after September 1941, see BA, NS3/1089, pp. 78–80. For the porcelain works, see Huber, *Allach-München.* See Allen ("SS Mid-Level Managers") for a general analysis of the ideological and economic motivations of SS mid-level managers.

35 ÖDMMA, A/8/1. A copy of this draft also exists in the Bundesarchiv, though without Speer's cover letter to the Economic Ministry claiming that he suggested the brickworks for Berlin: BA, R2/12163, pp. 79–80. For Speer's post-war manipulation of his involvement, see, e.g., Speer, *Infiltration*, pp. 153–7; cf. P. Jaskot, "Anti-Semitic Policy in Albert Speer's Plans for the Rebuilding of Berlin,"

Art Bulletin, 1996, vol. 77, pp. 622–32; M. Schmidt, *Albert Speer: The End of a Myth*, London, Harrap Limited, 1985.

36 See the renegotiated contract in BA, NS 3/36, pp. 199–203. For a brief summary of the early failure of the brickworks at Sachsenhausen, see BA, NS3/719, pp. 3–10. See also Chapter 4, this volume.

37 See the list of GBI payments for 1938, 1940 and 1941, respectively, in BA, R2/4499, R43II/1183, R120/729, pp. 66–70. For an overview of DEST's credit situation (22 August 1939), see BA, NS3/1532, pp. 1–11.

38 For budget statements and payments, see BA, NS3/1345, pp. 8–9; NS3/32, pp. 1–25; NS3/1009, pp. 4–6. Kaienburg acknowledges the absence of a study of the granite works of the SS, a gap which the present book attempts in part to fill. As a result of the schematic view of the granite works apparent in Kaienburg's text, he fails to account for (among other aspects) the early and sustained profits produced by the granite works in relation to the losses produced by the brickworks, which form the basis of his study. See, especially, Kaienburg, *"Vernichtung durch Arbeit,"* pp. 114–18.

39 For an overview of the literature and analysis of the German war economy, see P. Hayes, "Polycracy and Policy in the Third Reich: The Case of the Economy," in T. Childers and J. Caplan (eds), *Reevaluating the Third Reich*, New York, Holmes and Meier, 1993, pp. 190–210. For the forced-labor economy, see Herbert, "Labour and Extermination."

40 On the war economy, see W. Naasner, *Neue Machtzentren in der deutschen Kriegswirtschaft 1942–45*, Boppard am Rhein, Harald Boldt Verlag, 1994. For an overview of the process by which the prioritization of building projects into *"Dringlichkeitsstufen"* occurred, see A. Sander, "Baudringlichkeitsstufen und Dringlichkeitsstufen des Fertigungsprogramms der Wehrmacht," *Der Deutsche Baumeister*, June 1941, pp. 11–13.

41 A review of *Der Deutsche Baumeister* reveals the prioritization of wartime and monumental building projects as well as the focus on key wartime issues like material acquisition and labor policy. See, for example, J. Steffens, "Die gegenwärtigen und zukünftigen Möglichkeiten des Bauschaffens," *Der Deutsche Baumeister*, 1942, vol. 1, pp. 7–12. For a comprehensive overview of the use of prisoners of war, foreign workers and forced labor, see Herbert, "Labour and Extermination."

42 See Pohl's 1942 summary of the development and purpose of the DWB, in BA, NS3/1135, p. 5. For the taxing of the SS economic enterprises and need to offset DEST's losses, see Baier's report to Pohl of 22 April 1944, in BA, NS3/1004, pp. 10–25. See Allen's excellent discussion of the reorganization in these years and the ideological motivations of SS personnel in Allen, "Engineers and Modern Managers," pp. 153–84.

43 See the 1940 balance sheet, in BA, NS3/1009, p. 7. The 1940 DEST annual report (with Salpeter's remarks) and production statistics for Flossenbürg and Mauthausen can be found in BA, NS3/1346, pp. 56–67, 153–4. For a copy of the new GBI contract, see BA, NS3/36, pp. 199–200.

44 See the summary of DEST brickworks in BA, NS3/32, pp. 1–11. Georg, *Die wirtschaftlichen Unternehmungen*, pp. 47–53. Georg points out that, as the brickwork near Hamburg was acquired and then followed by a concentration camp, the SS planned its economic expansion first and then adapted the political function of the camps to these goals. Kaienburg argues the opposite, though his documentation substantiates Georg's claim that the economic function of constructing a brickwork to serve the needs of the rebuilding of Hamburg was a major impetus to develop KL Neuengamme.

45 For the inclusion of the eastern brickworks in the SS HAVW, see Pohl's report of 21 December 1939, in BA, NS3/1080, p. 6. A list of properties controlled can be found in Salpeter's report to Pohl of 8 May 1940, BA, NS3/1470, p. 74. In October 1940, the SS also took over the administration of a gravel works to take advantage of forced labor from KL Auschwitz. For a brief summary of Himmler's political authority in the east, see R. Breitman, *The Architect of Genocide. Himmler and the Final Solution*, New York, Alfred A. Knopf, 1991, pp. 77–84. For Himmler's economic plans for the east and the cultural aspirations of the SS, see D. Dwork and R. Jan van Pelt, *Auschwitz. 1270 to the Present*, New York, W.W. Norton and Company, 1996, pp. 127–59.

46 Hohberg discusses the quality of the various clay deposits for the camps in his letter to Reichsbankdirektor Puhl of August 1939, BA, NS3/1532, p. 3. For the debate that arose in the nineteenth century concerning the "Germanic" expressiveness of brick, see W. Hermann (ed. and trans.), *In What Style Should We Build?*, Santa Monica, Getty Center, 1992.

47 See the summary of DEST quarries, in BA, NS3/32, pp. 13–24.

48 Georg, *Die wirtschaftlichen Unternehmungen*, p. 56. Georg cites the statements made at the Nuremberg Tribunal by Schwarz and Mummenthey concerning Speer's involvement in choosing the location for Natzweiler and Gross-Rosen based on the type of stone. This is supported, particularly in reference to Natzweiler, through the documentation on the Nuremberg Party Rally Grounds presented in Chapter 3, this volume. For production statistics from 1939–40, see BA, NS3/1009, pp. 321–2.

49 From a Sipo order of 3 September 1939, cited in Pingel, *Häftlinge unter SS-Herrschaft*, p. 72.

50 See the Ministry of Finance report on the meeting, in BA, R2/12163, p. 84.

51 Production goals and progress report of 1941 in BA, NS3/1538, p. 8. Kaienburg also discusses the goals set by the SS, but he relies on the DEST-Geschäftsbericht that projects the total eventual production objectives rather than those that were set only for 1941. As a result, he is led more easily to conclude that the SS economic goals were "hardly realistic" because Himmler had ordered a 100,000 cbm increase in stone production as the final objective (i.e. more than the entire output of the German granite industry). Though Himmler's plan is clearly improbable for the short term when the best quarry at Flossenbürg was producing only 2,000–3,000 cbm per year, the HAVW was actively attempting to achieve these production goals through an incremental and realistic process as indicated by the discussion of the early 1941 report. Cf. Kaienburg, *"Vernichtung durch Arbeit,"* p. 115.

52 See the letter from Mummenthey and Salpeter to the Golddiskontbank, in BA, NS3/1532, pp. 17–19.

53 Production statistics for 1941 from DWB balance report, in BA, NS3/341, p. 25. For the brickworks, see Georg, *Die wirtschaftlichen Unternehmungen*, p. 56; Kaienburg, *"Vernichtung durch Arbeit,"* pp. 90–111, 190–8. For the letter from Salpeter to Mummenthey of May 1941, see BA, NS3/1532, p. 18v.

54 See the DEST 1941 annual report, in BA, NS3/341, p. 13. For statistics on the amount of business of the quarries in relation to the brickworks, see Georg, *Die wirtschaftlichen Unternehmungen*, p. 56.

55 See the two letters from Schondorff, in BA, R7/1240, pp. 185–6, 187–93. For discussion with the Finance Ministry of tax exemption in the summer of 1940, see BA, NS3/1244, p. 318.

56 For the rejection of DEST's claims, see the letter of 1 March 1941 from the Reichswirtschaftskammer, in BA, R7/1240, pp. 181–4.

57 Allen, "Engineers and Modern Managers," pp. 307–49; Kárný, "Das SS-Wirtschafts-Verwaltungshauptamt," pp. 153–69. For the reorganization of the HAVW in September 1941, see BA, NS3/1080, pp. 72–8. A description of the organization of DEST and Salpeter's transfer can be found in BA, NS3/1470, p. 42. Note that most historians treat the formation of the WVHA as the key to their explanation of SS economic interests. Such a limitation explains the focus of the literature on SS use of forced labor in the armaments industries as well as the lack of emphasis on DEST.

58 W. Durth, *Deutsche Architekten: Biographische Verflechtungen 1900–1970*, Braunschweig, Friedr. Vieweg & Sohn, 1987, pp. 195–8.

59 Summaries of the works at KL Stutthof and KL Auschwitz, in BA, NS3/32, pp. 8–12; NS3/1344, p. 277. For purchase of the Marburg property, see BA, NS3/1238, p. 67.

60 Georg, *Die wirtschaftlichen Unternehmungen*, p. 56. Absorption of losses by the DWB noted in auditors' report on DEST in BA, NS3/719, p. 38. For the success of the quarries and overview of DWB activity in 1942, see BA, NS3/1135, p. 10. Participation in the 1942 trade fair mentioned in BA, NS3/1347, p. 61.

61 See, e.g., Broszat, "Konzentrationslager 1933–1945." Georg, as the first systematic account of the SS economic activity, maintains that DEST did not move to armaments production significantly until 1943. As DEST was the largest economic concern of the SS and most often the focus of SS economic reports, I have maintained with Georg that 1943 is the more appropriate date for asserting an effective full-scale shift to armaments production, though plans were certainly being made and sometimes implemented in 1942. See Georg, *Die wirtschaftlichen Unternehmungen*, pp. 57–8. For a discussion of Speer's distortion of his role in influencing the SS entrance into the armaments industry, see Allen, "Engineers and Modern Managers," pp. 360–79; cf. Speer, *Infiltration*.

62 BA, NS3/719, p. 2 (emphasis in original).

63 See also the broader discussion of the use of forced labor in the German war economy in Herbert, "Labour and Extermination."

64 For the expansion of the brickwork at KL Neuengamme, see BA, NS3/1271, p. 5.

Kaienburg, *"Vernichtung durch Arbeit,"* pp. 262–72. See the summary of 1943 DEST activity, in BA, NS3/719, pp. 2–15. For discussion on the exempted status of DEST quarries and production statistics, see the draft of the 1943 report in BA, NS3/1238, pp. 32–4. For a list of clients of the various works, see BA, NS3/339, pp. 62–4.

65 See the WVHA report of 12 January 1943 outlining the implementation of Pohl's order, in BA, NS3/1133, pp. 4–6. For specific fees paid at Mauthausen, see BA, NS3/1168, p. 52. For population statistics, see Pingel, *Häftlinge unter SS-Herrschaft,* pp. 128–30. See also Speer's interpretation of this period of SS development, in Speer, *Infiltration.* Speer's account emphasizes the SS goal of capturing a dominant share of the armaments market and excludes evidence indicating the continued interest of the SS in building materials. Compare this to Naasner's analysis which sees an integration of the workings of the WVHA, Speer and Sauckel's staffs (Naasner, *Neue Machtzentren*).

66 See Fischer's letter of 9 September 1944 to Mummenthey discussing budgets in the first half of the year and turnover statistics, in BA, NS3/163, pp. 11, 18–20.

67 For the purchase of land near Zehlendorf and discussion of the quarry at Flossenbürg, see BA, NS3/1344, pp. 39–40, 103–7.

68 For information of the evacuations, see BA, NS3/138, pp. 37–53. On the experience of the death marches, see, for example, M. Gilbert, *The Holocaust: A History of the Jews of Europe during the Second World War*, New York, Henry Holt and Company, 1985, pp. 767–83; P. Heigl, *Konzentrationslager Flossenbürg*, Regensburg, Mittelbayerische Druckerei- und Verlags-Gesellschaft mbH, 1989, pp. 17–59.

69 In this sense, I would argue that Allen and others who see the "primacy of policing" as the only dominant condition in this stage of KL development have too narrow a focus. While there is no question that the commandants and camp guards saw their main goal as punishing the prisoners, this goal cannot be separated from the equally important influence on the prisoner's life of the attempt to gear forced labor to the production of building materials. Cf. Allen, "SS Mid-Level Managers," pp. 260–8.

70 H. Marsalek, *Die Geschichte des Konzentrationslagers Mauthausen,* Vienna, Österreichische Lagergemeinschaft Mauthausen, 1974, p. 3; G. Rabitsch, "Das KL Mauthausen," in *Studien zur Geschichte der Konzentrationslager,* Stuttgart, Deutsche Verlags-Anstalt, 1970, p. 50; T. Siegert, "Das Konzentrationslager Flossenbürg," in *Bayern in der NS-Zeit*, vol. 2, Munich, R. Oldenbourg Verlag, 1979, p. 434. Siegert bases the dating of the visit by Pohl, Eicke and Karl on the appointment calendar of the Forstamtdirektor in Flossenbürg, while Rabitsch and Marsalek both date the visit to May 1938 following Karl's testimony for the IMT. Siegert's data, coupled with Eigruber's speech reported in the *London Times*, indicates that March is the correct date. For a copy of the *London Times* report, see ÖDMMA, A/5/3.

71 For a description of the output at the camps and quality of stone, see BA, NS3/32, pp. 13–14, 19–20. For more on the SS negotiations with the city of Vienna, see DöW, 12.929.

72   A. Hitler, *Mein Kampf*, Ludwig Lore (trans.), New York, Stackpole Sons Publishers, 1939, pp. 257–63. For further discussion of the aesthetic of Speer and Hitler and the production at the concentration camps see Chapters 3 and 4, this volume. See, also, Scobie, *Hitler's State Architecture*. An investigation of the ideological debates surrounding the significance of materials in, e.g., nineteenth-century Germany can be found in M. Schwarzer, *German Architectural Theory and the Search for Modern Identity*, Cambridge, Cambridge University Press, 1995, pp. 167–214.

73   Broszat, "Konzentrationslager 1933-1945," pp. 46–55; Tuchel, *Konzentrationslager*, pp. 121–51. For a comprehensive discussion of limits placed on economic policy by the "primacy of policing" taught to camp personnel, see Allen, "SS Mid-Level Managers."

74   Broszat, "Konzentrationslager 1933–1945," pp. 57–66; Siegert, "Flossenbürg," p. 44. See also the psycho-historical analysis of camp commandants, in T. Segev, *Soldiers of Evil. The Commandants of the Nazi Concentration Camps,* New York, McGraw-Hill Book Company, 1987.

75   Pingel, *Häftlinge unter SS-Herrschaft*, pp. 102–17; Rabitsch, "Mauthausen," pp. 56–7.

76   Heigl, *Flossenbürg*, p. 121; Siegert, "Flossenbürg," pp. 437–49. For the appointment of Max Schubert as Werkleiter, see Salpeter's memorandum of 8 May 1940 to Pohl, in BA, NS3/1470, pp. 74–5. The documents at the Bundesarchiv also list SS-Mann Ronge as a work leader for DEST at Flossenbürg, though Ronge disappears from the lists by 1941 and Schubert remains. See also the SS personnel files on these individuals (especially Künstler) in the Berlin Document Center.

77   For a discussion of the social background of SS leaders, see H. Ziegler, *Nazi Germany's New Aristocracy. The SS Leadership, 1925–1939*, Princeton, Princeton University Press, 1989, pp. 116–24. For a discussion of the ideological motivations of camp personnel, see Allen, "Engineers and Modern Managers," pp. 230–59.

78   Siegert, "Flossenbürg," pp. 435–41. For production statistics up to the end of 1939, see BA, NS3/1346, p. 153.

79   Marsalek, *Mauthausen*, pp. 145–55; Rabitsch, "KL Mauthausen," p. 54. Work leaders listed in BA, NS3/1470, p. 75. For Walther's tasks at Mauthausen, see BA, NS3/1343, pp. 62, 110. An example of Richard Glücks (Inspekteur der KL after Eicke) complimenting Ziereis can be found in Segev, *Soldiers of Evil*, p. 157. See also the personnel files at the Berlin Document Center.

80   Rabitsch, "KL Mauthausen," pp. 51–9. As with Flossenbürg, much of the documentary evidence is lacking for a complete picture of Mauthausen because of papers destroyed by the SS, through air raids, etc. However, a selected list of prisoners who entered the camp from 1938 to 1945 does exist indicating the extent of the prison population, categorized by occupation and nationality. See AGKBZHwP, KL Mauthausen/3–16. For the early years of the camp and its relation to local social and economic conditions, see G. Horwitz, *In the Shadow of Death. Living Outside the Gates of Mauthausen*, New York, The Free Press, 1990, pp. 23–54.

81   Siegert, "Flossenbürg," pp. 461–70.

82 Rabitsch, "KL Mauthausen," pp. 61–73. See also Pike's discussion of the conditions for Spanish prisoners in D. Pike, *In the Service of Stalin. The Spanish Communists in Exile, 1939–1943*, Oxford, Clarendon Press, 1993.

83 See the summary of the development of and work at Flossenbürg through 1943, in BA, NS3/32, pp. 13–14. For production statistics (1940–1), see BA, NS3/341, p. 25. Discussion of the stone-mason program and mention of patrons for Mauthausen and Flossenbürg can be found in BA, NS3/1346, pp. 149–56. For more on Nuremberg and Berlin, see Chapters 3 and 4, this volume.

84 See also Allen's discussion of this dynamic in Allen, "SS Mid-Level Managers."

85 Letter from Schmitz, in KZ-Gedenkstätte Dachau Archiv, 15.927.

86 Siegert, "Flossenbürg," pp. 441–4.

87 Statistics on the New Reich Chancellery recorded in A. Schönberger, *Die Neue Reichskanzlei von Albert Speer*, Berlin, Gebr. Mann Verlag, 1981, pp. 162–3.

88 Siegert, "Flossenbürg," pp. 444–50. Though, as in the case of Flossenbürg, the shift to armaments production lowered the death rate, many historians rightly view this shift skeptically as to any real changes in the conditions prisoners faced. See, for example, Pingel, *Häftlinge unter SS-Herrschaft*, pp. 130–9.

89 For the post-1942 organization of the armaments industry and use of forced labor, see Naasner, *Neue Machtzentren*.

90 Heydrich's order of 1 January 1941 ranking the camp reprinted in Marsalek, *Mauthausen*, p. 22. For the redesign of Linz, see I. Sarlay, "Hitropolis," in B. Brock and A. Preiss (eds), *Kunst auf Befehl? Dreiunddreissig bis Fünfundvierzig*, Munich, Klinkhardt und Biermann, 1990, pp. 187–99.

91 Rabitsch, "KL Mauthausen," pp. 57–9. Production statistics for 1940–1, in BA, NS3/341, p. 25. A list of distribution and stone production of 7 December 1940 notes that production began in October. See BA, NS3/1346, p. 154. For a breakdown of the kinds of stone produced in each of the three quarries, see BA, NS3/1345, pp. 36–7. These statistics (from December 1939) indicate that the highest prices and highest turnover were attained by stone produced at the Gusen quarry.

92 Rabitsch, "KL Mauthausen," pp. 59–61. For a series of letters from late 1942 to early 1943 regarding the transfer of prisoner specialists to and from Mauthausen, see ÖDMMA, F7/Nr. 3. See the partial list of orders placed in 1943, in BA, NS3/339, pp. 63–4. Though, as Rabitsch notes, documents are particularly difficult to come by for this period of camp development, much information on production can be obtained from the DEST monthly reports of 1940–2 in BA, NS3/1346; NS3/1347.

93 Horwitz, *Shadow of Death*, pp. 23–6, 52–4; Marsalek, *Mauthausen*, pp. 30–71; Rabitsch, "KL Mauthausen," pp. 61–8. For a copy of the Himmler order transferring Soviet prisoners to the quarry, see ÖDMMA, P16/Nr. 14. See also Herbert's discussion of the variable use of forced labor depending on how the prisoner was politically or ideologically defined (Herbert, "Labour and Extermination").

94 ÖDMMA, U/3/1, pp. 9–10. For the situation of Jews in the camp, see B. Eckstein, "Jews in the Mauthausen Concentration Camp," in *The Nazi Concentration Camps*, Jerusalem, Yad Vashem, 1984, pp. 257–71.

95 Rabitsch, "KL Mauthausen," pp. 61–8. The experiment on prisoners is reported in

AGKBZHwP, KL Mauthausen/48. For the transition to armaments works, the opening in 1943 of multiple side-camps at Mauthausen and the conditions at such camps, see F. Freund, *Arbeitslager Zement. Das Konzentrationslager Ebensee und die Raketenrüstung*, Vienna, Verlag für Gesellschaftskritik, 1989, pp. 12–50, 119–253. See also Allen's discussion of Maurer's leadership of the SS-Arbeitseinsatz within the Inspekteur der KL. In this discussion, Allen sees Maurer's management as also emphasizing the medical and statistical analysis of the forced-labor population rather than any concern for the individual prisoner. Allen, "SS Mid-Level Managers," pp. 277–85.

96 Marsalek, *Mauthausen*, pp. 173–6; Pingel, *Häftlinge unter SS-Herrschaft*, pp. 79–80; Rabitsch, "KL Mauthausen," p. 65.

97 Marsalek, *Mauthausen*, pp. 71–2; Rabitsch, "KL Mauthausen," pp. 63–78, 89; Siegert, "Flossenbürg," pp. 441–4, 489–92. The death statistics are approximate because of the deliberate mystifications in the SS records and the inability to know exactly the extent of killings in the work camps. All historians who work on these camps acknowledge this fact, but, like Rabitsch and Siegert, realize they can also arrive at reasonably close and documentable estimations.

Chapter 3: THE PARTY RALLY GROUNDS AT NUREMBERG

1 In the last decade, several publications on the Party Rally Grounds have helped to explain the development and function of the rallies from the Weimar Republic through the National Socialist period. See, especially M. Diefenbacher (ed.), *Bauen in Nürnberg 1933–1945. Architektur und Bauformen im Nationalsozialismus*, Nuremberg, W. Tümmels Buchdruckerei und Verlag, 1995; A. Scobie, *Hitler's State Architecture. The Impact of Classical Antiquity*, University Park, Pennsylvania State University Press, 1990; S. Zelnhefer, *Die Reichsparteitage der NSDAP. Geschichte, Struktur und Bedeutung der Grössten Propagandafeste im nationalsozialistschen Feierjahr*, Nuremberg, Stadtarchiv Nürnberg, 1991. Zelnhefer treats each party rally as distinct, showing why they cannot be considered generically. However, relatively little attention is given to architecture. See also the brief essay and documentation on Nuremberg in J. Dülffer, J. Thies and J. Henke (eds), *Hitlers Städte: Baupolitik im Dritten Reich*, Cologne, Böhlan Verlag, 1978.

2 For an overview of the relationship between efficiency and productivity in the private German economy with a specific case study of armaments industries, see T. Siegel, "Rationalizing Industrial Relations: A Debate on the Control of Labor in German Shipyards in 1941," in T. Childers and J. Caplan (eds), *Reevaluating the Third Reich*, New York, Holmes and Meier, 1993, pp. 139–60.

3 For an assessment of the Party Rally Grounds in relation to Walter Benjamin's maxim of the aestheticization of politics, see B. Ogan, "Architektur als Weltanschauung: Ein Beitrag über die Ästhetisierung von Politik," in Centrum Industriekultur Nürnberg (ed.), *Kulissen der Gewalt: das Reichsparteitagsgelände in Nürnberg*, Munich, Hugendubel, 1992, pp. 123–40.

4 For the early history of the Party rallies and their use to introduce policy, see Zelnhefer, *Reichsparteitage*, pp. 9–59, 212–49. An overview of propaganda

techniques and the effectiveness of these techniques can be found in D. Welch, *The Third Reich. Politics and Propaganda*, London, Routledge, 1993.

5   K. Backes, *Hitler und die bildenden Künste: Kulturverständnis und Kunstpolitik im Dritten Reich*, Cologne, DuMont Buchverlag, 1988, pp. 159–60; Zelnhefer, *Reichsparteitage*, pp. 60–3. Quotation from Hitler cited in Zelnhefer.

6   A. Speer, *Inside the Third Reich*, New York, Macmillan Company, 1970, pp. 26–31. Though Speer's account of his later activity in the National Socialist state must be viewed skeptically (particularly in relation to his dealings with the SS), the portrayal of his earlier architectural successes has found general acceptance in the secondary literature. Matthias Schmidt, reliable for the most part in his critique of Speer, focuses on Speer's early work in Berlin. M. Schmidt, *Albert Speer: The End of a Myth*, London, Harrap Limited, 1985, pp. 38–44.

7   See Brugmann's personnel file in SAN, C 18/II PAN 390. See as well the published reports on building in the *Chronik der Stadt Nürnberg*, SAN, F2, pp. 45–7. For an analysis of the importance of social connections in relation to art policy and collecting, see J. Petropoulos, *Art as Politics in the Third Reich*, Chapel Hill, University of North Carolina Press, 1996.

8   B. Hinz, *Art in the Third Reich*, New York, Pantheon Books, 1979, pp. 189–95; Zelnhefer, *Reichsparteitage*, pp. 175–8. For a discussion of the increase in workers' housing resulting from the development of the armament and building industry in Nuremberg in the 1930s, see the report from Liebel's statistical office of 16 February 1939 in BA, R2/19435.

9   K. Förster, "Das Deutsche Stadion in Nürnberg. Planungsgeschichte und Funktion," Masters Thesis, Universität Göttingen, Göttingen, 1979, pp. 32–3; Speer, *Inside the Third Reich*, pp. 55–6; Zelnhefer, *Reichsparteitage*, pp. 76–9. See also Scobie's analysis of the Zeppelin Field in relation to the Pergamum Altar, in Scobie, *Hitler's State Architecture*, pp. 85–92. Franz Ruff, who had taken over his father's business after Ludwig Ruff's death in August 1934, signed the contract with the city for the completion of the Congress Hall. For mention of the date of the first designs for, financing of and contract concerning the Congress Hall, see BA, R2/11901. For Speer's contract (25 September 1935) that included control of all work except the Congress Hall, see BA, NS1/426/2, pp. 203–6.

10 Note that the integration of buildings into a complex around a central axis was an academic planning strategy typical of a variety of Nazi buildings irrespective of their stylistic variations. See U. Hartung, "Bauästhetik im Nationalsozialismus und die Frage der Denkmalwürdigkeit," in B. Faulenbach and F.-J. Jelich (eds), *Reaktionäre Modernität und Völkermord*, Essen, Klartext Verlag, 1994, pp. 71–84.

11 Zelnhefer, *Reichsparteitage*, pp. 78–9. See the presentation of 6 December 1934 of the city's case to State Secretary Fritz Reinhardt, Ministry of Finance, in BA, R2/11901.

12 Draft of law from the Ministry of the Interior under Wilhelm Frick (approved by Hitler), 13 March 1934, in BA, R2/11901.

13 Förster, "Deutsche Stadion," p. 41. For the protocol of the first meeting, see SAN, C 32 Z/RPT, 4.

14 *RGBl.*, 1935, vol. 1, p. 459. For the exchange involving the Ministry of Finance, see BA, R2/11901.

15 See financial reports for the period 1935–8, including a summary of costs produced for the Ministry of Finance on 22 June 1938, in BA, R2/11901. See also the discussion of public works in D. Silverman, *Hitler's Economy. Nazi Work Creation Programs, 1933–1936*, Cambridge, Massachusetts, Harvard University Press, 1998.

16 BA, R43II/1176a, p. 105; *RGBl.*, 1938, vol. 1, p. 379. See also the discussion of the significance of the law in J. Dülffer, "NS-Herrschaftssystem und Stadtgestaltung: Das Gesetz zur Neugestaltung deutscher Städte vom 4. Oktober 1937," *German Studies Review*, February 1989, vol. 12, pp. 69–89.

17 For Brugmann and his role, see his personnel file, in SAN, C 18/II PAN 390. While not every administration in Nazi Germany can be described as competitive, the polycratic nature of the building administration for Nuremberg is clear from Brugmann's role in the process.

18 For the ZRPT financial focus on these two projects, see the addendum to the 1935 Budget in BA, NS1/426/1.

19 SAN, C 32 Z/RPT, 8. The supplement to the third meeting in the SAN document noted that 11,000 cbm of stone would be necessary for the Zeppelin Field. At the time, the author (unnamed) of the text noted that this was a "colossal" amount. This amount, however, pales in relation to the later quantities of stone for the German Stadium and Congress Hall. The ZRPT could not anticipate the full extent of the plans as they grew over the years from Hitler's wishes and the needs of the Party and state.

20 Protocols from the third and fourth meeting of the ZRPT board in: BA, NS1/426/2.

21 Budget report from November 1937 in BA, NS1/426/2.

22 Förster, "Deutsche Stadion," pp. 49–50. For the 1937 budgets see BA, NS1/462/2. For the naming of the building in July and laying of the cornerstone in September, see SAN, C 32 Z/RPT, 970. Förster's work is an excellent dossier of much of the available archival information on the German Stadium. Notably, however, her presentation of building economy issues is limited.

23 See the discussion of the Greco-Roman precedents for the stadium in Scobie, *Hitler's State Architecture*, pp. 75–80. See also Hitler's well-known discussion of the state of contemporary German cities in comparison to the architecture of Greece, Rome and medieval Germany in A. Hitler, *Mein Kampf*, Ludwig Lore (trans.), New York, Stackpole Sons Publishers, 1939, pp. 257–63. For a discussion of the "artistic transformation of politics" evident in *Mein Kampf*, see O.K. Werckmeister, "Hitler the Artist," *Critical Inquiry*, 1997, vol. 23, pp. 280–2. It should be noted that Scobie, like many scholars on National Socialist architecture, treats Nazi ideology as relatively consistent rather than multivalent and, often, contradictory. The best overview of the competing ideological claims made for architecture in this period remains the first significant study of Nazi architecture's political function: B. Miller Lane, *Architecture and Politics in Germany 1918–1945*, Cambridge, Massachusetts, Harvard University Press, 1968, pp. 169–216. However, cf. Hartung, "Bauästhetik."

24 Many Nazi writers emphasized the relationship between the ideological significance of masonry construction and the militarist needs of the German building economy in the late 1930s and into the war. See, especially, E. Simon, "Baugestaltung und Bauwirtschaft," *Der Deutsche Baumeister*, March 1939, vol. 1, no. 3, pp. 5–8; A. Speer, "Stein statt Eisen," *Der Vierjahresplan*, 1937, vol. 1, pp. 135–7. For a discussion of the material needs of the West Wall and the political influence on the building materials market, see F. Seidler, *Die Organisation Todt: Bauen für Staat und Wehrmacht 1938–1945*, Koblenz, Bernhard & Graefe Verlag, 1987, pp. 15–18.

25 Budget report from November 1938 and cost summary for 1935–8 prepared in June 1938 for the Finance Ministry in, respectively, BA, NS1/426/2; R2/11901.

26 BA, R2/11901. Those present at the meeting included Kerrl, Liebel, Fritz Todt (head of the Organisation Todt), Speer, Brugmann, K.F. Liebermann (from the German Stadium) and representatives from the Party and the Bavarian land. It is unclear from the minutes of the meeting whether the participants other than Speer and Brugmann were aware that the model had already been constructed when funds were being requested.

27 Zelnhefer notes that this July meeting was the last official gathering of the board. See Zelnhefer, *Reichsparteitage*, pp. 87–90.

28 BA, R2/11901.

29 Two associations were formed: Arge Süd made up of Holzmann, Siemens Bauunion, Hochtief and Deutsche Bau; and Arge Nord with Heilmann & Littmann, Dyckerhoff & Widmann, Grün & Bilfinger, Stöhr and Boswau & Knauer.

30 Arge offers and contracts with the ZRPT can be found in SAN, C 32 Z/RPT, 954, 955, 982. For similar associations tending towards oligarchic market control, see, for example, P. Hayes, *Industry and Ideology: IG Farben in the Nazi Era*, Cambridge, Cambridge University Press, 1987; J. Petley, *Capital and Culture. German Cinema 1933–1945*, London, British Film Institute, 1979. Mason early on discussed this tendency in the fascist economy; see T. Mason, *Nazism, Fascism and the Working Class*, Cambridge, Cambridge University Press, 1995, pp. 63–9.

31 Zelnhefer, *Reichsparteitage*, pp. 82–6. Budget statements in BA, R2/11901; SAN, C 32 Z/RPT, 955. By 1939, the March Field budget was paid for by direct contributions from the armed forces.

32 BA, R2/11901.

33 See, for example, the discussion by Christian Koch which dates the "end" of work on the Party Rally Grounds as 1940 (C. Koch, "Bauen in Nürnberg 1933–1945," in Diefenbacher (ed.), *Bauen in Nürnberg*, p. 23).

34 BA, R2/11902.

35 For overviews of the use of labor (forced and unforced) from the occupied territories, see E. Homze, *Foreign Labor in Nazi Germany*, Princeton, Princeton University Press, 1967; U. Herbert, "Labour and Extermination: Economic Interest and the Primacy of *Weltanschauung* in National Socialism," *Past & Present*, 1993, no. 138, pp. 144–95.

36 See the report from the GBBau, in BA, R2/9242.

37 *Aktennotiz* from the Finanzverwaltungsamt der RPT in BA, NS1/38. Hitler's order to continue building in the "Hitler Cities" is reprinted in Dülffer, Thies, Henke, *Hitlers Städte*, p. 36.

38 Arge Nürnberg Annual Report in BA, R120/3941d, pp. 13–14.

39 Budget report from March 1941 in BA, R2/11902.

40 Förster, "Deutsche Stadion," p. 54; Zelnhefer, *Reichsparteitage*, pp. 80–5. For the Arge Nürnberg report concerning stone amounts and building at the site, see BA, R120/3941d. For requests for and approval of prisoners for the Deutsches Stadion-Arge Nord, see SAN, C 32 Z/RPT, 1154, 1156.

41 *Chronik der Stadt Nürnberg, 1936–1944*, SAN, F 2 47, p. 579. See the report of the Ministry of Economics law and Brugmann's position at GBBau in the GBI office journal, in BA, R3/1735, p. 42.

42 Zelnhefer, *Reichsparteitage*, pp. 80–6. Budget report from September 1942, in BA, R2/11902.

43 Arge Nürnberg report for 1942 in BA, R120/3941d. For the continuation of building in Berlin in these years, see Chapter 4, this volume.

44 1943 Arge Nürnberg report concerning stone orders and deliveries in BA, R120/3941d. For use of the site by the military and later stone contracts, see SAN, C 32 Z/RPT, 974, 1175.

45 See the DEST monthly report for August 1941, in BA, NS3/1346, p. 161.

46 For the SS and Speer's plans for Berlin, see Chapter 4, this volume.

47 See the stone test results, in SAN, C 32 Z/RPT, 238. For reports on finished work at Gross-Rosen and Natzweiler as well as an agreement between the German Stadium administrators and Flossenbürg, see BA, NS3/1225; NS3/1259; NS/1347, p. 195. See also the letter exchange between the ZRPT and the firm Diabaswerksteinbrüche from May to August 1940 in which ZRPT representative Wallraff stated the need for specific businesses such as DEST and the Diabaswerksteinbrüche to handle the production of exceptionally large stones (SAN, C 32 Z/RPT, 974).

48 BA, NS3/32, p. 22; NS3/1225. A brief overview of the camp's early history as well as population statistics can be found in W. Kirstein, *Das Konzentrationslager als Institution totalen Terrors. Das Beispiel des KL Natzweiler*, Pfaffenweiler, Centaurus-Verlagsgesellschaft, 1992, pp. 1–4, 60–70. While Kirstein's book offers an analysis of the social, psychological and punitive experience of the prisoners, he spends little time on the labor in the camp or its connection to SS economic interests. For DEST, he relies predominantly on E. Georg, *Die wirtschaftlichen Unternehmungen der SS*, Stuttgart, Deutsche Verlags-Anstalt, 1963, and additional secondary literature.

49 M. Broszat, "Nationalsozialistische Konzentrationslager 1933–1945," in *Anatomie des SS-Staates*, vol. 2, Munich, Deutscher Taschenbuch Verlag, 1967, pp. 95–6. The population statistics of prisoners used in individual camps were not broken down in the DEST budget reports until late 1941. For 1942 statistics, see BA, NS3/1347.

50 For a discussion of the signed contract, see Speer's letter of September 1941 to

Pohl, in BA, Potsdam, 46.06 GBI/25, p. 181. See also Georg, *Die wirtschaftlichen Unternehmungen*, p. 45. To this author's knowledge, the original contract no longer exists. In the letter to Pohl, Speer also offered to pursue the placement of the concern in *"Dringlichkeitstufe I"* (priority level one) of the GBBau and provided iron and wood from the GBI contingent for the construction of the necessary buildings.

51   For the planned output of Natzweiler and remarks on the total output of the German quarrying industry, see, respectively, BA, NS3/32, p. 22; NS3/1538, p. 8.

52   For a discussion of the SS practice of "destruction and work," see M.T. Allen, "The Banality of Evil Reconsidered: SS Mid-Level Managers of Extermination through Work," *Central European History*, 1998, vol. 30, pp. 253–94. See also the collection of essays on forced labor in H. Kaienburg (ed.), *Konzentrationslager und deutsche Wirtschaft 1939–1945*, Opladen, Leske + Budrich, 1996.

53   The best discussion of this variable implementation of political and economic policy is Allen, "SS Mid-Level Managers," pp. 260–8.

54   See, particularly, the post-war testimonials of witnesses and former inmates about life at Natzweiler in Series 136 of the National Archives and Records Administrations, Records of the Judge Advocate General, R Group 153. A copy of this record group can be found in the US Holocaust Memorial Museum, RG 04.030 M (Reel 1).

55   For Speer's travels in 1941, see the GBI reports in BA, R3/1735. Liebermann's visit is noted in Arge Nürnberg report, BA, R120/3941d.

56   For a brief overview of the training and history of stone-masonry, see *Der Steinmetz und Steinbildhauer*, Berlin, Lehrmittelzentrale des Amtes für Berufserziehung und Betriebsführung der Deutschen Arbeitsfront, 1937.

57   Reichsstand des Deutschen Handwerks report in BA, R43II/278, pp. 81–102.

58   Ibid. The report is authored by Reichshandwerksmeister Schramm and Generalsekretär Schüler from the Reichsstand des Deutschen Handwerks. I would like to thank Fred McKitrick for his help with finding sources and his comments on the trades in National Socialist Germany.

59   For the control of eastern industries and Himmler's political and ideological goals as Reich Kommissar, see M.T. Allen, "Engineers and Modern Managers in the SS: The Business Administration Main Office (*Wirtschaftsverwaltungshauptamt*)," PhD diss., University of Pennsylvania, 1995, pp. 185–202; R. Breitman, *The Architect of Genocide. Himmler and the Final Solution*, New York, Alfred A. Knopf, 1991, pp. 77–82; D. Dwork and R. Jan van Pelt, *Auschwitz. 1270 to the Present*, New York, W.W. Norton and Company, 1996, pp. 127–59.

60   For Himmler's response, see BA, R43II/278, pp. 75–9.

61   For statistics on the stone-mason industry, see the report from the Reich Guild Union of Sculptors and Stone-Masons (Reichsinnungsverband Bildhauer und Steinmetzen) from February 1941 and protocol from meeting of the Reichsinnungsverband board from September 1942 in, respectively, BA, R97I/24; R97I/21.

62   For their own building plans in the east, see Allen, "Engineers and Modern Managers," pp. 260–306.

63 See, e.g., H. Kaienburg, *"Vernichtung durch Arbeit". Der Fall Neuengamme*, Bonn, Verlag J.H.W. Dietz, 1990, p. 115. Georg does read the document as an attempt by the SS to enact its goals realistically. However, Georg does not consider the letter in terms of the relation of SS goals to the monumental building plans of the Party and state. See Georg, *Die wirtschaftlichen Unternehmungen*, pp. 110–13.

64 BA, NS4 GR/6. The order for the 100,000 cbm of stone, to the present author's knowledge, has not survived.

65 See, for example, the three case studies of forced labor and big business by Peter Hayes, Karl Heinz Roth and Birgit Weitz in Kaienburg (ed.), *Konzentrationslager*, pp. 129–95.

66 For a copy of the leaflet, see IfZ, Fa 183/1, pp. 95–6.

67 For the chronology of stone-mason programs and their effectiveness, see the DEST monthly reports, in BA, NS3/1346, pp. 36–8, 150. For an overview of conditions in the camps, see F. Pingel, *Häftlinge unter SS-Herrschaft. Widerstand, Selbstbehauptung und Vernichtung im Konzentrationslager*, Hamburg, Hoffmann und Campe, 1978.

68 See discussions of contracts and prison populations in monthly reports of 1942 and 1943, in BA, NS3/1346, pp. 60, 150, 187; NS3/1347, pp. 6, 195, 236. Report from Amt C I, WVHA, from 12 February 1942, in BA, NS4 FL/34. Report from Amt II-Bauten, HAVW, from 12 October 1940, in BA, NS4 FL/40.

69 Report on new plans for KL Flossenbürg, 20 February 1941, in BA, NS4 FL/67. For induction of Soviets to the stone-mason program, see BA, NS3/1347, 236. An overview of the training of stone-masons can be found in *Der Steinmetz und Steinbildhauer*. For a particular analysis of the symbolic significance of stone and the stone trade, especially in the Weimar Republic, see C. Fuhrmeister, "Beton, Klinker, Granit – Die Politische Bedeutung des Materials von Denkmälern in der Weimarer Republik und im Nationalsozialismus," PhD diss., University of Hamburg, 1998. Thanks to Christian Fuhrmeister for his help on finding stone-mason sources.

70 Report on new plans for KL Flossenbürg, 20 February 1941, in BA, NS4 FL/67. See also Aly and Heim's discussion of the relation of Nazi economic and political interests, particularly in reference to the exploitation and destruction of European Jewry. (G. Aly and S. Heim, "The Economics of the Final Solution: A Case Study from the General Government," *Simon Wiesenthal Center Annual*, 1988, vol. 5, pp. 3–48.)

71 April 1942 report to DEST, in BA, NS3/1475, p. 8.

72 BA, NS3/1475, pp. 1–4.

73 BA, NS19/2065.

74 For an overview of forced prostitution in Nazi Germany, see C. Wickert, "Das grosse Schweigen: Zwangsprostitution im Dritten Reich," *Werkstatt Geschichte*, 1996, vol. 13, pp. 90–5.

75 See the overview of the 1943 camps, in BA, NS3/32, p. 22.

76 Cited from a report of November 1940 describing workers at Gross-Rosen, in BA, NS3/1346, p. 158.

Chapter 4: THE REBUILDING OF BERLIN

1 A. Speer, *Inside the Third Reich,* New York, Macmillan Company, 1970, p. 33.

2 The moral judgment clear in the question of culpability is most thoroughly treated in G. Sereny, *Albert Speer: His Battle with Truth*, New York, Alfred A. Knopf, 1995. See also M. Schmidt, *Albert Speer: The End of a Myth*, London, Harrap Limited, 1985. For a brief overview of the reception and the attempted rehabilitation of Speer's architectural activity, see W. Nerdinger, "Baustile im Nationalsozialismus: Zwischen Klassizismus und Regionalismus," in D. Ades *et al.* (eds), *Kunst und Macht*, London, Hayward Gallery, 1996, pp. 322–3.

3 Speer's antipathy towards Himmler is well documented, beginning with his own post-war writings. See, e.g., Speer, *Inside the Third Reich*, pp. 330–42.

4 For the development of the Berlin plan, see H. Reichhardt and W. Schäche, *Von Berlin nach Germania. Über die Zerstörungen der Reichshauptstadt durch Albert Speers Neugestaltungsplanungen*, Berlin, Transit Buchverlag, 1986; A. Scobie, *Hitler's State Architecture. The Impact of Classical Antiquity*, University Park, Pennsylvania State University Press, 1990, pp. 97–108. See also S. Helmer, *Hitler's Berlin: The Speer Plans for Reshaping the Central City*, Ann Arbor, University of Michigan Research Press, 1985.

5 For an overview of Berlin in the Weimar Republic, see E. Busche, "Laboratorium: Wohnen und Weltstadt," in J. Kleihues (ed.), *750 Jahre Architektur und Städtebau in Berlin*, Stuttgart, Verlag Gerd Hatje, 1987, pp. 153–82. On the ideological treatment of Wagner and other modernist architects in the National Socialist press, the crucial text remains B. Miller Lane, *Architecture and Politics in Germany 1918–1945*, Cambridge, Massachusetts, Harvard University Press, 1968, pp. 125–67. See also L. Scarpa, *Martin Wagner und Berlin*, Braunschweig, Friedr. Vieweg und Sohn, 1986, pp. 148–51. The most extensive analysis of the city's building administration in this early period is W. Schäche, *Architektur und Städtebau in Berlin zwischen 1933 und 1945: Planen und Bauen unter der Ägide der Stadtverwaltung*, Berlin, Gebr. Mann Verlag, 1991, pp. 96–138. For the anti-Semitic process of purging the civil service, especially in relation to cultural administrations, see A. Steinweis, *Art, Ideology, and Economics in Nazi Germany. The Reich Chambers of Music, Theater, and the Visual Arts*, Chapel Hill, University of North Carolina Press, 1993, pp. 103–46.

6 Schäche, *Städtebau*, pp. 101–38; W. Schäche, "Von Berlin nach 'Germania'," in D. Ades *et al.* (eds), *Kunst und Macht*, p. 326; Speer, *Inside the Third Reich*, p. 80. See also the discussion of how Hitler's political and architectural goals developed in relation to one another in O.K. Werckmeister, "Hitler the Artist," *Critical Inquiry*, 1997, vol. 23, pp. 270–97.

7 See Reichhardt and Schäche, *Berlin nach Germania*, p. 68. For an overview of Hitler's role in the question of funding, see K. Backes, *Hitler und die bildenden Künste: Kulturverständnis und Kunstpolitik im Dritten Reich*, Cologne, DuMont Buchverlag, 1988, p. 124.

8 Schäche, "Berlin nach 'Germania'," p. 326; A. Schönberger, *Die Neue Reichs–kanzlei von Albert Speer: zum Zusammenhang von nationalsozialistischer*

Architektur und Ideologie, Berlin, Mann Verlag, 1981, pp. 22–35.

9 *RGBl.,* 1937, vol. 1, p. 103.

10 Ibid., p. 1054.

11 J. Dülffer, "NS-Herrschaftssystem und Stadtgestaltung: Das Gesetz zur Neugestaltung deutscher Städte vom 4. Oktober 1937," *German Studies Review,* February 1989, vol. 12, pp. 69–90. For the order designating Berlin, see *RGBl.,* 1937, vol. 1, p. 1162. For a listing of Neugestaltung cities named, those seeking nomination and Hitler's response to requests, see the report from the Reich Chancery from 4 December 1938, in BA, R43II/1176a, p. 105. See also the analysis of the development of the "Hitler Cities" in J. Dülffer, J. Thies and J. Henke (eds), *Hitlers Städte: Baupolitik im Dritten Reich,* Cologne, Böhlan Verlag, 1978, esp. pp. 3–8 and documents.

12 See below for discussion of the "exceptional" case of Jewish property and the lack of rights for Jewish tenants.

13 See the documents on financing and compensation of owners displaced from their property in BA, R43II/1176a. For a summary of the jurisdictional authority of the GBI over the city of Berlin, see Reichhardt and Schäche, *Berlin nach Germania,* pp. 47–9.

14 Schönberger, *Reichskanzlei,* pp. 42–3, 162–70; A. Speer, "Stein statt Eisen," *Der Vierjahresplan,* 1937, vol. 1, pp. 135–7. For the Four Year Plan, see H.-E. Volkmann, "Die NS-Wirtschaft in Vorbereitung des Krieges," in W. Deist *et al.* (eds), *Ursachen und Voraussetzungen des Zweiten Weltkrieges,* Frankfurt am Main, Fischer Taschenbuch Verlag GmbH, 1989, pp. 211–435. In an otherwise notable essay, Iain Boyd Whyte points to the Neue Reichskanzlei as an example of SS interest in the building economy by claiming that stone from KL Flossenbürg was produced for the building (Whyte cites no source for this claim). However, as we have seen, Flossenbürg was not producing stone until the end of 1939, well after the completion of the building's construction. While it is possible that small amounts of stone were produced at Flossenbürg to finish details on the building, this project was not the major focus of production at the camp, as we shall see. A careful attention to the chronological development of DEST works allows us to make more specific assertions about the connection of oppressive camp policies and monumental architectural projects. See I. Whyte, "Der Nationalsozialismus und die Moderne," in D. Ades *et al.* (eds), *Kunst und Macht,* p. 263.

15 For an extended analysis of the formulation of an anti-Semitic policy within the GBI, see P. Jaskot, "Anti-Semitic Policy in Albert Speer's Plans for the Rebuilding of Berlin," *Art Bulletin,* 1996, vol. 77, pp. 622–32. Notably, the GBI anti-Semitic housing policy makes no appearance in the post-war writings of Speer. As Gitta Sereny indicates, Speer maneuvered greatly in the post-war period to clear his record (and historical documents like his GBI office journal) of any hint of active anti-Semitism, with some success, one might add. Even with Schmidt's and Sereny's works, art historians continue to rely on Speer's own words rather than the administrative record of his architectural career. See Schmidt, *Albert Speer,* pp. 181–4; Sereny, *Albert Speer,* pp. 219–30.

16 A. Barkai, *From Boycott to Annihilation. The Economic Struggle of German Jews, 1933–1943*, Hanover, New Hampshire, University Press of New England, 1989, pp. 130–3. For some sense of the complicated dynamics and jurisdictions over the Nazi decision-making process concerning the Jews (1939–41), see C. Browning, "Beyond 'Intentionalism' and 'Functionalism': A Reassessment of Nazi Jewish Policy from 1939 to 1941," in T. Childers and J. Caplan (eds), *Reevaluating the Third Reich*, New York, Holmes and Meier, 1993, pp. 211–33.

17 See protocols for both meetings in, respectively, BA, Potsdam, 46.06 GBI/702; 46.06 GBI/157, pp. 195–7.

18 Jaskot, "Anti-Semitic Policy," pp. 626–8.

19 *RGBl.*, 1939, vol. 1, pp. 864–5. For the meeting of 12 November 1938, see the minutes in documents from the International Military Tribunal at Nuremberg, PS.1816, pp. 41ff. See also R. Hilberg, *The Destruction of the European Jews*, revised and abridged, New York, Holmes and Meier Publishers Inc., 1985, pp. 49–50; Barkai, *Boycott to Annihilation*, p. 130.

20 For Göring's letter, see BA, Potsdam, 46.06 GBI/157, p. 145. A brief discussion of the resettlement office in the GBI and the Gestapo can be found in Schmidt, *Albert Speer*, pp. 182–3.

21 See, for example, *Berliner Lokal-Anzeiger*, 28 January 1938, vol. 56, p. 1, as cited in Reichhardt and Schäche, *Berlin nach Germania*, p. 48.

22 See, Wolters' memo to Speer in BA, Potsdam, 46.06 GBI/1202. See also the discussion of Nazi city planning and historical precedents for the North–South Axis in, respectively: Scobie, *Hitler's State Architecture*, pp. 37–68; Schäche, *Städtebau*, pp. 132–8.

23 See Werckmeister's discussion of the political import of Hitler's drawings in Werckmeister, "Hitler the Artist," pp. 282–7.

24 For Kreis, see the series of essays in W. Nerdinger and E. Mai (eds), *Wilhelm Kreis. Architekt zwischen Kaiserreich und Demokratie 1873–1955*, Munich, Klinkhardt und Biermann, 1994. See, in particular, Nerdinger's overview of Kreis' career in this volume. The significance of the Hochschulstadt competition is discussed in Schäche, "Berlin nach 'Germania'," pp. 327–8. In reference to Rimpl, it should be noted that his office also included architects active in the modernist movement during the Weimar Republic. As long as these architects did not openly disagree with National Socialist policy, it appears that Rimpl tolerated and at times encouraged their presence. See W. Durth, *Deutsche Architekten: Biographische Verflechtungen 1900–1970*, Braunschweig, Friedr. Vieweg & Sohn, 1987, pp. 95–9.

25 Mai discusses this "instrumentalization of death" in relation to a variety of Kreis' Nazi-era designs in E. Mai, "Von 1930 bis 1945: Ehrenmäler und Totenburgen," in Nerdinger and Mai (eds), *Wilhelm Kreis*, pp. 162–7.

26 The following is based on the contract for the OKH complex signed by Speer and Kreis in BA, R120/3955, pp. 2–8.

27 For the derivation of the Soldiers' Hall, see K. Arndt, "Problematischer Ruhm – die Großaufträge in Berlin 1937–1943," in Nerdinger and Mai (eds), *Wilhelm Kreis*, pp. 182–3. The contract also lists the terms of payment to the architect (2 per cent

of the entire building costs). Kreis and his design staff were allowed to continue to accept payments until March 1945 at which point they had received RM 2,690,000 in remuneration. For payments to Kreis, see BA, R120/1651, p. 23.

28 See Reichhardt and Schäche, *Berlin nach Germania*, pp. 37, 42–3. In this section of their exhibition catalog, Schäche implies that both Brugmann and Liebermann were in their positions at the GBI by the end of 1938. While Brugmann held much influence with Speer and his plans, he was not officially appointed to head the GBI Bauleitung until 1940. See Chapter 3, this volume.

29 See the GBI protocol from 2 May 1939 in BA, Potsdam, 46.06 GBI/75, p. 531. The dating of the final designs can be attributed through, for example, the view from the North–South Axis of the Soldiers' Hall façade in the Bundesarchiv. The plan is dated 3.11.39 but indicates that it shows minor changes from the design of 23.11.38 (BA, Potsdam, 46.06 GBI/KS 3700, No. 60). Helmer, *Hitler's Berlin*, also illustrates a photo from the Library of Congress from July 1938 showing the finished foundation outline on the plan and dates the formulation of this design from November 1936; Arndt "Problematischer . . ." follows Helmer. However, a drawing with the same date in Helmer does not indicate the same ground plan. Based on this evidence, an accurate dating of the finished form of the Soldiers' Hall can be deduced as the latter half of 1938.

30 For Speer's advice to Kreis, see the GBI report 6 May 1939, in BA, Potsdam, 46.06 GBI/772, p. 26. See, for the protocol of the meeting from 26 May 1939, BA, Potsdam, 46.06 GBI/75, p. 328. In addition to the type of stone to be used, details about the production of stone were also outlined. Kreis reported that twenty-four firms were ready to start deliveries for the project and twenty others (which were already producing stone for the German Stadium) should also soon be ready.

31 Reichhardt and Schäche, *Berlin nach Germania*, pp. 73-7.

32 For the Kreis report, see BA, Potsdam, 46.06 GBI/772, p. 19.

33 See the discussion of wartime curtailment of the building process in the protocol from a meeting between Clahes and the city official, Dr. Pade, 4 September 1939, in LA, Pr. Br. Rep. 107/278/1.

34 Reichhardt and Schäche, *Berlin nach Germania*, p. 58.

35 BA, Potsdam, 46.06 GBI/772, p. 13.

36 See statistics in a letter from Lang to Wehrkreisverwaltung III, in BA, R120/3941a. As has been noted previously, labor acquisition was key to a focus on output and the GBI was already in a difficult situation in this regard before the outbreak of war. This difficulty was intensified with the need for soldiers during the war. Such a scenario was typical of many labor-intensive industries where pressure on the labor market (after full employment was reached in 1936) was exacerbated by additional labor needs caused by the war. See, for example, the analysis of the mining industry in J. Gillingham, *Industry and Politics in the Third Reich. Ruhr Coal, Hitler and Europe*, London, Methuen, 1985, pp. 49–67, 112–38.

37 See the multiple files from February–March 1940 in BA, R120/3941a. For a detailed list of property on the site and the date for the four major site clearings planned (beginning with the Soldiers' Hall), see BA, R120/3905. This list was finalized with

the decision to clear away Emil Fahrenkamp's Shellhaus in October 1941 (BA, R120/1651, pp. 2–12).

38 Arge Nürnberg's 1940 annual report, in BA, R120/3941d. The following account of stone production for the Soldiers' Hall is taken from this report. The report thanked Hitler for the success of the quarries: "Dem Führer ist es zu verdanken, dass auch während des Krieges die Naturwerksteinindustrie weiterarbeiten kann." For Nuremberg, see Chapter 3, this volume.

39 Schäche also argues for an analysis of architecture that includes an integration of the expansionist wartime goals and architectural policy. In this sense, he is one of the few architectural historians who attempts to document the continuation of design and construction into the war. See Schäche, "Berlin nach 'Germania'," pp. 328–9.

40 Quotation from Wolters' GBI journal, in BA, R3/1735, p. 83. For an October 1940 decree extending the authority of the GBI, see: *RGBl.*, 1940, vol. 1, p. 1387. Giesler's influence over rebuilding in Munich is documented in H.-P. Rasp, *Eine Stadt für tausend Jahre. München – Bauten und Projekte für die Hauptstadt der Bewegung*, Munich, Süddeutscher Verlag GmbH, 1981.

41 See the discussion of stone firms and contracts in BA, R3/1735, pp. 15–87. The Ministry of Economics exempted the stone-quarrying industry from shifting its production over to wartime needs. The exemption status was not lifted until 3 March 1944. See the Arge Nürnberg report dated 1 September 1944 in BA, R120/3941d. For Mummenthey joining the Arge Nürnberg board, see the 1941 Annual Report, in BA, R120/3941d. For further discussion of the integration of Hitler's militarist and architectural goals, see Werckmeister, "Hitler the Artist."

42 See, e.g., Browning, "'Intentionalism' and 'Functionalism';" U. Herbert, "Labour and Extermination: Economic Interest and the Primacy of *Weltanschauung* in National Socialism," *Past & Present*, 1993, no. 138, pp. 144–95; J. Thies, *Architekt der Weltherrschaft: Die "Endziele" Hitlers*, Düsseldorf, Droste Verlag, 1976, pp. 149–87.

43 The plans for the Soldiers' Hall in the Bundesarchiv indicate that the latest changes to the plan were made by November 1940, perhaps affecting the working drawings and stone orders in the early part of 1941. See, for example, BA, Potsdam, 46.06 GBI/KS 3700, plan 98.

44 For stone orders and deliveries, see the Arge Nürnberg 1941 annual report, in BA, R120/3941d. See also Chapter 3, this volume, for statistics on Nuremberg in this period.

45 See the description of the numerous pressures on the German economy (including transportation of materials) due to the Four Year Plan in Volkmann, "Die NS-Wirtschaft in Vorbereitung des Krieges," pp. 429–35.

46 See the *Gesellschaftsvertrag* in LA, Pr. Br. Rep. 107/141/5. See, for an example of the use of the Soldiers' Hall to justify the business, the letter from Lang to the OKH from June 1940, in BA, R120/3941a. For the purchase of the land by the OKH and examples of GBI contracts with shipping firms to deliver stone from, among others, DEST, see BA, R120/3940b.

47 Information from the GBI journal, in BA, R3/1735, pp. 82–6. As Herbert points out, the status of a laborer (POW, foreign worker, KL forced laborer) and her or his ethnicity were key factors in distinguishing the use and abuse of workers in the German economy. Such distinctions seem lost on the GBI in its attempt to maximize production through mobilizing labor capacity at all costs. See Herbert, "Labour and Extermination," pp. 148–9.

48 GBI journal, in BA, R3/1735, p. 87. See also Herbert's summary of the use of Soviet prisoners in Herbert, "Labour and Extermination," pp. 165–8.

49 GBI journal, in BA, R3/1735, pp. 82–6. See also documents on the creation of bordellos for foreign workers in order to increase productivity, in BA, R2/4500.

50 Reported in the GBI journal, in BA, R3/1735, pp. 85–6. Speer's ability to make the most of maneuvering for authority is indicated by his earlier refusal of SS-Gruppenführer Karl Hermann Frank (Heydrich's assistant in Prague), who had also requested advice concerning the redesign of Prague. Frank was apparently not in a key position to give Speer the help he needed, but Heydrich certainly was. See Speer's letter to Frank of 31 July 1941, in BA, Potsdam, 46.06 GBI/24, p. 180.

51 See Speer's letter to Dietrich of 22 May 1941, in BA, Potsdam, 46.06 GBI/24, p. 151 (emphasis in original). Speer states in the letter that the military has given him the prisoners and he waits only on getting the required guard personnel.

52 See the memorandum of 29 September 1940, in BA, Potsdam, 46.06 GBI/78, p. 88. For Speer's claims of authorship of the policy (cited below), see BA, Potsdam, 46.06 GBI/24, p. 57. See, also, Jaskot, "Anti-Semitic Policy," pp. 630–1.

53 *RGBl.*, 1941, vol. 1, p. 218. Unlike Speer, it remains unclear whether Giesler ever made use of this new authority. On the distortions of the archival version of the GBI journal and the editing by Speer of such words as "crammed" from the original, see, e.g., Schmidt, *Albert Speer*, p. 183; Sereny, *Albert Speer*, pp. 216–30. For a brief overview of the attack on Jewish property rights and partial centralization of Jewish urban populations during this period (1939–42), see Barkai, *Boycott to Annihilation*, pp. 167–74.

54 See, for example, the letter of 2 May 1941 from the Reich Labor Ministry to the Finance Ministry concerning the double need of the population under siege and the architectural policy of the state, in BA, R2/19435. The location of new housing amongst other Jews and, later, the drawing up of lists of those Jews who were to be "relocated" (i.e. sent to the death camps) was carried out by the Jüdisches Gemeinde für Berlin, efficiently and with little resistance. For a discussion of this difficult moment in the history of the destruction of the European Jews, see R. Hilberg, *The Destruction of the European Jews*, Chicago, Quadrangle Books, 1967, pp. 122–5.

55 For the protocol, see BA, R120/1975, pp. 144–8. Sereny writes the following about Hettlage: "With Dr. Hettlage, an elegant, gently humorous and perceptive man, one had the distinct impression of someone who had nothing to regret, unlike so many Germans of the period" (Sereny, *Albert Speer*, p. 155). This post-war impression could only be based on the avoidance of historians in critically analyzing the actions of such mid-level bureaucrats in the GBI.

56 BA, Potsdam, 46.06 GBI/24, p. 57.

57 Hilberg, *Destruction*, revised, pp. 174–86; Schmidt, *Albert Speer*, pp. 187–8.

58 For stone statistics and the description of Soldiers' Hall activity, see the Arge Nürnberg 1942 annual report, in BA, R120/3941d.

59 See Wolters' report, in BA, R120/1446. The reorganization of the OKH Building Administration can be found in a report of 9 February 1944 by Doblin, in BA, R120/1651, pp. 27–8. For the order changing the exemption status of stone quarries, see the introduction to the Arge Nürnberg annual report for budget year 1943, in BA, R120/3941d.

60 Arge Nürnberg, 1943 annual report, in BA, R120/3941d.

61 See the (undated) list of GBI stone orders, in BA, R120/3282, p. 15. The date of February 1944 is based on other indicative documents in this file.

62 BA, R120/1651, pp. 57–8.

63 See the letter from 22 January 1945 from the OKH Building Administration, in BA, R120/3282, p. 61.

64 Cf. the relatively small amounts of stone procurement for, e.g., the headquarters of the Oberkommando der Luftwaffe (across the street from the Soldiers' Hall on the North–South Axis), in BA, R120/741. For GBI budget reports, see BA, R120/741; R120/1651.

65 Cf. M.T. Allen, "Engineers and Modern Managers in the SS: The Business Administration Main Office (*Wirtschaftsverwaltungshauptamt*)," PhD diss., University of Pennsylvania, 1995, pp. 107–52.

66 For an insightful study of how successful National Socialism was in its attempts to politicize the government bureaucracy, see D. Silverman, "Nazification of the German Bureaucracy Reconsidered: A Case Study," *Journal of Modern History*, 1988, vol. 60, pp. 496–539.

67 For Ahrens' dealings with the GBI, see, for example, BA, Potsdam, 46.06 GBI/3449, pp. 57–60, 95–100.

68 See the contract draft, in ÖDMMA, A/8/1.

69 See the discussion of brick-making techniques and Sachsenhausen in Allen, "Engineers and Modern Managers," pp. 123–8. My thanks to Allen for our multiple conversations on this subject and for sharing his expertise in the technological history of SS concerns.

70 See the summary of business up to 11 January 1939 from a GBI protocol in BA, Potsdam, 46.06 GBI/3449, pp. 57–60. See also Speer's view of the factory's problems and financing, after the fact, in a letter of 17 January 1942 to Pohl, in BA, Potsdam, 46.06 GBI/28, pp. 103–9. In his over 500-page long post-war autobiography, Speer spends all of two paragraphs on SS interest in the building materials business. Both are devoted to ridiculing the ignorance of SS managers and Himmler in their business knowledge, and one paragraph specifically targets the failure at Sachsenhausen. Needless to say, Speer's account is selective and extremely dubious in relation to GBI involvement with clean-up efforts at the camp. Speer, *Inside the Third Reich*, p. 144.

71 H. Kaienburg, *"Vernichtung durch Arbeit". Der Fall Neuengamme*, Bonn, Verlag

J.H.W. Dietz, 1990, pp. 93–7. See also Speer's letter to Pohl from 17 January 1942 where he lists the amount lost by the reorientation of the concern, in BA, Potsdam, 46.06 GBI/28, p. 106. For Pohl's reaction to Ahrens, see his letter of 16 June 1939 to Oranienburg managers, in BA, NS3/880, p. 40. Schondorff's biography can be found in his file at the Berlin Document Center. Allen analyses Schondorff's education and expertise in Allen, "Engineers and Modern Managers," pp. 155–60.

72 BA, Potsdam, 46.06 GBI/28, p. 108.

73 Ibid., p. 109.

74 LA, Pr. Br. Rep. 107/123/2 Oranienburg.

75 BA, R120/1585, pp. 38–40. The date on the contract is unclear, though it refers to meetings and agreements from late 1940 and is marked by an unnamed GBI reader in August 1941. Hence, I have dated the contract as mid-1941. Also in the contract, the SS repeats that the GBI came to it and on 4 September 1940 gave instructions (*den Auftrag erteilt*) to build the stone-processing center near the Oranienburg brickworks. However, in the margins are two question marks (next to those sections where the SS indicates that the GBI was the active agent) and the words "im Gegenteil!" written to question the phrasing. Whether or not the SS was originally responsible for the plan, the GBI (as in the protocol cited above) represented itself as the instigator of the work.

76 DEST financial reports to the GBI, in BA, R120/1585, pp. 48–50, 60. See also the discussion above of Transportflotte Speer and the redirection of the building materials economy to the use of water transport in 1941–2. For a description of the project, see Jelkmann's report of 20 September 1940, in BA, R120/1585, pp. 6–9.

77 See Schwarz's letter, in BA, R120/1585, pp. 62–4.

78 See the description of the *Kriegsbauprogramm* and the contract, in BA, R120/1585, pp. 70–1, 94–5. A sum of moneys spent on Oranienburg II, prepared on 24 March 1944, can be found in BA, R120/1585, pp. 132–3.

79 Kaienburg, "*Vernichtung durch Arbeit*", pp. 116–18.

80 As noted in Chapter 2, this volume, the years of greatest quarrying activity also corresponded to the years when the work conditions at the camp were at their worst.

81 See summaries of sales from Mauthausen and Flossenbürg 1938–40, in BA, NS3/1346, pp. 153–4. See the summary of 1940 production authored by Schwarz, in BA, NS3/1009, pp. 321–2.

82 See summary of total production for the DEST stone works including the gravel concern at Auschwitz 1940–1, in BA, NS3/341, p. 25. For 1942, see BA, NS3/1347. The statistics for 1942 are taken from the DEST monthly reports. These reports do not break down the type of stone produced in relation to the quantity until June 1942. Hence, it is impossible to ascertain exactly what percentage of granite was quarried in relation to other types of stone production (e.g. street building material). As production could shift depending on weather conditions and wartime demands, these numbers should be treated as approximate.

83 The data here and in the following paragraph comes from a report by DEST's Schwarz in the HAVW, Amt III A, a copy of which can be found in BA, NS4 FL/67.

84   Ibid. KL Flossenbürg, unlike the Oranienburg Brickworks and Oranienburg II, was not on a waterway and thus could not easily take advantage of the Transportflotte Speer.

85   Ibid. (emphasis in original). For a discussion of this document in terms of the stone-mason programs, see Chapter 3, this volume.

86   Compare the discussion of rationalization of labor potential and anti-Semitic ideological considerations in the use and abuse of Jewish forced labor in G. Aly and S. Heim, "The Economics of the Final Solution: A Case Study from the General Gouvernement," *Simon Wiesenthal Center Annual*, 1988, vol. 5, pp. 3–48.

87   See statistics in Table 1 (p. 41) and in the Schwarz memorandum.

88   List of stone remaining at the quarries for the OKH complex at the end of the war, in BA, R3, Anhang/172, pp. 20–30. It is probable that the numbers for DEST are also low given that these enterprises, too, stored stone at the Fürstenberg site. See, for example, the October 1941 list of deliveries from ten firms (including 70 cbm from KL Gross-Rosen) to the GBI facility in R120/3940b. To this author's knowledge, no complete list broken down by firms exists for stone deliveries to Fürstenberg.

Chapter 5: THE POLITICAL FUNCTION OF SS ARCHITECTURE

1   H. Himmler, "Deutsche Burgen im Osten," *Das Schwarze Korps*, January 1941, vol. 4, p. 4.

2   J. Ackermann, *Heinrich Himmler als Ideologe*, Göttingen, Musterschmidt, 1970, pp. 60–2. See, also, K.J. Leyser, "Henry I and the Beginnings of the Saxon Empire," in *Medieval Germany and its Neighbors 900–1250*, London, The Hambledon Press, 1982, pp. 11–42.

3   SS institutional architecture and, above all, the architecture of the concentration camps has become the subject of increasing scholarly interest in the past decade. However, most scholars continue to explore the sites for their relation to the politics of post-war German memory rather than as products of Nazi architectural considerations. See, e.g., H. Marcuse, *Legacies of Dachau: The Uses and Abuses of a Concentration Camp, 1933–2000*, Cambridge, Cambridge University Press, forthcoming 1999; J. Young, *The Texture of Memory. Holocaust Memorials and Meaning*, New Haven, Yale University Press, 1993. For a notable exception, see the first systematic architectural account of the design of a concentration camp in D. Dwork and R. Jan van Pelt, *Auschwitz. 1270 to the Present*, New York, W.W. Norton and Company, 1996.

4   See the city documents and letters from Pohl in SAN, C7/VIII KR Nr. 4311. Considering the size, location and importance of the patrons, it is surprising how little attention has been paid to the SS Barracks by architectural historians. Koch mentions the building only in passing in his summary of Nuremberg during the Nazi era (C. Koch, "Bauen in Nürnberg 1933–1945," in M. Diefenbacher [ed.], *Bauen in Nürnberg 1933–1945*, Nuremberg, W. Tümmels Buchdruckerei und Verlag, 1995, p. 29).

5   Petropoulos cites multiple examples of the use of art to establish social and political

relationships between the Nazi elite. See, especially, the discussion of Himmler's use of art and patronage in J. Petropoulos, *Art as Politics in the Third Reich*, Chapel Hill, University of North Carolina Press, 1996, pp. 212–20.

6   For Himmler's view of the project, the suggestion of Ruff and Hitler's interest in SS projects, see Pohl's letter to the Ministry of Finance, in BA, R2/27481, pp. 9–11. Mention of Hitler's drawing for the layout of the complex can also be found in this file. See ibid., p. 31.

7   The general significance of referencing Roman Imperial architecture is discussed in A. Scobie, *Hitler's State Architecture. The Impact of Classical Antiquity*, University Park, Pennsylvania State University Press, 1990. For changes in the design, see Ruff's report of 20 August 1937 to the Finance Ministry, in BA, R2/27481. Further information on the design process is indicated in a memorandum from the Finance Ministry, October 1937, in BA, R2/27482. Notably, work on the SS Barracks was also partly carried out during the war by inmates from KL Flossenbürg. See the payment request of 17 August 1943 for use of prisoners from the Flossenbürg building administration, in BA, NS4 FL/48.

8   Pohl's participation is well documented in numerous memoranda in SAN, C7/VIII KR Nr. 4311, 4324. This file also records the tension between the architect Ruff and city administrators, especially the chief administrator Dr Walter Eickemeyer, head of Directorate B with oversight of the building administration. In September 1937, Eickemeyer physically threatened Ruff if he did not meet the construction deadlines. Ruff complained to Himmler, Himmler to Liebel, Liebel passed it on to Eickemeyer, Himmler responded through Pohl. Eickemeyer claimed it was a joke, Ruff claimed he thought it was serious. Ultimately, the whole affair was dismissed with no resolution but clear resentment on each side.

9   See the correspondence from the HAHuB (6 July 1939) and from Pohl and his staff (August 1938) to the building administration at Flossenbürg, in BA, NS4 FL/33. The NS4 FL series of documents includes over seventy boxes of unsorted material concerning the concentration camp at Flossenbürg. Many historians have overlooked the source because the majority of the documents stem from the camp's building administration (SS Bauleitung). As such, however, this material provides crucial evidence for the present study.

10   For the building office's description, see BA, NS3/183, 45. The original plans, as described in this account, were not contained in this file.

11   For a brief overview of the development of several concentration camp sites, see Young, *Texture of Memory*, pp. 49–79.

12   Pohl's letter of 15 September 1937 to Eicke, in BA, NS3/183, p. 42. A small drawing of the building showing alterations as per Pohl's demands can be found in BA, NS3/375, p. 34. The completed structure has a wooden two-storied midsection with a tower topped by a clock in the cupola and plain, plaster-walled wings to each side.

13   *Das Schwarze Korps*, 21 January 1937, p. 12. The passage is illustrated with the Brandenburg Gate.

14   R. Breitman, *The Architect of Genocide. Himmler and the Final Solution*, New York,

Alfred A. Knopf, 1991, pp. 33–45. Marriages and "Aryan" heritages were handled by the office of the SS Race and Settlement Main Office, headed by Richard-Walther Darré who promoted the infamous "Blood and Soil" theory for German racial purity. See also R. Koehl, *The Black Corps: The Structure and Power Struggles of the Nazi SS*, Madison, University of Wisconsin Press, 1983, pp. 79–83. For an overview of Quedlinburg's history and the involvement of the SS, see H. Fuhrmann, "Vom einstigen Glanz Quedlinburgs," in *Das Quedlinburger Evangeliar,* Munich, Prestel Verlag, 1991, pp. 13–22.

15   E. Georg, *Die wirtschaftlichen Unternehmungen der SS*, Stuttgart, Deutsche Verlags-Anstalt, 1963, pp. 21–3; K. Hüser, *Wewelsburg 1933 bis 1945. SS-Kult- und Terrorstätte*, Paderborn, Verlag Bonifatius Druckerei, 1982, pp. 1–13. Concerning Himmler and Henry I, see also Ackermann, *Himmler*, pp. 202–3.

16   Hüser, *Wewelsburg*, pp. 5–8, 16–19.

17   Hüser, *Wewelsburg*, pp. 69–106. For a summary of work done on the north tower by prisoners up to the end of 1941, see BA, NS3/430, pp. 35–6. DEST balance drafts for 1941 and 1942 in BA, NS3/1222. For Speer's intercession on behalf of building at Wewelsburg, see BA, NS3/430, p. 64.

18   Hüser, *Wewelsburg*, pp. 61–8. For an overview of the use of medieval revival architecture and its nationalist connotations in Germany, see B. Miller Lane, "National Romanticism in Modern German Architecture," in *Nationalism in the Visual Arts*, Washington, DC, National Gallery of Art, 1991, pp. 111–47. Note that Himmler's interest in medieval German culture extended beyond architecture and artworks to include a variety of different areas. In folklore studies, for example, he competed with Rosenberg over control of the discipline between 1937 and 1939, as both leaders wanted to control the promotion of pre-modern Germanic society. (H. Lixfeld, *Folklore and Fascism: The Reich Institute for German Volkskunde*, Bloomington, Indiana University Press, 1994, pp. 105–20.)

19   For Himmler's political plans in the East and their dependence on pre-modern agricultural settlements, see, respectively, Breitman, *Architect of Genocide*, pp. 167–87; Dwork and van Pelt, *Auschwitz*, pp. 127–59. See also J. Wolschke-Bulmahn and G. Gröning, "The National Socialist Garden and Landscape Ideal: *Bodenständigkeit* (Rootedness in the Soil)," in R. Etlin (ed.), *Culture and the Nazis*, Chicago, University of Chicago Press, forthcoming.

20   For an analysis of the development of early penal and institutional architectural types in modern Europe and the US, see T. Markus, *Buildings and Power*, London, Routledge, 1993, pp. 95–145.

21   Concerning the barracks in the camps, see, for example, the agreement of 28 September 1938 from the firm Kämper und Seeberg to deliver seventeen barracks ordered by the SS building administration at Flossenbürg, BA, NS4 FL/40.

22   For the SS building administration hierarchy, see BA, NS3/555 (Anhang), p. 16. See also the letter from the HAHuB, Amt II C, 10 December 1940, in BA, NS4 FL/40. For information on Kammler, see his SS file at the Berlin Document Center. For the professionalization of the SS building administration, see M.T. Allen, "Engineers and Modern Managers in the SS: The Business Administration Main Office

(*Wirtschaftsverwaltungshauptamt*)," PhD diss., University of Pennsylvania, 1995, pp. 260–97. In February 1942, when the SS economic administration combined its two major offices into the WVHA, construction tasks were reorganized under the newly created Amt C.

23 An example of the early organization of the approval and creation of designs can be found in a description by the building administrator Georg Mayrl from 7 September 1938 in BA, NS4 FL/58. For Pohl's involvement in approving architectural projects, see his letter of 31 August 1938 to Eicke, in BA, NS4 FL/59. For the appointment of Blaschek as the leader of the building inspectors of Bauleitung Süd (memo of 30 January 1942) and Busching's demand from July 1942 that the building administrators at Flossenbürg direct all correspondence to his office, see BA, NS4 FL/37. See also Blaschek's file in the Berlin Document Center.

24 Description of housing construction in report from Seiz (July 1942) in BA, NS4 FL/29. Meeting of Salpeter, Weiseborn, Eckstein and Mayrl reported in letter from Mayrl (7 September 1938) in BA, NS4 FL/58. For DEST structures built in 1938, see BA, NS3/1345, pp. 11–14.

25 See the Bauleitung report of work at Flossenbürg from 1940 to 1942 in BA, NS4 FL/38. See Kuiper's description (12 November 1940) of the changes for the camp in BA, NS4 FL/55.

26 Summary of the construction at Flossenbürg and building costs 1940–2 in the report from the Bauleitung (20 October 1942), BA, NS4 FL/38.

27 See the description of 15 October 1942 by Ernest Seiz (Bauleitung) of the ground and buildings, in BA, NS4 FL/52. Mayrl report in BA, NS4 FL/50.

28 For Hauser's orders, recorded in an exchange between Mayrl and the HAHuB, see BA, NS4 FL/59.

29 Stone prices for one watch tower and multiple receipts in BA, NS4 FL/35. For the confirmation of an oral contract between DEST and the camp (23 July 1940), the billing from DEST for the carting of stone to the building site (22 November 1940), and the letter chastising the Bauleitung (8 December 1941), see BA, NS4 FL/40.

30 For construction at Auschwitz, see Dwork and van Pelt, *Auschwitz*, pp. 163ff. The "effectiveness" of Auschwitz at projecting the institutional authority of the SS is evidenced in the architecture of the camp becoming the main postwar symbol of the brutality of the fascist regime. See D. Hoffmann, "Auschwitz im visuellen Gedächtnis. Das Chaos des Verbrechens und die symbolische Ordnung der Bilder," in *Auschwitz: Geschichte, Rezeption und Wirkung*, Frankfurt am Main, Campus Verlag, 1996, pp. 223–57.

31 DEST to Mayrl, 24 April 1940, concerning replacement of technical drawer sent back to Dachau, in BA, NS4 FL/53.

32 Report on prisoner architects and draftsmen from Amt II, 9 February 1942, in BA, NS4 FL/34. Appointment of three prisoners, 15 December 1942, in BA, NS4 FL/40.

33 W. Benjamin, "Theses on the Philosophy of History," in H. Arendt (ed.), *Illuminations*, New York, Schocken Books, 1969, p. 256.

34 For the Heydrich order from January 1941, see H. Marsalek, *Die Geschichte des*

Konzentrationslagers Mauthausen, Vienna, Österreichische Lagergemeinschaft Mauthausen, 1974, p. 22.

35 Marsalek, *Mauthausen*, pp. 15–16.

36 G. Horwitz, *In the Shadow of Death. Living Outside the Gates of Mauthausen*, New York, The Free Press, 1990, p. 28. Horwitz analyzes the effect of the camp on the townspeople and the advantages and disadvantages derived from its presence by the local businesses (particularly the stone-quarry enterprise owned by the Poschacher family).

37 For the ground plan, see BA, NS4 MA/54. For a discussion of the use of medieval models in Weimar and National Socialist Germany, see Miller Lane, "National Romanticism," pp. 130–6.

38 Speer, on visiting KL Mauthausen in 1943, commented on the too "grandiose" building plans (particularly the wall), criticizing the SS for diverting the work of the prisoners towards construction at a time of war. The brief disagreement between Speer's staff and Himmler's led finally to the clarification that, while the walls were impressive, the work had been done mostly before 1943. Speer could thus rest assured that the orderly transfer of forced labor from building tasks to armaments had been completed. See the exchange between Speer and Himmler's staff, in BA, NS19/1542.

39 Marsalek, *Mauthausen*, pp. 68–84, 114–19.

40 See, for example, ÖDMMA, U/3/1, pp. 9–10. For a testimonial of an inmate who worked outside of the quarry, see S. Gorondowski, "Bericht über Mauthausen," *Dachauer Hefte*, 1986, vol. 2, pp. 123–32.

41 Whether National Socialist officials valued or did not value Jewish labor is subject to debate in Nazi studies. However, convincing arguments have been brought forth to suggest that Jewish forced labor was variably valued depending on the location of the Jewish population and the changing needs of the German war economy. See, for example, G. Aly and S. Heim, "The Economics of the Final Solution: A Case Study from the General Gouvernement," *Simon Wiesenthal Center Annual*, 1988, vol. 5, pp. 3–48. But cf. U. Herbert, "Labour and Extermination: Economic Interest and the Primacy of *Weltanschauung* in National Socialism," *Past & Present*, 1993, no. 138, pp. 153–65.

42 Horwitz, *Mauthausen*, pp. 13–14; D. Pike, *In the Service of Stalin. The Spanish Communists in Exile, 1939–1943*, Oxford, Clarendon Press, 1993. For SS records on the number and place of origin of prisoners arriving from 1940 through 1942, see AGKBZHwP, KL Mauthausen, 5–7. The increased ability for an individual to survive the camp based on his or her pre-camp experiences is convincingly argued by F. Pingel, *Häftlinge unter SS-Herrschaft. Widerstand, Selbstbehauptung und Vernichtung im Konzentrationslager*, Hamburg, Hoffmann und Campe, 1978, esp. pp. 10–13. A testimony of one individual's experience from the civil war to the freeing of the camp is given in M. Constante, *Les Années rouges. De Guernica à Mauthausen*, Paris, Mercure de France, 1971.

43 Mena's narrative in M. Razola and M. Constante (eds), *Triangle bleu. Les républicains espagnols à Mauthausen 1940–1945*, Paris, Editions Gallimard, 1969, p. 76.

44 Razola narrative in Razola and Constante, *Triangle bleu*, pp. 62–3.

45 Navarro's narrative in Razola and Constante, *Triangle bleu*, p. 68.

46 See Leyser, "Henry I," pp. 14–25.

Chapter 6: CONCLUSION

 1 Speer letter of 15 May 1945, BA, R3/1587. See also Sereny's discussion of these days in G. Sereny, *Albert Speer: His Battle with Truth*, New York, Alfred A. Knopf, 1995, pp. 546–7.

 2 On Speer's participation in the Dönitz government and the presentation of his case at the Nuremberg Tribunals, see M. Schmidt, *Albert Speer: The End of a Myth*, London, Harrap Limited, 1985, pp. 132–68. Petropoulos also notes that, even after his appointment as Minister of Armaments in 1942, Speer continued to emphasize his role as architect, especially when dealing with Hitler. Nevertheless, these wartime projections of his artistic role were not separated by Speer from his abilities as a cabinet minister; such a separation began in earnest with his post-war testimony and writings. See J. Petropoulos, *Art as Politics in the Third Reich*, Chapel Hill, University of North Carolina Press, 1996, pp. 166–9.

 3 More recently, a limited number of scholars have taken exception to this dominant theory. See, e.g., A. Steinweis, *Art, Ideology, and Economics in Nazi Germany. The Reich Chambers of Music, Theater, and the Visual Arts*, Chapel Hill, University of North Carolina Press, 1993; J. Van Dyke, "Franz Radziwill. 'Die Gemeinschaft' und die nationalsozialistische 'Revolution' in der Kunst," in *Georges-Bloch-Jahrbuch des Kunstgeschichtlichen Seminars der Universität Zürich*, vol. 4, Zurich, Kunstgeschichtlichen Seminars der Universität Zürich, 1997, pp. 135–63.

 4 See the discussion of the legal formulation of the four counts of indictment in T. Taylor, *The Anatomy of the Nuremberg Trials*, New York, Alfred A. Knopf, 1992, pp. 78–115.

 5 *Trial of the Major War Criminals before the International Military Tribunal*, vol. 17, Nuremberg, 1948, p. 25.

 6 Ibid., p. 244.

 7 B. Smith, *Reaching Judgment at Nuremberg*, New York, Basic Books, 1977, p. 220. Certainly, not all Allied representatives were so disposed towards Speer. However, he, of all of the defendants, made the most favorable and "gentlemanly" impression on many interrogators and guards. See, for example, the account of his time leading up to Nuremberg in Sereny, *Albert Speer*, pp. 545–61.

 8 *Trials of War Criminals before the Nuernberg Military Tribunals*, "The Pohl Case," vol. 5, Washington, DC, United States Government Printing Office, 1950, p. 331.

 9 Ibid., p. 327.

10 Ibid., p. 568.

11 In describing the transformation of DEST concerns to armaments tasks, Mummenthey pushed this idea of conflict even further:

In that period [after 1942], the struggle of the DEST for economic matters on the one hand and for political power on the other hand with the commandants continued without a break . . . [T]he DEST, and I shall speak about that in detail later, for economic reasons had a vital interest in speaking up for the inmates." (Ibid., p. 570)

See also Allen's discussion of the post-war trial of WVHA engineers and business managers in M.T. Allen, "Engineers and Modern Managers in the SS: The Business Administration Main Office (*Wirtschaftsverwaltungshauptamt*)", PhD diss., University of Pennsylvania, 1995, pp. 543–9.

12 For a discussion of how the debate on "fascist" form continues in contemporary Germany, see G. Rosenfeld, "The Architects' Debate. Architectural Discourse and the Memory of Nazism in the Federal Republic of Germany, 1977–1997," *History and Memory*, 1997, vol. 9, nos. 1/2, pp. 189–225.

13 W. Durth, *Deutsche Architekten: Biographische Verflechtungen 1900–1970*, Braunschweig, Friedr. Vieweg & Sohn, 1987, pp. 252–4. Durth and his colleague, Niels Gutschow, have been crucial in defining the renewed interest in studying the generational continuities between Weimar, National Socialist and West German architectural personnel. The following section is indebted to their research.

14 Ibid., pp. 277–98.

15 The Architektenring modeled itself on the earlier "ring" of artistically and politically avant-garde architects around Bruno Taut formed in the early Weimar Republic. See I. Whyte, *Bruno Taut and the Architecture of Activism*, Cambridge, Cambridge University Press, 1982.

16 Durth, *Deutsche Architekten*, pp. 297–302.

17 Ibid., pp. 303–5.

Bibliography

ARCHIVES CONSULTED

Archivum Glowna Komisja Badonia Zbrodni Hitlerowskich w Polse (Warsaw)
Berlin Document Center (Berlin)
Bundesarchiv (Berlin; formerly Koblenz)
Bundesarchiv, Abteilung Potsdam (Berlin; formerly Potsdam)
Dokumentationsarchiv des österreichischen Widerstandes (Vienna)
Institut für Zeitgeschichte (Munich)
KZ-Gedenkstätte Dachau Archiv (Dachau)
Landesarchiv (Berlin)
Öffentliches Denkmal und Museum Mauthausen Archiv (Vienna)
Stadtarchiv Nürnberg (Nuremberg)
US Holocaust Memorial Museum (Washington)

SELECT BIBLIOGRAPHY

Ackermann, J., *Heinrich Himmler als Ideologe*, Göttingen, Musterschmidt, 1970.
Adam, P., *Art of the Third Reich*, New York, Harry N. Abrams Inc., 1992.
Ades, D., Benton, T., Elliott, D. and Whyte, I. (eds), *Kunst und Macht*, London, Hayward Gallery, 1996.
Allen, M.T., "Engineers and Modern Managers in the SS: The Business Administration Main Office (*Wirtschaftsverwaltungshauptamt*)," PhD diss., University of Pennsylvania, 1995.
——— "The Banality of Evil Reconsidered: SS Mid-Level Managers of Extermination through Work," *Central European History*, 1998, vol. 30, no. 2, pp. 253–94.
d'Alquen, G., *Die SS. Geschichte, Aufgabe und Organisation der Schutzstaffel der NSDAP*, Berlin, Junker und Dünnhaupt Verlag, 1939.
Aly, G. and Heim, S., "The Economics of the Final Solution: A Case Study from the

General Gouvernment," *Simon Wiesenthal Center Annual*, 1988, vol. 5, pp. 3–48.

Arndt, K., "Architektur und Politik," in *Albert Speer. Architektur-Arbeiten 1933–1942*, Berlin, Propylaen, 1978, pp. 113–50.

—— "Problematischer Ruhm – die Großaufträge in Berlin 1937–1943," in W. Nerdinger and E. Mai (eds), *Wilhelm Kreis. Architekt zwischen Kaiserreich und Demokratie 1873–1955*, Munich, Klinkhardt und Biermann, 1994, pp. 168–87.

Ayçoberry, P., *The Nazi Question: An Essay on the Interpretations of National Socialism (1922–1975)*, trans. R. Hurley, New York, Pantheon Books, 1981.

Backes, K., *Hitler und die bildenden Künste: Kulturverständnis und Kunstpolitik im Dritten Reich*, Cologne, Dumont Buchverlag, 1988.

Balfour, A., *Berlin. The Politics of Order 1737–1989*, New York, Rizzoli International Publications Inc., 1990.

Barkai, A., *Das Wirtschaftssystem des Nationalsozialismus: Der historische und ideologische Hintergrund 1933–1936*, Cologne, Verlag Wissenschaft und Politik, 1977.

—— *From Boycott to Annihilation. The Economic Struggle of German Jews, 1933–1943*, trans. W. Templer, Hanover, New Hampshire, University Press of New England, 1989.

Bartov, O., *Murder in our Midst. The Holocaust, Industrial Killing, and Representation*, Oxford, Oxford University Press, 1996.

Behrenbeck, S., "Festarchitektur im Dritten Reich," in B. Brock and A. Preiss (eds), *Kunst auf Befehl?*, Munich, Klinkhardt & Biermann Verlagsbuchhandlung GmbH, 1990, pp. 201–52.

Benjamin, W., "Theses on the Philosophy of History," in H. Arendt (ed.), *Illuminations*, New York, Schocken Books, 1969, pp. 253–64.

Bernett, H., "Zur Grundsteinlegung vor 50 Jahren: Das 'Deutsche Stadion' in Nürnberg – ein Phantom nationalsozialistischen Grössenwahns," *Sozial- und Zeitgeschichte des Sports*, 1987, vol. 1, no. 3, pp. 14–40.

Billig, J., *Les Camps de concentration dans l'économie du Reich Hitlérien*, Paris, Presses Universitaires de France, 1973.

Blaich, F., *Wirtschaft und Rüstung im "Dritten Reich"*, Düsseldorf, Pädagogischer Verlag Schwann-Bagel GmbH, 1987.

Botz, G., "National Socialist Vienna: Antisemitism as a Housing Policy," in M. Marrus (ed.), *The Nazi Holocaust. Historical Articles on the Destruction of European Jews*, vol. 2, Westport, Meckler Corporation, 1989, pp. 640–57.

Breitman, R., *The Architect of Genocide. Himmler and the Final Solution*, New York, Alfred A. Knopf, 1991.

Brenner, H., *Die Kunstpolitik des Nationalsozialismus*, Reinbeck bei Hamburg, Rowohlt Taschenbuch Verlag, 1963.

Broszat, M., "Nationalsozialistische Konzentrationslager 1933–1945," in *Anatomie des SS-Staates*, vol. 2, Munich, Deutscher Taschenbuch Verlag, 1967, pp. 11–133.

——— *The Hitler State*, trans. J. Hiden, New York, Longman Inc., 1981.

Browning, C., "Beyond 'Intentionalism' and 'Functionalism': A Reassessment of Nazi Jewish Policy from 1939 to 1941," in T. Childers and J. Caplan (eds), *Reevaluating the Third Reich*, New York, Holmes and Meier, 1993, pp. 211–33.

Buchheim, H., "Die SS – das Herrschaftsinstrument," in *Anatomie des SS-Staates*, vol. 1, Munich, Deutscher Taschenbuch Verlag, 1979, pp. 15–214.

Busche, E., "Laboratorium: Wohnen und Weltstadt," in J. Kleihues (ed.), *750 Jahre Architektur und Städtebau in Berlin*, Stuttgart, Verlag Gerd Hatje, 1987, pp. 153–82.

Centrum Industriekultur Nürnberg (ed.), *Kulissen der Gewalt: das Reichsparteitagsgelände in Nürnberg*, Munich, Hugendubel, 1992.

Childers, T. and Caplan, J. (eds), *Reevaluating the Third Reich*, New York, Holmes and Meier, 1993.

Constante, M., *Les Années rouges. De Guernica à Mauthausen*, Paris, Mercure de France, 1971.

Deist, W., Messerschmidt, M., Volkmann, H.-E. and Wette, W., *Ursachen und Voraussetzungen des Zweiten Weltkrieges*, Frankfurt am Main, Fischer Taschenbuch Verlag GmbH, 1989.

Diefenbacher, M. (ed.), *Bauen in Nürnberg 1933–1945. Architektur und Bauformen im Nationalsozialismus*, Nuremberg, W. Tümmels Buchdruckerei und Verlag, 1995.

Drobisch, K., "Hinter der Torinschrift 'Arbeit macht frei.' Häftlingsarbeit, wirtschaftliche Nutzung und Finanzierung der Konzentrationslager 1933 bis 1939," in H. Kaienburg (ed.), *Konzentrationslager und deutsche Wirtschaft 1939–1945*, Opladen, Leske + Budrich, 1996, pp. 17–27.

Dülffer, J., "NS-Herrschaftssystem und Stadtgestaltung: Das Gesetz zur Neugestaltung deutscher Städte vom 4. Oktober 1937," *German Studies Review*, February 1989, vol. 12, pp. 69–89.

Dülffer, J., Thies, J. and Henke, J. (eds), *Hitlers Städte: Baupolitik im Dritten Reich*, Cologne, Böhlan Verlag, 1978.

Durth, W., *Deutsche Architekten: Biographische Verflechtungen 1900–1970*, Braunschweig, Friedr. Vieweg & Sohn, 1987.

Durth, W. and Gutschow, N., *Träume in Trümmern. Planungen zum Wiederaufbau zerstörter Städte im Westen Deutschlands 1940–1950*, Braunschweig, Friedr. Vieweg & Sohn, 1988.

Dwork, D. and van Pelt, R. Jan, *Auschwitz. 1270 to the Present*, New York, W.W. Norton and Company, 1996.

Eckstein, B., "Jews in the Mauthausen Concentration Camp," in *The Nazi Concentration Camps*, Jerusalem, Yad Vashem, 1984, pp. 257–71.

"Entwicklung der Baustoffpreise und Baukosten im Jahre 1935," *Beilage zum "Baumeister,"* August 1936, p. B166.

Ferencz, B., *Less than Slaves: Jewish Forced Labor and the Quest for Compensation*, Cambridge, Massachusetts, Harvard University Press, 1979.

Förster, K., "Das Deutsche Stadion in Nürnberg. Planungsgeschichte und

Funktion," Masters Thesis, Universität Göttingen, Göttingen, 1979.

———— "Staatsaufträge an Bildhauer für das Reichsparteitagsgelände in Nürnberg," in *Entmachtung der Kunst. Architektur, Bildhauerei und ihre Institutionalisierung 1920 bis 1960*, Berlin, 1985, pp. 156–82.

Frank, H. (ed.), *Faschistische Architekturen: Planen und Bauen in Europa 1930 bis 1945*, Hamburg, Hans Christians Verlag, 1985.

Freund, F., *Arbeitslager Zement. Das Konzentrationslager Ebensee und die Raketenrüstung*, Vienna, Verlag für Gesellschaftskritik, 1989.

Fuhrmann, H., "Vom einstigen Glanz Quedlinburgs," in *Das Quedlinburger Evangeliar*, Munich, Prestel Verlag, 1991, pp. 13–22.

Fuhrmeister, C., "Beton, Klinker, Granit – Die politische Bedeutung des Materials von Denkmälern in der Weimarer Republik und im Nationalsozialismus," PhD diss., University of Hamburg, 1998.

Gellately, R., *The Gestapo and German Society. Enforcing Racial Policy 1933–1945*, Oxford, Clarendon Press, 1990.

———— "Situating the 'SS-State' in a Social-Historical Context: Recent Histories of the SS, the Police, and the Courts in the Third Reich," *Journal of Modern History*, 1992, vol. 64, pp. 338–65.

Georg, E., *Die wirtschaftlichen Unternehmungen der SS*, Stuttgart, Deutsche Verlags-Anstalt, 1963.

Gilbert, M., *The Holocaust: A History of the Jews of Europe during the Second World War*, New York, Henry Holt and Company, 1985.

Gillingham, J., *Industry and Politics in the Third Reich. Ruhr Coal, Hitler and Europe*, London, Methuen, 1985.

Gorondowski, S., "Bericht über Mauthausen," *Dachauer Hefte*, 1986, vol. 2, pp. 123–32.

"Günstige Aussichten für das Bauwesen im Jahre 1936," *Beilage zum "Baumeister*," March 1933, p. B57.

Harlander, T. and Fehl, G. (eds), *Hitlers sozialer Wohnungsbau 1940–1945: Wohnungspolitik, Baugestaltung und Siedlungsplanung*, Hamburg, Hans Christians Verlag, 1986.

Hartung, U., "Bauästhetik im Nationalsozialismus und die Frage der Denkmalwürdigkeit," in B. Faulenbach and F.-J. Jelich (eds), *Reaktionäre Modernität und Völkermord*, Essen, Klartext Verlag, 1994, pp. 71–84.

Hayes, P., *Industry and Ideology: IG Farben in the Nazi Era*, Cambridge, Cambridge University Press, 1987.

———— "Polycracy and Policy in the Third Reich: The Case of the Economy," in T. Childers and J. Caplan (eds), *Reevaluating the Third Reich*, New York, Holmes and Meier, 1993, pp. 190–210.

———— "Die IG Farben und die Zwangsarbeit von KZ-Häftlingen im Werk Auschwitz," in H. Kaienburg (ed.), *Konzentrationslager und deutsche Wirtschaft 1939–1945*, Opladen, Leske + Budrich, 1996, pp. 129–48.

Heger, H., *The Men with the Pink Triangle*, trans. D. Fernbach, Boston, Alyson Publications Inc., 1980.

Heigl, P., *Konzentrationslager Flossenbürg*, Regensburg, Mittelbayerische Druckerei- und Verlags-Gesellschaft mbH, 1989.

Helmer, S., *Hitler's Berlin: The Speer Plans for Reshaping the Central City*, Ann Arbor, University of Michigan Research Press, 1985.

Henke, J., "Von den Grenzen der SS-Macht. Eine Fallstudie zur Tätigkeit des SS-Wirtschafts-Verwaltungshauptamtes," in D. Rebentisch (ed.), *Verwaltung contra Menschenführung im Staat Hitlers*, Göttingen, Vandenhoeck & Ruprecht, 1986, pp. 255–77.

———— "Die Reichsparteitage der NSDAP in Nürnberg 1933–1938. – Planung, Organisation, Propaganda," in *Aus der Arbeit des Bundesarchivs*, Boppard am Rhein, Harald Boldt Verlag, 1977, pp. 398–422.

Herbert, U., "Arbeit und Vernichtung. Ökonomisches Interesse und Primat der 'Weltanschauung' im Nationalsozialismus," in *Ist der Nationalsozialismus Geschichte?*, Frankfurt am Main, Fischer Taschenbuch Verlag, 1987, pp. 198–236.

———— "Labour and Extermination: Economic Interest and the Primacy of *Weltanschauung* in National Socialism," *Past & Present*, 1993, no. 138, pp. 144–95.

Hermann, W. (ed. and trans.), *In What Style Should We Build?*, Santa Monica, Getty Center, 1992.

Hilberg, R., *The Destruction of the European Jews*, Chicago, Quadrangle Books, 1967.

———— *The Destruction of the European Jews*, second edition, revised and abridged, New York, Holmes and Meier Publishers Inc., 1985.

Himmler, H., "Deutsche Burgen im Osten," *Das Schwarze Korps*, January 1941, vol. 4, p. 4.

Hinz, B., *Art in the Third Reich*, New York, Pantheon Books, 1979.

———— (ed.), *Die Dekoration der Gewalt. Kunst und Medien im Faschismus*, Giessen, Anabas-Verlag Günter Kämpf KG, 1979.

———— "1933/45: Ein Kapitel Kunstgeschichtlicher Forschung seit 1945," *Kritische Berichte*, 1986, vol. 14, no. 4, pp. 18–33.

Hitler, A., *Mein Kampf*, trans. L. Lore, New York, Stackpole Sons Publishers, 1939.

Hochman, E., *Architects of Fortune. Mies van der Rohe and the Third Reich*, New York, Fromm International Publishing Corporation, 1990.

Hoffmann, D., "Auschwitz im visuellen Gedächtnis. Das Chaos des Verbrechens und die symbolische Ordnung der Bilder," in Fritz Bauer Institut (ed.), *Auschwitz: Geschichte, Rezeption und Wirkung*, Frankfurt am Main, Campus Verlag, 1996, pp. 223–57.

Hoffmann-Curtius, K., "Die Frau in ihrem Element. Adolf Zieglers Triptychon der 'Naturgesetzlichkeit'," in B. Hinz (ed.), *NS-Kunst: 50 Jahre danach*, Marburg, Jonas Verlag, 1989, pp. 9–34.

Homze, E., *Foreign Labor in Nazi Germany*, Princeton, Princeton University Press, 1967.

Höhne, H., *The Order of the Death's Head: The Story of Hitler's S.S.*, trans. R. Barry, London, Secker and Warburg, 1969.

Horwitz, G., *In the Shadow of Death. Living Outside the Gates of Mauthausen*, New York, The Free Press, 1990.

Huber, G., *Die Porzellan-Manufaktur Allach-München GmbH*, Marburg, Jonas Verlag, 1992.

Hüser, K., *Wewelsburg 1933 bis 1945. SS-Kult- und Terrorstätte*, Paderborn, Verlag Bonifatius Druckerei, 1987.

"Die internationale Baukrisis in Zahlen," *Der Baumeister*, January 1933, pp. B6–7.

Janssen, G., *Das Ministerium Speer. Deutschlands Rüstung im Krieg*, Berlin, Ullstein, 1968.

Jaskot, P., "Anti-Semitic Policy in Albert Speer's Plans for the Rebuilding of Berlin," *Art Bulletin*, 1996, vol. 77, no. 4, pp. 622–32.

Johe, W., *Neuengamme. Zur Geschichte der Konzentrationslager in Hamburg*, Hamburg, Landeszentrale für politische Bildung, 1986.

Kaienburg, H., *"Vernichtung durch Arbeit". Der Fall Neuengamme*, Bonn, Verlag J.H.W. Dietz, 1990.

—— (ed.), *Konzentrationslager und deutsche Wirtschaft 1939–1945*, Opladen, Leske + Budrich, 1996.

Kaiser, P., "Monopolprofit und Massenmord im Faschismus. Zur ökonomischen Funktion der Konzentrations- und Vernichtungslager im faschistischen Deutschland," *Blätter für deutsche und internationale Politik*, 1975, vol. 20, no. 5, pp. 552–77.

Kárný, M., "'Vernichtung durch Arbeit.' Sterblichkeit in den NS-Konzentrationslagern," in *Sozialpolitik und Judenvernichtung. Gibt es eine Ökonomie der Endlösung?*, Berlin, Rotbuch Verlag Berlin, 1983, pp. 133–58.

—— "Das SS-Wirtschafts-Verwaltungshauptamt. Verwalter der KZ-Häftlingsarbeitskräfte und Zentrale des SS-Wirtschaftskonzerns," in *"Deutsche Wirtschaft." Zwangsarbeit von KZ-Häftlingen für Industrie und Behörden*, Hamburg, VSA-Verlag, 1991, pp. 153–69.

Kershaw, I., *Popular Opinion and Political Dissent in the Third Reich*, Oxford, Clarendon Press, 1983.

—— "Ideology, Propaganda, and the Rise of the Nazi Party," in P. Stachura (ed.), *The Nazi Machtergreifung*, London, George Allen and Unwin, 1983, pp. 162–81.

—— *The Nazi Dictatorship*, London, Edward Arnold (Publishers) Ltd., 1985.

Kirstein, W., *Das Konzentrationslager als Institution totalen Terrors. Das Beispiel des KL Natzweiler*, Pfaffenweiler, Centaurus-Verlagsgesellschaft, 1992.

Koch, C., "Bauen in Nürnberg 1933–1945," in M. Diefenbacher (ed.), *Bauen in Nürnberg 1933–1945*, Nuremberg, W. Tümmels Buchdruckerei und Verlag, 1995, pp. 14–113.

Koch, P. (ed.), *Himmlers Graue Eminenz – Oswald Pohl und das Wirtschaftsverwaltungshauptamt der SS*, Hamburg, Facta Oblita Verlag, 1988.

Koehl, R., *The Black Corps: The Structure and Power Struggles of the Nazi SS*, Madison, University of Wisconsin Press, 1983.

Kogon, E., *Der SS-Staat. Das System der deutschen Konzentrationslager*, Munich, Wilhelm Heyne Verlag, 1974.

Konieczny, A., "Das Konzentrationslager Groß-Rosen," *Dachauer Hefte*, 1989, vol. 5, pp. 15–27.

Konzentrationslager Buchenwald. Post Weimar/Thur., Buchenwald, Nationale Mahn- und Gedenkstätte Buchenwald, 1990.

Koonz, C., *Mothers in the Fatherland*, New York, St Martin's Press, 1987.

Krier, L. (ed.), *Albert Speer: Architecture 1932–1942*, Brussels, Archives d'Architecture Moderne, 1985.

"Die Lenkung des Baumarktes," *Beilage zum "Baumeister,"* 1937, no. 6, pp. B132–3.

Leyser, K.J., "Henry I and the Beginnings of the Saxon Empire," in *Medieval Germany and its Neighbors 900–1250*, London, The Hambledon Press, 1982, pp. 11–42.

Lixfeld, H., *Folklore and Fascism: The Reich Institute for German Volkskunde*, Bloomington, Indiana University Press, 1994.

Lotz, W., "Das Deutsche Stadion in Nürnberg," *Kunst und Volk*, 1937, vol. 5, pp. 256–7.

Mai, E., "Von 1930 bis 1945: Ehrenmäler und Totenburgen," in W. Nerdinger and E. Mai (eds), *Wilhelm Kreis. Architekt zwischen Kaiserreich und Demokratie 1873–1955*, Munich, Klinkhardt und Biermann, 1994, pp. 156–67.

Maier, C., *In Search of Stability: Explorations in Historical Political Economy*, Cambridge, Cambridge University Press, 1987.

Marcuse, H., *Legacies of Dachau: The Uses and Abuses of a Concentration Camp, 1933–2000*, Cambridge, Cambridge University Press, forthcoming 1999.

Marsalek, H., *Die Geschichte des Konzentrationslagers Mauthausen*, Vienna, Österreichische Lagergemeinschaft Mauthausen, 1974.

Mason, T., *Sozialpolitik im Dritten Reich*, Opladen, Westdeutscher Verlag, 1978.

—— *Nazism, Fascism and the Working Class*, J. Caplan (ed.), Cambridge, Cambridge University Press, 1995.

Miller Lane, B., *Architecture and Politics in Germany 1918–1945*, Cambridge, Massachusetts, Harvard University Press, 1968.

—— "National Romanticism in Modern German Architecture," in R. Etlin (ed.), *Nationalism in the Visual Arts*, Washington, DC, National Gallery of Art, 1991, pp. 11–47.

Müller, R.-D., *Hitlers Ostkrieg und die deutsche Siedlungspolitik. Die Zusammenarbeit von Wehrmacht, Wirtschaft und SS*, Frankfurt am Main, Fischer Taschenbuch Verlag, 1991.

Naasner, W., *Neue Machtzentren in der deutschen Kriegswirtschaft 1942–45. Die Wirtschaftsorganisation der SS, das Amt des Generalbevollmächtigten für den Arbeitseinsatz und das Reichsministerium für Bewaffnung und Munition/ Reichsministerium für Rüstungs- und Kriegsproduktion im nationalsozialistischen Herrschaftssystem*, Boppard am Rhein, Harald Boldt Verlag, 1994.

Nerdinger, W., "Wilhelm Kreis – Repräsentant der deutschen Architektur im 20. Jahrhundert," in W. Nerdinger and E. Mai (eds), *Wilhelm Kreis. Architekt zwischen Kaiserreich und Demokratie 1873–1955*, Munich, Klinkhardt und Biermann, 1994, pp. 8–27.

———— "Baustile im Nationalsozialismus: Zwischen Klassizismus und Regionalismus," in D. Ades, T. Benton, D. Elliott and I. Whyte (eds), *Kunst und Macht*,
London, Hayward Gallery, 1996, pp. 322–5.

Nerdinger, W. and Mai, E. (eds), *Wilhelm Kreis. Architekt zwischen Kaiserreich und
Demokratie 1873–1955*, Munich, Klinkhardt und Biermann, 1994.

Neumann, D., "'The Century's Triumph in Lighting': The Luxfer Prism Companies
and their Contribution to Early Modern Architecture," *Journal of the Society of
Architectural Historians*, 1995, vol. 54, no. 1, pp. 24–53.

Neumann, F., *Behemoth: The Structure and Practice of National Socialism*, London,
Victor Gollancz Ltd., 1943.

Ogan, B., "Architektur als Weltanschauung: Ein Beitrag über die Ästhetisierung
von Politik," in *Kulissen der Gewalt: das Reichsparteitagsgelände in Nürnberg*,
Munich, Hugendubel, 1992, pp. 123–40.

Overy, R., *The Nazi Economic Recovery, 1932–1938*, London, Macmillan, 1982.

———— *Goering, the Iron Man*, Boston, Routledge and Kegan Paul, 1984.

———— "Unemployment in the Third Reich," *Business History*, 1987, vol. 29, no. 3,
pp. 253–82.

———— *The Nazi Economic Recovery, 1932–1938*, second edition, revised,
Cambridge, Cambridge University Press, 1996.

Petley, J., *Capital and Culture. German Cinema 1933–1945*, London, British Film
Institute, 1979.

Petropoulos, J., *Art as Politics in the Third Reich*, Chapel Hill, University of North
Carolina Press, 1996.

Petsch, J., *Baukunst und Stadtplanung im Dritten Reich: Herleitung/
Bestandsaufnahme/Entwicklung/Nachfolge*, Munich, Carl Hanser Verlag, 1976.

Petsch, J. and Schäche, W., "Architektur im deutschen Faschismus: Grundzüge und
Charakter der nationalsozialistischen 'Baukunst'," in *Realismus: 1919–1939 –
zwischen Revolution und Reaktion*, Munich, Prestel Verlag, 1981, pp. 396–495.

Pike, D., *In the Service of Stalin. The Spanish Communists in Exile, 1939–1943*,
Oxford, Clarendon Press, 1993.

Pingel, F., *Häftlinge unter SS-Herrschaft. Widerstand, Selbstbehauptung und
Vernichtung im Konzentrationslager*, Hamburg, Hoffmann und Campe, 1978.

Preiss, A., "Nazikunst und Kunstmuseum. Museumsentwürfe und -konzepte im
'Dritten Reich' als Beitrag zu einer aktuellen Diskussion," in B. Hinz (ed.),
NS-Kunst: 50 Jahre danach, Marburg, Jonas Verlag, 1989, pp. 80–94.

Rabitsch, G., "Das KL Mauthausen," in *Studien zur Geschichte der Konzentrationslager*, Stuttgart, Deutsche Verlags-Anstalt, 1970, pp. 50–92.

Rasp, H.-P., *Eine Stadt für tausend Jahre. München – Bauten und Projekte für die
Hauptstadt der Bewegung*, Munich, Süddeutscher Verlag GmbH, 1981.

Razola, M. and Constante, M. (eds), *Triangle bleu. Les républicains espagnols à
Mauthausen 1940–1945*, Paris, Editions Gallimard, 1969.

Reichel, P., *Der schöne Schein des Dritten Reiches. Faszination und Gewalt des
Faschismus*, Munich, Carl Hanser Verlag, 1991.

Reichhardt, H. and Schäche, W., *Von Berlin nach Germania. Über die Zerstörungen der Reichshauptstadt durch Albert Speers Neugestaltungsplanungen*, Berlin, Transit Buchverlag, 1986.

Rosenfeld, G., "The Architects' Debate. Architectural Discourse and the Memory of Nazism in the Federal Republic of Germany, 1977–1997," *History and Memory*, 1997, vol. 9, nos. 1–2, pp. 189–225.

Roth, K., "Zwangsarbeit im Siemens-Konzern (1938–1945): Fakten – Kontroversen – Probleme," in H. Kaienburg, *Konzentrationslager und deutsche Wirtschaft 1939–1945*, Opladen, Leske + Budrich, 1996, pp. 149–68.

Sander, A., "Baudringlichkeitsstufen und Dringlichkeitsstufen des Fertigungs-programms der Wehrmacht," *Der Deutsche Baumeister*, June 1941, pp. 11–13.

Sarlay, I., "Hitropolis," in B. Brock and A. Preiss (eds), *Kunst auf Befehl? Dreiunddreissig bis Fünfundvierzig*, Munich, Klinkhardt und Biermann, 1990, pp. 187–99.

Scarpa, L., *Martin Wagner und Berlin*, Braunschweig, Friedr. Vieweg und Sohn, 1986.

Schäche, W., "Albert Speer," in W. Ribbe and W. Schäche (eds), *Baumeister, Architekten, Stadtplaner. Biographien zur baulichen Entwicklung Berlins*, Berlin, Stapp Verlag, 1987, pp. 511–28.

——— "Bauen im Nationalsozialismus: Dekoration der Gewalt," in J. Kleihues (ed.), *750 Jahre Architektur und Städtebau in Berlin*, Stuttgart, Verlag Gerd Hatje, 1987, pp. 183–212.

——— *Architektur und Städtebau in Berlin zwischen 1933 und 1945: Planen und Bauen unter der Ägide der Stadtverwaltung*, Berlin, Gebr. Mann Verlag, 1991.

——— "Von Berlin nach 'Germania'," in D. Ades, T. Benton, D. Elliott and I. Whyte (eds), *Kunst und Macht*, London, Hayward Gallery, 1996, pp. 326–9.

Schmidt, M., *Albert Speer: The End of a Myth*, trans. J. Neugroschel, London, Harrap Limited, 1985.

Schönberger, A., *Die Neue Reichskanzlei von Albert Speer: zum Zusammenhang von nationalsozialistischer Architektur und Ideologie*, Berlin, Mann Verlag, 1981.

Schwarzer, M., *German Architectural Theory and the Search for Modern Identity*, Cambridge, Cambridge University Press, 1995.

Scobie, A., *Hitler's State Architecture. The Impact of Classical Antiquity*, University Park, Pennsylvania State University Press, 1990.

Segev, T., *Soldiers of Evil. The Commandants of the Nazi Concentration Camps*, trans. H. Watzman, New York, McGraw-Hill Book Company, 1987.

Seidler, F., *Fritz Todt: Baumeister des Dritten Reiches*, Munich, F.A. Herbig Verlagsbuchhandlung, 1986.

——— *Die Organisation Todt: Bauen für Staat und Wehrmacht 1938–1945*, Koblenz, Bernhard & Graefe Verlag, 1987.

Sereny, G., *Albert Speer: His Battle with Truth*, New York, Alfred A. Knopf, 1995.

Siegel, T., "Rationalizing Industrial Relations: A Debate on the Control of Labor in German Shipyards in 1941," in T. Childers and J. Caplan (eds), *Reevaluating the Third Reich*, New York, Holmes and Meier, 1993, pp. 139–60.

Siegert, T., "Das Konzentrationslager Flossenbürg," in *Bayern in der NS-Zeit*, vol. 2, Munich, R. Oldenbourg Verlag, 1979, pp. 429–99.

Silverman, D., "Nazification of the German Bureaucracy Reconsidered: A Case Study," *Journal of Modern History*, 1988, vol. 60, no. 3, pp. 496–539.

—— *Hitler's Economy. Nazi Work Creation Programs, 1933–1936*, Cambridge, Massachusetts, Harvard University Press, 1998.

Simon, E., "Baugestaltung und Bauwirtschaft," *Der Deutsche Baumeister*, 1939, vol. 1, no. 3, pp. 5–8.

Smith, B., *Reaching Judgment at Nuremberg*, New York, Basic Books, 1977.

Smith, T., "A State of Seeing, Unsighted: Notes on the Visual in Nazi War Culture," *Block*, 1986–7, vol. 12, pp. 50–70.

Sofsky, W., *Die Ordnung des Terrors: Das Konzentrationslager*, Frankfurt am Main, S. Fischer Verlag, 1993.

Speer, A., "Stein statt Eisen," *Der Vierjahresplan*, 1937, vol. 1, pp. 135–7.

—— *Inside the Third Reich*, trans. C. and R. Winston, New York, Macmillan Company, 1970.

—— *Infiltration: How Heinrich Himmler Schemed to Build an SS Industrial Empire*, trans. J. Neugroschel, New York, Macmillan Publishing Co. Inc., 1981.

Steffens, J., "Die gegenwärtigen und zukünftigen Möglichkeiten des Bauschaffens," *Der Deutsche Baumeister*, 1942, no. 1, pp. 7–12.

Steinlein, G., "Vorkommen, Eigenschaften und Verwendungsarten deutscher natürlicher Gesteine," *Beilage zum "Baumeister,"* 1936, no. 5, pp. B91–3.

Der Steinmetz und Steinbildhauer, Berlin, Lehrmittelzentrale des Amtes für Berufserziehung und Betriebsführung der Deutschen Arbeitsfront, 1937.

Steinweis, A., *Art, Ideology, and Economics in Nazi Germany. The Reich Chambers of Music, Theater, and the Visual Arts*, Chapel Hill, University of North Carolina Press, 1993.

Syrup, F., "Arbeitseinsatz in der Bauwirtschaft," *Der Deutsche Baumeister*, 1940, no. 8, pp. 3–4.

Tafuri, M., "'Radical' Architecture and the City," in *Architecture and Utopia. Design and Capitalist Development*, trans. B. Luigia La Penta, Cambridge, Massachusetts, MIT Press, 1976, pp. 104–24.

Taylor, R., *The Word in Stone*, Berkeley, University of California Press, 1974.

Taylor, T., *The Anatomy of the Nuremberg Trials*, New York, Alfred A. Knopf, 1992.

Teut, A., *Architektur im Dritten Reich 1933–1945*, Frankfurt am Main, Verlag Ullstein GmbH, 1967.

Thies, J., *Architekt der Weltherrschaft: Die "Endziele" Hitlers*, Düsseldorf, Droste Verlag, 1976.

Trial of the Major War Criminals before the International Military Tribunal, 42 vols., Nuremberg, 1947–9.

Trials of War Criminals before the Nuernberg Military Tribunals, "The Pohl Case," vol. 5, Washington, DC, United States Government Printing Office, 1950, pp. 195–1256.

Triska, J., "'Work Redeems': Concentration Camp Labor and the Nazi German

Economy," *Journal of Central European Affairs*, 1959, vol. 19, no. 1, pp. 3–22.

Tuchel, J., *Konzentrationslager. Organisationsgeschichte und Funktion der "Inspektion der Konzentrationslager" 1934–1938*, Boppard am Rhein, Harald Boldt Verlag, 1991.

———— "Die Systematisierung der Gewalt. Vom KZ Oranienburg zum KZ Sachsenhausen," in G. Morsch (ed.), *Konzentrationslager Oranienburg*, Oranienburg, Edition Hentrich, 1994, pp. 117–28.

Umbreit, H., "Auf dem Weg zur Kontinentalherrschaft," in *Das Deutsche Reich und der Zweite Weltkrieg*, vol. 5, Stuttgart, Deutsche Verlags-Anstalt, 1988, pp. 3–345.

Van Dyke, J., "Franz Radziwill. 'Die Gemeinschaft' und die nationalsozialistische 'Revolution' in der Kunst," in *Georges-Bloch-Jahrbuch des Kunstgeschichtlichen Seminars der Universität Zürich*, Zurich, Kunstgeschichtlichen Seminars der Universität Zürich, 1997, vol. 4, pp. 135–63.

"Vierjahresplan und Bauwesen," *Beilage zum "Baumeister,"* 1937, no. 1, p. B14.

Vögler, E., "Die Bauwirtschaft macht mit," *Der Deutsche Baumeister*, 1939, no. 3, pp. 9–11.

Welch, D., *The Third Reich. Politics and Propaganda*, London, Routledge, 1993.

Weitz, B., "Der Einsatz von KZ-Häftlingen und jüdischen Zwangsarbeiten bei der Daimler-Benz AG (1941–1945). Ein Überblick," in H. Kaienburg (ed.), *Konzentrationslager und deutsche Wirtschaft 1939–1945*, Opladen, Leske + Budrich, 1996, pp. 169–95.

Werckmeister, O.K., "Hitler the Artist," *Critical Inquiry*, Winter 1997, vol. 23, pp. 270–97.

Whyte, I., *Bruno Taut and the Architecture of Activism*, Cambridge, Cambridge University Press, 1982.

———— "Der Nationalsozialismus und die Moderne," in D. Ades, T. Benton, D. Elliott and I. Whyte (eds), *Kunst und Macht*, London, Hayward Gallery, 1996, pp. 258–68.

Wickert, C., "Das grosse Schweigen: Zwangsprostitution im Dritten Reich," *Werkstatt Geschichte*, 1996, vol. 13, pp. 90–5.

"Wirtschaftliche Dienstpflicht," *Beilage zum "Baumeister,"* 1938, no. 8, p. B222.

Wolschke-Bulmahn, J. and Gröning, G., "The National Socialist Garden and Landscape Ideal: *Bodenständigkeit* (Rootedness in the Soil)," in R. Etlin (ed.), *Culture and the Nazis*, Chicago, University of Chicago Press, forthcoming.

Wolters, R., "Wilhelm Kreis und die Bauten des Oberkommandos des Heeres," *Die Kunst im Dritten Reich*, February 1939, vol. 2, edition B, pp. 46–63.

———— *Albert Speer*, Oldenburg, Gerhard Stalling Verlag, 1943.

Young, J., *The Texture of Memory. Holocaust Memorials and Meaning*, New Haven, Yale University Press, 1993.

"10 Jahre Bauproduktion in Deutschland," *Der Baumeister*, 1933, no. 6, p. B81.

Zelnhefer, S., *Die Reichsparteitage der NSDAP. Geschichte, Struktur und Bedeutung der grössten Propagandafeste im nationalsozialistschen Feierjahr*, Nuremberg, Stadtarchiv Nürnberg, 1991.

Ziegler, H., *Nazi Germany's New Aristocracy. The SS Leadership, 1925–1939*, Princeton, Princeton University Press, 1989.

Ziereis, F., *Beichte des Lagerkommandanten von Mauthausen SS-Standartenführer Franz Ziereis*, Baden-Baden, Arbeitsgemeinschaft "Das Licht," 1947.

Index